THE SHAKESPEARE PARALLEL TEXT SERIES

P9-CRB-782

HAMLET

Edited by
John Richetti
Rutgers University

THE PERFECTION FORM COMPANY
Logan, Iowa

A NOTE FROM THE PUBLISHER

The purpose of the Parallel Text Series of Shakespeare's plays is to assist the reader in understanding and appreciating the work of the foremost poet and dramatist of the English language. That there are considerable difficulties in reading and understanding this language is apparent from a casual glance through the many modern editions of the plays, which are accompanied by copious notes on each page of the text. Even these heavily annotated editions often fail to go far enough in illuminating the richly poetic and elliptical language that in large part demonstrates Shakespeare's genius and primacy, and constitutes our frequent perplexity.

In providing a line-by-line, contemporary prose paraphrase of the play on facing pages we have, in a sense, merely carried the convention of using explanatory notes to its logical conclusion. No attempt has been made to translate Shakespeare into modern poetry — a presumptuous and virtually impossible task. Instead, we have tried to render the often unfamiliar and remote Elizabethan language into a neutral and comprehensible modern equivalent. By its very nature, this task sometimes neglects the richness and complexity of the text, which is, in part, created by Shakespeare's magnificent and original use of language. Thus, the paraphrase is offered as an aid to understanding, not as a substitute for reading the original. The reader will find that referring to the paraphrase will often clarify the surface of the text, but the rewards to be found in reading Shakespeare yield themselves only to the careful and dedicated student of the original.

The Past is Prologue

Shakespeare lives! So writes his most eminent biographer, S. Schoenbaum, in the prologue to *Shakespeare: The Globe and the World* (New York: Oxford University Press, 1979). And the evidence is all around us.

We find it in the language we use. When we lament that "the course of true love never did run smooth," whether we are conscious of it or not, we are quoting from *A Midsummer Night's Dream*. When we observe that a well-intended law or regulation is "more honor'd in the breach than the observance," we are applying — or perhaps misapplying — a phrase from *Hamlet*. When we inscribe "What's past is prologue" on the National Archives building in our nation's capital, we are dignifying a minor line from *The Tempest*. Often without realizing it, we find ourselves speaking, if only momentarily, in the accents of a Portia or a Polonius, a Macbeth or a Mercutio. And when we *do* realize it — when we are conscious of the Shakespearean idiom embedded in so much of our daily speech — we take pleasure in those subtle turns of phrase that continue to enrich our discourse. A veteran gardener recently observed, for example, that anyone who calls a rose by any other name has probably been pruning.

Alongside the Greek classics and the King James version of the Bible, Shakespeare's words and works offer a cultural treasure chest from which English-speaking peoples have been drawing, in one way or another, for more than three and a half centuries. Folks have been

following the advice given in *Kiss Me Kate* — brushing up on their Shakespeare — for quite some time.

But Shakespeare's presence is also reflected in a number of other ways. Consider, for example, the more than 800 operatic and symphonic compositions deriving from such plays as *The Merry Wives of Windsor*, *The Taming of the Shrew*, and *Othello*. Or Broadway musicals, such as *The Boys from Syracuse* (a take-off on *The Comedy of Errors*) and *West Side Story* (Leonard Bernstein's New York gang-war updating of *Romeo and Juliet*). Or literary works such as William Faulkner's *The Sound and the Fury*, a sustained allusion to Macbeth's "tomorrow and tomorrow and tomorrow" speech. Here in the United States, Shakespeare has been part of our lives since the earliest days of the republic — even on the frontier, where spinoffs and parodies of Shakespeare helped while away many an hour in the nineteenth century. We've all delighted in the fractured Shakespeare offered up by the Duke and the King in Mark Twain's *Huckleberry Finn*. Ah yes, numerous — but not always sweet — are the uses of Shakespeare.

Nor is there any reason to think that Shakespeare's influence will be any less vital in the future than in the past. In most of the countries of the world, Shakespeare continues to maintain his position as the most frequently performed playwright. Every summer in the United States, for example, Shakespeare festivals highlight the vacation map from Maine to Texas, from Alabama to Oregon.

Ben Jonson was right, then, when he prefaced the first collected edition of Shakespeare's plays with the words "he was not of an age, but for all time!"

The Stratford Years

But if Shakespeare was a man for all time, he was also very much a man of his own age. Christened at Holy Trinity Church in Stratford-upon-Avon in April, 1564, he grew up, the son of illiterate parents, in a small Warwickshire town more noted for its wool and leather goods than for its literary cultivation. His mother, Mary Arden, was the daughter of a well-to-do farmer. His father, John Shakespeare, was a successful glovemaker who held several important borough offices in Stratford before he suffered financial reverses during William's teen years. The birthplace house still stands.

It seems all but certain that young Shakespeare spent most of his weekdays at the nearby Stratford grammar school, where, having learned his ABCs and the Lord's Prayer from a hornbook, he would have gone on to study Latin

Holy Trinity Church, Stratford-on-Avon

Shakespeare's House, Stratford-on-Avon

under the supervision of a stern schoolmaster.
Sundays he would have attended religious
services, studying the catechism of the newly
re-established Church of England and worshiping
in accordance with *The Book of Common Prayer.*

It was a rigorous upbringing, and it equipped
Shakespeare with enough background to become
one of the most widely educated men who ever
lived — despite the fact that he never attended a
day at a college or university.

Judging from his plays and poems, we may
infer that Shakespeare was interested in virtually
every aspect of human life — in professions such
as law, medicine, religion, and teaching; in everyday occupations such as farming, sheepherding,
tailoring, and shopkeeping; in skills such as
fishing, gardening, and cooking. Much of what
Shakespeare knew about these and countless
other subjects he would have acquired from
books. He must have been a voracious reader.

But he would have learned a great deal, also, from simply being alert to all that went on around him. He would have observed the plant and animal life of the nearby woods that he would later immortalize, in *As You Like It*, as the Forest of Arden. While there, he may have hunted from time to time; one legend has it that he left Stratford because he had been caught poaching deer from the estate of a powerful squire four miles upstream. He probably learned to swim as a youth, skinny-dipping in the river Avon. He may have participated in the kinds of athletic competition that were popular in the Elizabethan equivalent of the Olympics, the Cotswold Games. Chances are, too, that he would have been familiar with indoor recreations such as hazard (a popular dice game), or chess, or any of a number of card games. His works make it clear that he was fully at home with a broad spectrum of pastimes characteristic of the daily life of Elizabethan England.

Once his schooldays ended, Shakespeare married, at the age of eighteen, a woman who was eight years his senior. Anne Hathaway was pregnant when the wedding vows were solemnized. That it was a forced marriage is unlikely. But we shall never know how close the couple were. What we do know is that a daughter, Susanna, was baptized in Holy Trinity in May of 1583, followed less than two years later by the christening of twins, Hamnet and Judith. Sometime thereafter, certainly by the late 1580s, the father was in London.

The London Years

London was approximately a hundred miles distant. Shakespeare may have traveled there by way of the spires of Oxford, as do most visitors returning from Stratford to London today. But why he went, or when, history does not tell us. It has been plausibly suggested that he joined an acting troupe that was one player short when it toured Stratford in 1587. All we know for certain is that by 1592 Shakespeare had established himself as an actor and had written at least three plays. One of these — the third part of *Henry VI* — was alluded to in that year in a testament by a dying poet and playwright. Robert Greene warned his fellow playwrights to beware of the "upstart crow" who, not content with being a mere player, was aspiring to a share of the livelihood that had previously been the exclusive province of professional writers such as "the University Wits."

If we look at what Shakespeare had written by the early 1590s, we see that he had already become thoroughly familiar with the daily round of what was rapidly developing into one of the great capitals of Europe. Shakespeare knew St. Paul's Cathedral, famous not only as a house of worship but also as the marketplace where books were bought and sold. He knew the Inns of Court, where aspiring young lawyers studied for the bar. He knew the river Thames,

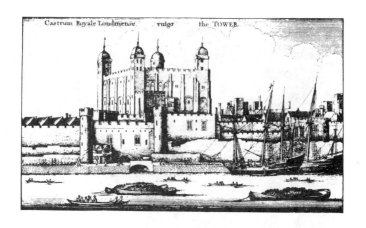

Castrum Royale Londinense. vulgo the TOWER.

spanned by the ever-busy, ever-fascinating London Bridge. He knew the Tower, where so many of the characters he would depict in his history plays had met their deaths, and where in his own lifetime, such prominent noblemen as the Earl of Essex and Sir Walter Raleigh would be imprisoned prior to their executions. He knew Westminster, where Parliament met when summoned by the Queen, and where the Queen herself kept her court at Whitehall Palace. He knew the harbor, where English ships, having won control of the seas by defeating the "invincible" Spanish Armada in 1588, had begun in earnest to explore the New World.

In Shakespeare's day, London was a vigorous city of approximately 160,000. If in its more majestic aspects it was dominated by the court of Queen Elizabeth — the sovereign most historians regard as the greatest monarch in English history — in its everyday affairs it was accented by the hustle-bustle of getting and spending. Its Royal Exchange was one of the forerunners of today's stock exchanges. Its many marketplaces offered a variety of goods for a variety of tastes.

Its crowded streets presented a colorful pageant of Elizabethan modes of transport and dress, ranging from countrywomen in homespun to elegant ladies in apparel as decorative as their husbands' wealth — and the Queen's edicts on clothing — would allow. Its inns and taverns afforded a robust diversity of vivid personalities— eating, drinking, talking, and enjoying games of all kinds.

London was, in short, a stimulating social and cultural environment for the poet whose works would later be praised as the very "mirror of life." And the young playwright took full advantage of the opportunity to observe humanity in all its facets. Without the broadening that London provided, it is doubtful that Shakespeare could ever have created such breathtakingly real characters as Falstaff, Prince Hal, and "all the good lads in Eastcheap."

Not that all was always well. Like any major city, London also had its unpleasant aspects. For one thing, it was riddled with conflict. Preachers were constantly denouncing the excessive use of cosmetics by women of the period. Even Hamlet speaks out against "your paintings," telling Ophelia "God has given you one face, and you make yourselves another."

In a similar vein, the city's Puritan authorities, regarding the theatres as dens of iniquity, closed them down on any available pretext, particularly during periods when the plague was rampant.

But even with the theatres closed, London was not free of vice and crime. In the Bankside district, prostitution abounded, as did gambling and drunkenness. Pickpockets, vagabonds, and other members of the fraternity of urban lowlife lay in wait for "conies" or unsuspecting victims. With so many "notorious villainies" for the "Belman of London" to bring to light, it is not surprising that some of the most interesting pamphlets of the period were muckraking tracts from reformers outraged by the sinfulness of the modern metropolis.

In such a setting did Shakespeare write and perform the greatest dramatic works the world has ever seen. And he did so in an area of the city that was accustomed to entertainments we would regard as the very antithesis of the sweet Swan of Avon's poetic sublimity. For if Bankside was to blossom into the finest theatrical center of that or any other age, it was also, for better or worse, the seedbed for such crude and cruel spectator sports as bear-baiting, bull-baiting, and cock-fighting. This may help account for the blood and violence one often sees on the Elizabethan stage, even in such Shakespearean works as *Titus Andronicus*, *Julius Caesar*, and *King Lear*.

But of course there was more than murder and mayhem in the "wooden O" that served as amphitheatre for Shakespeare's works. On a stage largely devoid of scenery, the playwright and the actor made splendid use of language and gesture to establish locale, atmosphere, and meaning. And because the stage was surrounded on three sides by nearby spectators, the playwright and the actor benefited from a more intimate relationship with the audience than is customary in present-day theatres fitted with a curtain and a proscenium arch. For Shakespeare, this meant that he could allow a character to confide in the audience through asides, as does Iago in *Othello*, or to be overheard as he meditates in solitude, as does Hamlet in his celebrated "To be or not to be" soliloquy.

The limitations of the Globe and similar Elizabethan theatres are obvious to us today. For one thing, they were exposed to the sky and thus could not operate comfortably in inclement weather or in darkness. For another, lacking spotlights and other modern paraphernalia, they could not achieve some of the special effects we have come to take for granted in the theatre of our own day. What we sometimes forget, however, is that these limitations could be liberating for the playwright and the actor, making possible a kind of dramatic invention and flexibility difficult to duplicate in the more "advanced" theatre of the twentieth century.

The same was probably true in the Blackfriars and other private indoor theatres of the period, not to mention the halls at Court or the great palaces of the nobility. For it is well to remember that many of Shakespeare's plays were performed in theatrical settings other than the Globe, or its predecessor, the Theatre, or other amphitheatres of the period. Shakespeare's company was known as the Lord Chamberlain's Men from 1594 to 1603, when Queen Elizabeth died; after the accession of King James I, from 1603 on, it was known as the King's Men. Both designations implied a special relationship with the Court, and Shakespeare and his colleagues were invited to perform before the monarch more often than all the other acting troupes in the realm combined.

Shakespeare's real bread and butter, however, came from the immense cross section of the English populace who thronged to Bankside to see his plays performed. Despite the occasional caviling of such rival playwrights as Ben Jonson (whose admiration for Shakespeare was at times "this side idolatry"), we have reason to believe

Interior of Holy Trinity Church

that Shakespeare's dramatic works were immediately recognized for their artistic merits. By 1598, a critic named Francis Meres was comparing Shakespeare's genius to that of the greatest poets of antiquity — Ovid, Plautus, and Seneca — and finding the contemporary playwright superior to his classical predecessors. But unlike many great writers, Shakespeare was also a popular success in his own lifetime. He earned a generous amount of money, invested it wisely in real estate, both in London and in Stratford, and around 1613, eased into a gentleman's retirement — the owner of New Place, the second largest house in his native town.

There, three years later, he died. Fittingly, his death date, like the date tradition has agreed upon for his birth date, was April 23, the day England celebrated its patron saint. In the four centuries since the poet's birth, it seems no exaggeration to say that he has eclipsed even the heroic St. George in glory.

Epilogue

Shakespeare was laid to rest where fifty-two years earlier he had been christened. Shortly thereafter, a monument to his memory was erected above the tomb in Holy Trinity, and that monument is still in place for Shakespeare admirers to see today. But an even greater monument to his memory was produced several years later, when his theatrical colleagues assembled a large volume of his plays. The First Folio of 1623 was a labor of love, compiled as "an office to the dead, to procure his orphans' guardians" and "to keep the memory of so worthy a friend and fellow alive as was our Shakespeare." To that end, it was an unparalleled success, a publication that has aptly been summed up as "incomparably the most important work in the English language."

Among other things, the First Folio preserves what is generally considered the most reliable portrait of Shakespeare, the title-page engraving by Martin Droeshout. In dedicatory verses opposite the portrait, Ben Jonson attests to its authenticity. But quite properly, he then goes on to observe that though the engraver has "hit his face," he has been unable to draw "his wit." For that — for the mastery of language, of character, of poetic drama, of all that reminds us that, after all is said and done, "the play's the thing" — Jonson tells the reader, "look not on his picture but his book."

And so, for more than three and a half centuries, we have. We have read, and studied, and memorized, and performed — and yes, we have worshiped — the man Jonson praised as "Soul of the Age! The applause, delight, the wonder of our stage!"

Bardolatry — the word we use to refer to Shakespeare-worship — has had many manifestations over the intervening centuries. It has animated hundreds of Shakespeare festivals and celebrations, of which undoubtedly the most famous was the great Shakespeare Jubilee of 1769. On that occasion, thousands braved rainy Stratford weather to participate in ceremonies presided over by the principal actor of the eighteenth century, David Garrick. In a somewhat inverted form, Bardolatry has given rise to the notion that someone other than the son of ill-educated, small-town parents wrote the plays we attribute to William Shakespeare. Hence Francis Bacon, the Earl of Oxford, and other members of the nobility have been proposed as the "true" author of the works we still securely hold to be Shakespeare's. And Bardolatry has also occasioned an unceasing cavalcade of Shakespearean curios and knickknacks: everything from ceramic figurines and mulberry-wood chests to Shakespeare-lovers' poker cloths and Superbard T-shirts.

On the more serious side, appreciation of Shakespeare has inspired notable works of art by painters as diverse as Thomas Rowlandson, George Romney, Henry Fuseli, Eugene Delacroix, George Cruikshank, Arthur Rackham, Pablo Picasso, Salvador Dali, and David Hockney. His works have provided the basis of hundreds of musical tributes, by composers ranging from Beethoven to Mendelssohn, Tchaikovsky to Verdi. And of course his plays continue to be performed in theatres, in movie houses, and on television screens.

The Bard is in our bones. Shakespeare lives.

John F. Andrews
Former Editor Shakespeare Quarterly
Folger Shakespeare Library

GOOD FREND FOR IESVS SAKE FORBEARE,
TO DIGG THE DVST ENCLOASED HEARE:
BLESE BE Y MAN Y SPARES HES STONES
AND CVRST BE HE Y MOVES MY BONES

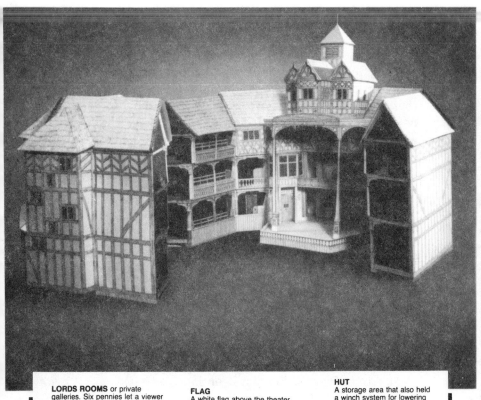

LORDS ROOMS or private galleries. Six pennies let a viewer sit here, or sometimes on stage.

FLAG
A white flag above the theater meant a show that day.

HUT
A storage area that also held a winch system for lowering characters to the stage.

MIDDLE GALLERY
The seats here were higher priced.

TRAP DOOR
Leading to the Hell area where a winch elevator was located.

THE HEAVENS
So identified by being painted with the zodiac signs.

ENTRANCE
Point leading to the staircase and upper galleries.

WARDROBE
An essential storage area.

GALLERY
Located above the stage to house musicians or spectators.

CORRIDOR
A passageway serving the middle gallery.

DRESSING ROOMS
Rooms where actors were 'attired' and awaited their cues.

MAIN ENTRANCE
Here the doorkeeper collected penny admission.

INNER STAGE
A recessed playing area often curtained off except as needed.

THE PIT
Sometimes referred to as 'The Yard' where the 'groundlings' watched.

TIRING-HOUSE DOOR
The rear entrance or 'stage door' for actors or privileged spectators.

STAGE
Major playing area jutting into the Pit, creating a sense of intimacy.

HELL
The area under the stage, used for ghostly comings and goings or for storage.

STAIRS
Theatergoers reached the galleries by staircases enclosed by stairwells.

STAGE DOORS
Doors opening into the Tiring-House.

TIRING-HOUSE
Backstage area provided space for storage and business.

HAMLET

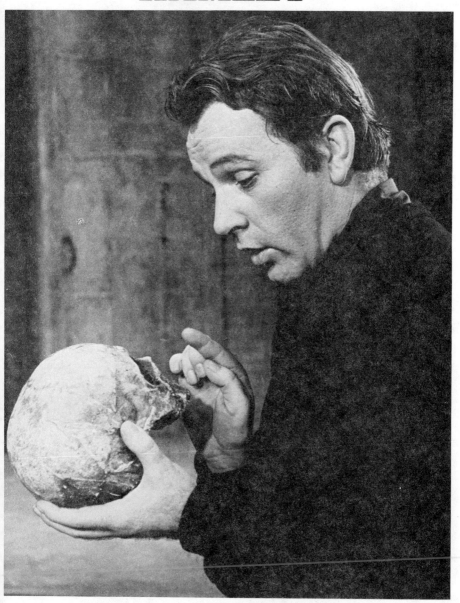

Richard Burton as Hamlet, in the 1964 production.
directed by John Gielgud.

The Tragedy of Hamlet
Prince of Denmark

Act I, Scene i: A guard platform of the castle. Enter BARNARDO
and FRANCISCO, *two sentinels.*

BARNARDO
Who's there?
FRANCISCO
Nay, answer me. Stand and unfold yourself.
BARNARDO
Long live the King!
FRANCISCO
Barnardo?
BARNARDO
5   He.
FRANCISCO
You come most carefully upon your hour.
BARNARDO
'Tis now struck twelve. Get thee to bed, Francisco.
FRANCISCO
For this relief much thanks. 'Tis bitter cold,
And I am sick at heart.
BARNARDO
Have you had quiet guard?
FRANCISCO
10   Not a mouse stirring.
BARNARDO
Well, good night.
If you do meet Horatio and Marcellus,
The rivals of my watch, bid them make haste.
Enter HORATIO *and* MARCELLUS.

2

The Tragedy of Hamlet
Prince of Denmark

Act I, Scene i: A guard platform of the castle. Enter from different directions BARNARDO *and* FRANCISCO, *two soldiers on guard duty.*

BARNARDO
  Who's there?
FRANCISCO
  No, you answer me. Stand still and tell me who you are.
BARNARDO
  Long live the King!
FRANCISCO
  Barnardo?
BARNARDO
5 Yes, it's me.
FRANCISCO
  You've come exactly on time.
BARNARDO
  The clock has just struck twelve. Go to bed, Francisco.
FRANCISCO
  Thanks a lot for coming to relieve me. It's bitter cold,
  and I've been scared stiff.
BARNARDO
  Has your guard duty been quiet?
FRANCISCO
10 Not a mouse stirring.
BARNARDO
  Well, good night.
  If you happen to meet Horatio and Marcellus,
  my partners on guard duty, tell them to hurry.
      Enter HORATIO *and* MARCELLUS.

3

FRANCISCO
I think I hear them. Stand, ho! Who is there?

HORATIO
Friends to this ground.

MARCELLUS
15   And liegemen to the Dane.

FRANCISCO
Give you good night.

MARCELLUS
                        O, farewell, honest soldier.
Who hath relieved you?

FRANCISCO
                        Barnardo hath my place.
Give you good night.
          Exit FRANCISCO.

MARCELLUS
                        Holla, Barnardo!

BARNARDO
                                        Say——
What, is Horatio there?

HORATIO
                        A piece of him.

BARNARDO
20   Welcome, Horatio. Welcome, good Marcellus.

MARCELLUS
What, has this thing appeared again tonight?

BARNARDO
I have seen nothing.

MARCELLUS
Horatio says 'tis but our fantasy,
And will not let belief take hold of him
25   Touching this dreaded sight twice seen of us;
Therefore I have entreated him along
With us to watch the minutes of this night,
That, if again this apparition come,
He may approve our eyes and speak to it.

FRANCISCO
I think I hear them. Stand still, you! Who goes there?

HORATIO
We are friends.

MARCELLUS
15   And loyal subjects of the King of Denmark.

FRANCISCO
God give you a good night's watch.

MARCELLUS
Goodnight to you, worthy soldier.
Who has taken over your watch?

FRANCISCO
Barnardo is in my place.
God give you a good night's watch.
        Exit FRANCISCO.

MARCELLUS
Hey there, Barnardo!

BARNARDO
Right—
What, is that Horatio there?

HORATIO
You see a part of him (the rest is frozen stiff).

BARNARDO
20   Welcome, Horatio. Welcome, good old Marcellus.

MARCELLUS
Don't tell me, has this thing appeared again tonight?

BARNARDO
I have seen nothing.

MARCELLUS
Horatio says that it's only our imagination,
and he refuses to allow himself to believe
25   that this terrifying sight we have seen twice is real.
So I have asked him to come along
with us and stand guard through this night;
so that if this ghost comes again,
Horatio can confirm what we have seen and speak to it.

HORATIO
  Tush, tush, 'twill not appear.
BARNARDO
30   Sit down awhile,
  And let us once again assail your ears,
  That are so fortified against our story,
  What we have two nights seen.
HORATIO
                                  Well, sit we down,
  And let us hear Barnardo speak of this.
BARNARDO
35   Last night of all,
  When yond same star that's westward from the pole
  Had made his course t' illume that part of heaven
  Where now it burns, Marcellus and myself,
  The bell then beating one——
          Enter GHOST.
MARCELLUS
40   Peace, break thee off. Look where it comes again.
BARNARDO
  In the same figure like the king that's dead.
MARCELLUS
  Thou art a scholar;* speak to it, Horatio.
BARNARDO
  Looks 'a not like the king? Mark it, Horatio.
HORATIO
  Most like: it harrows me with fear and wonder.
BARNARDO
  It would be spoke to.
MARCELLUS
45   Speak to it, Horatio.
HORATIO
  What art thou that usurp'st this time of night,
  Together with that fair and warlike form
  In which the majesty of buried Denmark
  Did sometimes march? By heaven I charge thee, speak.
MARCELLUS
  It is offended.
BARNARDO
50   See, it stalks away.

---

42 *scholar* exorcisms were performed in Latin, and therefore only a
scholar could properly speak to an evil spirit.

HORATIO
Oh, nonsense, it won't appear.

BARNARDO
30   Sit down for a bit,
and let us try once again to convince you,
since you're so set against believing our story,
of what we've seen these two nights.

HORATIO
All right, let's sit down,
and let's hear what Barnardo can say about this.

BARNARDO
35   Last night,
when that star over there to the west of the north star
had arrived to light up that part of the sky
where it now shines, Marcellus and myself,
the bell then striking one o'clock—
        Enter GHOST.

MARCELLUS
40   Quiet, stop talking. Look where it comes again.

BARNARDO
It looks exactly like the dead king, Hamlet.

MARCELLUS
You are an educated man, speak to it, Horatio.

BARNARDO
Doesn't it look like the king? Look closely, Horatio.

HORATIO
Just like him. It rips through me with fear and amazement.

BARNARDO
It wants to be spoken to.

MARCELLUS
45   Speak to it, Horatio.

HORATIO
What are you? Why do you take over this time of night
and appropriate that handsome and military appearance
in which the buried king of Denmark
used to march? In heaven's name, I order you, speak.

MARCELLUS
It is offended by what you say.

BARNARDO
50   Look, it marches away.

HORATIO
> Stay! Speak, speak! I charge thee, speak!
>   *Exit* GHOST.

MARCELLUS
> 'Tis gone and will not answer.

BARNARDO
> How now, Horatio? You tremble and look pale.
> Is not this something more than fantasy?
55 What think you on't?

HORATIO
> Before my God, I might not this believe
> Without the sensible and true avouch
> Of mine own eyes.

MARCELLUS
>   Is it not like the King?

HORATIO
> As thou art to thyself.
60 Such was the very armor he had on
> When he the ambitious Norway combated:
> So frowned he once, when, in an angry parle,
> He smote the sledded Polacks on the ice.
> 'Tis strange.

MARCELLUS
65 Thus twice before, and jump at this dead hour,
> With martial stalk hath he gone by our watch.

HORATIO
> In what particular thought to work I know not;
> But, in the gross and scope of my opinion,
> This bodes some strange eruption to our state.

MARCELLUS
70 Good now, sit down, and tell me he that knows,
> Why this same strict and most observant watch
> So nightly toils the subject of the land,
> And why such daily cast of brazen cannon
> And foreign mart for implements of war,

HORATIO
>Stay here! Speak, speak! I order you, speak!
>*Exit* GHOST.

MARCELLUS
>It's gone and won't answer our questions.

BARNARDO
>How are you, Horatio? You tremble and look pale.
>Isn't this something more than our imagination?
55   What do you think of it?

HORATIO
>I swear to God, I wouldn't believe this
>unless I could vouch for it by the report
>of my own eyes.

MARCELLUS
>Doesn't it look like the King?

HORATIO
>As you are like yourself.
60   That was the same armor he wore
>when he fought the ambitious king of Norway.
>He frowned that way once during an angry discussion of
>   truce terms,
>when he defeated the Poles in their sleds on the ice.
>It's strange.

MARCELLUS
65   Just that same way twice before and exactly at this still time
>   of night,
>he's marched by us as we stood watch.

HORATIO
>I don't know what particular meaning I can come up with
>   for this,
>but my general view is that
>this is a sign of some strange outbreak of violence about to take
>   place in our country.

MARCELLUS
70   All right now, let's sit down, and I want whoever knows
>   to tell me
>why such a strict and very careful guard
>forces the Danish people to work day and night.
>Why are bronze cannons cast every day?
>Why is there such trade with foreign nations for military
>   supplies?

75 Why such impress of shipwrights, whose sore task
Does not divide the Sunday from the week,
What might be toward that this sweaty haste
Doth make the night joint-laborer with the day?
Who is't that can inform me?
HORATIO
                                        That can I.
At least the whisper goes so: our last king,
80 Whose image even but now appeared to us,
Was, as you know, by Fortinbras of Norway,
Thereto pricked on by a most emulate pride,
Dared to the combat; in which our valiant Hamlet
(For so this side of our known world esteemed him)
85 Did slay this Fortinbras, who, by a sealed compact
Well ratified by law and heraldry,
Did forfeit, with his life, all those his lands
Which he stood seized of, to the conqueror;
Against the which a moiety competent
90 Was gagèd by our King, which had returned
To the inheritance of Fortinbras,
Had he been vanquisher, as, by the same comart
And carriage of the article designed,
His fell to Hamlet. Now, sir, young Fortinbras,
95 Of unimprovèd mettle hot and full,
Hath in the skirts of Norway here and there
Sharked up a list of lawless resolutes,
For food and diet, to some enterprise
That hath a stomach in't; which is no other,
100 As it doth well appear unto our state,
But to recover of us by strong hand
And terms compulsatory, those foresaid lands
So by his father lost; and this, I take it,
Is the main motive of our preparations,
105 The source of this our watch, and the chief head
Of this posthaste and romage in the land.
BARNARDO
I think it be no other but e'en so;
Well may it sort that this portentous figure

Why are so many ship builders forced into service and made
to work every day of the week, including Sunday?

75

What are we preparing for in such a sweaty hurry
that the night is turned into a fellow worker with the day?
Which of you can tell me why?

HORATIO

I can do that.
This at least is the rumor. Our last king,

80

whose likeness has just this minute appeared to us,
was as you know challenged to battle by Fortinbras of Norway,
who was provoked by jealous pride.
And in that battle our brave Hamlet
(for that's how everyone here in our part of the world thought
    of him)

85

killed this Fortinbras. By the terms of their sealed agreement
and according to the law and the custom of heraldry,
Fortinbras gave up to his conqueror not only his life but also
    the lands
he possessed.
Matching those, an equal portion of land

90

had been staked by our king, and that land would have been ceded
to Fortinbras and his heirs
if he had been the winner, that by the same terms of the
    agreement
and according to the meaning of the contract
passed to Hamlet. Now, sir, young Fortinbras,

95

eager and full of untested courage,
here and there along the borders of Norway
has recklessly picked up an army of lawless and desperate men.
He offered them their keep if they would take part in an enterprise
that requires courage, which is no other

100

(as our leaders can plainly see)
than to take back from us by force
those lands I mentioned before
that his father lost. And this, I believe,
is the chief reason for our preparations,

105

what lies behind this guard duty we're on, and the root cause
of this great hurry and bustle in the land.

BARNARDO

I think that's just what it is.
It fits in well with everything—this threatening figure

110   Comes armèd through our watch so like the King
       That was and is the question of these wars.

HORATIO
       A mote it is to trouble the mind's eye:
       In the most high and palmy state of Rome,
       A little ere the mightiest Julius fell,
115   The graves stood tenantless, and the sheeted dead
       Did squeak and gibber in the Roman streets;*
       As stars with trains of fire and dews of blood,
       Disasters in the sun; and the moist star,
       Upon whose influence Neptune's empire stands,
120   Was sick almost to doomsday with eclipse.
       And even the like precurse of feared events,
       As harbingers preceding still the fates
       And prologue to the omen coming on,
       Have heaven and earth together demonstrated
125   Unto our climatures and countrymen.
                Enter GHOST.
       But soft, behold, lo where it comes again!
       I'll cross it,* though it blast me.—Stay, illusion.
                He spreads his arms.
       If thou hast any sound or use of voice,
       Speak to me.
130   If there be any good thing to be done
       That may to thee do ease and grace to me,
       Speak to me.
       If thou art privy to thy country's fate,
       Which happily foreknowing may avoid,
135   O, speak!
       Or if thou hast uphoarded in thy life
       Extorted treasure in the womb of earth,
       For which, they say, you spirits oft walk in death,
                The cock crows.
       Speak of it. Stay and speak. Stop it, Marcellus.

MARCELLUS
140   Shall I strike at it with my partisan?*

---

       116 *Roman streets* one or more lines seem to have been lost between
       lines 116-17.
       127 *cross it* Horatio puts himself in the Ghost's path and holds out
       his arms to form a cross, a means of protecting himself from an evil spirit.

110   who marches in armor as we stand guard, who looks just like
     the King
who was and still is the issue behind these wars.

HORATIO
It is like a speck of dust which makes the eye of the mind blink
     and wonder.
During the greatest and most triumphant days of Rome,
just before that most powerful Julius Caesar was killed,
115   the graves were emptied, and the dead in their shrouds
shrieked and babbled in the streets of Rome.
Stars were seen with fiery tails like comets, there were
     blood-red dews
and threatening signs in the sun. And the moon,
whose force controls the oceans,
120   was almost eclipsed, as it will be at the end of the world.
And similar predictions of events we fear,
forerunners which always precede what is fated to happen,
announcements of the disaster which is coming,
have been evident here in heaven and on earth and clearly shown
125   to Denmark and our fellow Danes.
     Enter GHOST.
But wait, look, see where it comes again!
I'll stop it, even if it destroys me. Halt, phantom.
     (*Horatio spreads his arms, forming a cross.*)
If you can make any sound or use your voice,
speak to me.
130   If I can do any good deed
which will help you and earn grace for me,
speak to me.
If you know the secret of your country's fate,
which if we know we may avoid,
135   O, speak!
Or, if during your lifetime, you have hoarded up
ill-gotten treasure in an underground hiding place,
for which it is said you ghosts are often forced to wander
     after death, speak of it. Stay here
and talk. (*Ghost begins to move away.*) Stop it, Marcellus.
     (*A cock crows, a sign that dawn is approaching.*)

MARCELLUS
140   Shall I try to hit it with my partisan?

---

140 *partisan* a weapon made of a long wooden shaft topped by a blade
with broad, horizontally projecting cutting edges.

HORATIO
Do, if it will not stand.

BARNARDO
'Tis here.

HORATIO
'Tis here.

Exit GHOST.

MARCELLUS
'Tis gone.
We do it wrong, being so majestical,
To offer it the show of violence,
145   For it is as the air, invulnerable,
And our vain blows malicious mockery.

BARNARDO
It was about to speak when the cock crew.

HORATIO
And then it started, like a guilty thing
Upon a fearful summons. I have heard,
150   The cock, that is the trumpet to the morn,
Doth with his lofty and shrill-sounding throat
Awake the god of day, and at his warning,
Whether in sea or fire, in earth or air,*
Th' extravagant and erring spirit hies
155   To his confine; and of the truth herein
This present object made probation.

MARCELLUS
It faded on the crowing of the cock.
Some say that ever 'gainst that season comes
Wherein our Savior's birth is celebrated,
160   This bird of dawning singeth all night long,
And then, they say, no spirit dare stir abroad,
The nights are wholesome,* then no planets strike,
No fairy takes, nor witch hath power to charm:
So hallowed and so gracious is that time.

HORATIO
165   So have I heard and do in part believe it.
But look, the morn in russet mantle clad
Walks o'er the dew of yon high eastward hill.

---

153 *air* refers to the belief that the world was composed of four
"elements" — earth, water, air, and fire.

HORATIO
Yes, if it doesn't stay here.

BARNARDO
It's over here.

HORATIO
It's here.
        Exit GHOST.

MARCELLUS
It's gone.
We have offended it, since it is so majestic a creature,
by trying to force it by violence,
145   for it is like the air and cannot be hurt.
Our useless blows mock our own hasty and ill-willed foolishness.

BARNARDO
It was going to talk just as the cock crowed.

HORATIO
And then it was startled, like a guilty thing
which was summoned by a call it fears. I have heard
150   that the cock, which is the trumpet that announces morning,
with his exalted and high-pitched voice
awakens the god of day. And when he gives that warning,
whether it is in the sea or in fire, in the earth or in the air,
the wandering ghost which is far from its proper place hurries
        back
155   to its prison. This display we have just seen
proves the truth of that.

MARCELLUS
It faded away just when the cock crowed.
There are some who say that just before that time of year
when our Savior's birth is celebrated (i.e., Christmas),
160   this bird of the dawn sings all night long.
And then, they say, no ghost dares go out,
then nights are healthy, then no planets exert an evil force,
no fairy plays its mischievous tricks, nor has any witch the
        power to cast a spell—
so holy and full of grace is that time of year.

HORATIO
165   I have heard that before, and I partly believe it.
But look, dressed in a reddish cloak, the morning
walks on the dew that covers that high hill over there to the east.

---

162 *wholesome* in the medical beliefs of the time, the night air was
considered unhealthy.

Break we our watch up, and by my advice
Let us impart what we have seen tonight
170   Unto young Hamlet, for upon my life
This spirit, dumb to us, will speak to him.
Do you consent we shall acquaint him with it,
As needful in our loves, fitting our duty?

MARCELLUS
Let's do't, I pray, and I this morning know
175   Where we shall find him most convenient.
                    Exeunt.

Scene ii: The castle. Flourish. Enter CLAUDIUS, *King of Denmark,*
GERTRUDE *the Queen, Councilors,* POLONIUS *and his son* LAERTES,
HAMLET, *cum aliis [including* VOLTEMAND *and* CORNELIUS].

KING
Though yet of Hamlet our* dear brother's death
The memory be green, and that it us befitted
To bear our hearts in grief, and our whole kingdom
To be contracted in one brow of woe,
5   Yet so far hath discretion fought with nature
That we with wisest sorrow think on him
Together with remembrance of ourselves.
Therefore our sometime sister, now our Queen,
Th' imperial jointress of this warlike state,
10   Have we, as 'twere, with a defeated joy,
With an auspicious and a dropping eye,
With mirth in funeral, and with dirge in marriage,
In equal scale weighing delight and dole,
Taken to wife. Nor have we herein barred
15   Your better wisdoms, which have freely gone
With this affair along. For all, our thanks.
Now follows that you know young Fortinbras,
Holding a weak supposal of our worth,
Or thinking by our late dear brother's death
20   Our state to be disjoint and out of frame,
Colleaguèd with this dream of his advantage,

---

1 *our*   the King consistently uses the royal "we" in speaking about himself. The paraphrase converts this to the normal first person singular, "I," and "me," and so on.

Let's disband our watch, and my advice is
that we should tell what we have seen tonight
170   to young Hamlet, for by my life
this ghost, silent to us, will speak to him.
Do you all agree that we should tell him about it,
and that our friendship for him and our duty as soldiers require
     us to?

MARCELLUS
Let's do it, I agree. And I know this morning
175   where we can find him most conveniently.
          They exit.

Act I, Scene ii: The castle. A fanfare of trumpets. Enter CLAU-
DIUS, *King of Denmark;* GERTRUDE, *the Queen;* HAMLET,
POLONIUS, LAERTES, VOLTEMAND, CORNELIUS, *and vari-
ous counsellors and courtiers.*

KING
Although the memory of my dear brother Hamlet's death
is still fresh, and although it was proper for me
to grieve and to keep my whole kingdom
drawn up in a total state of mourning,
5   practical wisdom has modified my natural tendencies
so that I think about him with the wisest kind of sorrow
and consider my own affairs and necessities as well.
Therefore, my former sister-in-law and now my queen,
the imperial partner in ruling this warlike country,
10   I have with a defeated happiness, so to speak,
with a joyful and with a sad eye,
with laughter during the funeral, and with mourning during the
     marriage ceremony,
equally balancing pleasure and pain,
taken as a wife. (*To the counsellors*) Nor have I done this against
15   your considered judgment, for you have freely consented
to this matter. For all this, I give you my thanks.
Now, you should also know that young Fortinbras,
who supposes that I am weak,
or thinks that because of my late dear brother's death
20   my country is confused and in disorder,
has put those notions together with what he imagines is his own
     superiority.

He hath not failed to pester us with message,
Importing the surrender of those lands
Lost by his father, with all bonds of law,
25   To our most valiant brother. So much for him.
Now for ourself and for this time of meeting.
Thus much the business is: we have here writ
To Norway, uncle of young Fortinbras—
Who, impotent and bedrid, scarcely hears
30   Of this his nephew's purpose—to suppress
His further gait herein, in that the levies,
The lists, and full proportions are all made
Out of his subject; and we here dispatch
You, good Cornelius, and you, Voltemand,
35   For bearers of this greeting to old Norway,
Giving to you no further personal power
To business with the King, more than the scope
Of these delated articles allow.
Farewell, and let your haste commend your duty.

CORNELIUS, VOLTEMAND
40   In that, and all things, we will show our duty.

KING
We doubt it nothing. Heartily farewell.

    Exit VOLTEMAND *and* CORNELIUS.
And now, Laertes, what's the news with you?
You told us of some suit. What is't, Laertes?
You cannot speak of reason to the Dane
45   And lose your voice. What wouldst thou beg, Laertes,
That shall not be my offer, not thy asking?
The head is not more native to the heart,
The hand more instrumental to the mouth,
Than is the throne of Denmark to thy father.
What wouldst thou have, Laertes?

LAERTES
50   My dread lord,
Your leave and favor to return to France,
From whence, though willingly I came to Denmark
To show my duty in your coronation,
Yet now I must confess, that duty done,

He hasn't failed to pester me with frequent messages
that I should give up those lands his father lost under a lawful
agreement
25 to my brave brother. So much for him.
Now, what I have done and the reason for this meeting
is as follows : I have written
to the King of Norway, young Fortinbras' uncle—
who is weak and bedridden and only knows a little
30 of his nephew's intention—and to prevent
Fortinbras from going any further with his plan have told
Norway that the money,
the soldiers, with all their supplies, are all taken
by Fortinbras from Norway's own subjects. And I here send
you, good Cornelius, and you, Voltemand,
35 as messengers to the old King of Norway,
giving you no more personal authority
to deal with the King than is set out
in these detailed documents.
Goodbye, and swiftness in execution will make your duty
praiseworthy.

CORNELIUS, VOLTEMAND
40 In that and in all things, we will do as you wish.

KING
I don't doubt it at all. I wish you a hearty farewell.
Exit CORNELIUS *and* VOLTEMAND.
And now, Laertes, what do you have to say?
You told me you had some request. What is it, Laertes?
You cannot make a reasonable request to the King of Denmark
45 and speak in vain. Is there anything you can ask for, Laertes,
that I will not give you freely, rather than because you ask?
The head is not more closely related to the heart,
the hand (in eating) not more useful to the mouth,
than is the King of Denmark to your father.
What would you like, Laertes?

LAERTES
50 My mighty ruler,
your permission to return to France,
for although I came to Denmark from there willingly
to show my loyalty at your coronation,
yet now I must admit that since I have done that duty

55   My thoughts and wishes bend again toward France
      And bow them to your gracious leave and pardon.
KING
      Have you your father's leave? What says Polonius?
POLONIUS
      He hath, my lord, wrung from me my slow leave
      By laborsome petition, and at last
60   Upon his will I sealed my hard consent.
      I do beseech you give him leave to go.
KING
      Take thy fair hour, Laertes. Time be thine,
      And thy best graces spend it at thy will.
      But now, my cousin Hamlet, and my son——
HAMLET [*Aside*]
65   A little more than kin, and less than kind!*
KING
      How is it that the clouds still hang on you?
HAMLET
      Not so, my lord. I am too much in the sun.*
QUEEN
      Good Hamlet, cast thy nighted color off,
      And let thine eye look like a friend on Denmark.
70   Do not forever with thy vailèd lids
      Seek for thy noble father in the dust.
      Thou know'st 'tis common; all that lives must die,
      Passing through nature to eternity.
HAMLET
      Ay, madam, it is common.*
QUEEN
                                If it be,
75   Why seems it so particular with thee?
HAMLET
      Seems, madam? Nay, it is. I know not "seems."
      'Tis not alone my inky cloak, good mother,
      Nor customary suits of solemn black,
      Nor windy suspiration of forced breath,
80   No, nor the fruitful river in the eye,

---

65 *less than kind* Hamlet is "more than kin" because he is closer to
Claudius than a nephew, but "less than kind" because he doesn't feel kindly
toward him, the way a son should by nature (or "kind").

67 *sun* wordplay on "son/sun." Hamlet may mean that he is suffering
from too much exposure to the sunshine of the King's royal presence, and

55   my thoughts and wishes are to return to France.
        And I submit them for your gracious permission and indulgence.
        KING
        Do you have your father's permission? What do you say,
            Polonius?
        POLONIUS
        He has, my lord, slowly squeezed from me my permission
        by persistent requests, and finally
60   I gave my reluctant consent to his desire.
        I humbly ask you to give him permission to go.
        KING
        Leave when you like, Laertes. Do as you please,
        and I hope your virtues will help you use your time well.
        But now, my kinsman Hamlet, and my son—
        HAMLET *(to the audience)*
65   I am somewhat closer to you than a kinsman and I feel
            less than kindly toward you.
        KING
        Why do the clouds still hover over you?
        HAMLET
        Not so, my lord. I've spent too much time in the royal sunshine
            of your favor.
        QUEEN
        Good Hamlet, get rid of your black mourning clothes,
        and be friendly with the King of Denmark.
70   Don't keep your eyes downcast all the time,
        looking for your noble father in his grave.
        You know that it happens to everyone; all that lives must die,
        passing through this world to eternity.
        HAMLET
        Yes, madam, it happens to everyone, it's ordinary.
        QUEEN
        If that's true,
75   why do you seem to take it so personally (as if it were unique
            to you)?
        HAMLET
        "Seem," madam? No, it *is*. I'm not capable of pretending.
        It isn't just my black suit, dear mother,
        nor the traditional solemn black mourning clothes,
        nor heavy and labored sighing,
80   no, nor shedding a river full of tears,

---

that he is forced to play the "son" to a father he dislikes.

74 *common* Hamlet's echo of his mother's term looks two ways: death
is common because it is universal, but also common because it is ordinary
and even vulgar.

Nor the dejected havior of the visage,
Together with all forms, moods, shapes of grief,
That can denote me truly. These indeed seem,
For they are actions that a man might play,
85   But I have that within which passes show;
These but the trappings and the suits of woe.

KING
'Tis sweet and commendable in your nature, Hamlet,
To give these mourning duties to your father,
But you must know your father lost a father,
90   That father lost, lost his, and the survivor bound
In filial obligation for some term
To do obsequious sorrow. But to persever
In obstinate condolement is a course
Of impious stubbornness. 'Tis unmanly grief.
95   It shows a will most incorrect to heaven,
A heart unfortified, a mind impatient,
An understanding simple and unschooled.
For what we know must be and is as common
As any the most vulgar thing to sense,
100   Why should we in our peevish opposition
Take it to heart? Fie, 'tis a fault to heaven,
A fault against the dead, a fault to nature,
To reason most absurd, whose common theme
Is death of fathers, and who still hath cried,
105   From the first corse* till he that died today,
"This must be so." We pray you throw to earth
This unprevailing woe, and think of us
As of a father, for let the world take note
You are the most immediate to our throne,
110   And with no less nobility of love
Than that which dearest father bears his son
Do I impart toward you. For your intent
In going back to school in Wittenberg,
It is most retrograde to our desire,
115   And we beseech you, bend you to remain

---

105 *first corse* Abel, who was killed by his brother, Cain. See Genesis 4:1-16.

nor a downcast and mournful face.
No, not all these things combined with all the forms, moods, and
    shapes that mourning takes
can give a true picture of what I feel. These things are only
    a show,
since they are actions with which a man can pretend.
85 But I have feelings that are too deep for mere external display.
What I show now are only the outward signs of my grief.

KING
It shows how sweet and honorable your character is, Hamlet,
that you mourn so faithfully for your father.
But you must be aware that your father lost his father,
90 his father lost a father, and the survivor in each case was bound
to do his duty as a son by spending some time
in suitable mourning. But to continue
mourning for so long shows
only blasphemous stubbornness. This grief is not proper for
    a man.
95 It shows that your will is not resigned to heaven's wishes,
your heart is unprepared for suffering, and you have a turbulent
    and restless spirit,
your grasp of reality is simple-minded and inexperienced.
For when we know that something must happen—that it is as
    universal
as any of the most obvious things we experience—
100 why should we, with spiteful resentment against God's will,
take it personally? Oh no, it's an offense to heaven,
an offense against the dead, an offense to nature,
absurd to common sense, which always has to deal
with the death of fathers, and which has always cried out,
105 from the first corpse until the one that died today,
"This must be so." I entreat you to discard
this useless sorrow, and to think of me
as a father. For let everyone take notice:
you are the next in line for my throne,
110 and no less than the noble love
which a dearest father has for his son
is what I offer you. As for your intention
to go back to the university in Wittenberg,
it is very much against my wishes,
115 and I ask you most earnestly to remain,

Here in the cheer and comfort of our eye,
Our chiefest courtier, cousin, and our son.

QUEEN
Let not thy mother lose her prayers, Hamlet.
I pray thee stay with us, go not to Wittenberg.

HAMLET
120   I shall in all my best obey you, madam.

KING
Why, 'tis a loving and a fair reply.
Be as ourself in Denmark. Madam, come.
This gentle and unforced accord of Hamlet
Sits smiling to my heart, in grace whereof
125   No jocund health that Denmark drinks today,
But the great cannon to the clouds shall tell,
And the King's rouse the heaven shall bruit again,
Respeaking earthly thunder. Come away.
         Flourish. Exeunt all but HAMLET.

HAMLET
O that this too too solid flesh would melt,
130   Thaw, and resolve itself into a dew,
Or that the Everlasting had not fixed
His canon 'gainst self-slaughter. O God, O God!
How weary, stale, flat, and unprofitable
Seem to me all the uses of this world!
135   Fie on't, ah, fie, 'tis an unweeded garden
That grows to seed. Things rank and gross in nature
Possess it merely. That it should come to this:
But two months dead, nay, not so much, not two,
So excellent a king, that was to this
140   Hyperion to a satyr;* so loving to my mother
That he might not beteem the winds of heaven
Visit her face too roughly. Heaven and earth,
Must I remember? Why, she would hang on him
As if increase of appetite had grown
145   By what it fed on; and yet within a month—
Let me not think on't; frailty, thy name is woman—
A little month, or ere those shoes were old

---

140 *Hyperion to a satyr* Hyperion was the Greek god of the sun and a
model of manly beauty. Satyrs were spirits with the pointed ears, legs, and

to stay here in my consoling and comforting presence
as my chief courtier, my close relative, and my son.

QUEEN

Don't let your mother's prayers go unanswered, Hamlet.
I beg you to stay with us; don't go to Wittenberg.

HAMLET

120   I will always, madam, obey you to the best of my ability.

KING

Why, that's a loving and charming answer.
Consider yourself my equal in Denmark. Madam, come.
This polite and willing agreement of Hamlet
makes me glad, and to celebrate it,

125   I won't drink a single carefree toast today
without accompanying it with a great cannon blast to the sky.
And the King's toast shall be sounded again by the heavens,
echoing the thunder thus made on earth. Come, let's go.

Exit the KING *and* QUEEN *and all the court, to the sound
of trumpet flourishes.* HAMLET *is left alone.*

HAMLET

O if only this far too solid body of mine would melt,

130   thaw, and turn itself into dew,
or that God had not established
his prohibition against suicide. O God, O God!
How weary, stale, boring, and worthless
seem to me all the ways of this world!

135   To hell with it all! It's an unweeded garden
that goes to seed. Things that are overgrown and monstrous
      in their nature
have completely taken it over. That it should turn out this way:
only two months dead—no, not that long, not quite two—
and my father, who was so excellent a king, that compared to
      Claudius,

140   he was like the sun god set beside a filthy satyr. He was so loving
      to my mother
that he tried to keep the winds of heaven
from blowing too roughly on her face. O heaven and earth,
do I have to remember? Why, she used to hang on him
as if her appetite for him grew

145   the more she satisfied it with him. And yet within a month—
let me not think about it, the fickle weakness of women—
a little month, before those shoes were worn out

---

short horns of a goat and were commonly associated with lecherous behavior.

With which she followed my poor father's body
Like Niobe,* all tears, why she, even she—
150   O God, a beast that wants discourse of reason
Would have mourned longer—married with my uncle,
My father's brother, but no more like my father
Than I to Hercules.* Within a month,
Ere yet the salt of most unrighteous tears
155   Had left the flushing in her gallèd eyes,
She married. O, most wicked speed, to post
With such dexterity to incestuous* sheets!
It is not, nor it cannot come to good.
But break my heart, for I must hold my tongue.

Enter HORATIO, MARCELLUS, *and* BARNARDO.

HORATIO
Hail to your lordship!

HAMLET
160   I am glad to see you well.
Horatio—or I do forget myself.

HORATIO
The same, my lord, and your poor servant ever.

HAMLET
Sir, my good friend. I'll change that name with you.
And what make you from Wittenberg, Horatio?
165   Marcellus.

MARCELLUS
My good lord!

HAMLET
I am very glad to see you.
[*To Barnardo*] Good even, sir.
But what, in faith, make you from Wittenberg?

HORATIO
A truant disposition, good my lord.

HAMLET
170   I would not hear your enemy say so,
Nor shall you do my ear that violence
To make it truster of your own report
Against yourself. I know you are no truant.

---

149 *Niobe* punished by the gods with the death of her children, the grief-stricken mother was changed into a stone which wept forever.

153 *Hercules* not only a superman in Greek and Roman mythology, but in Shakespeare's time a figure who represented moral decisiveness and resolute action.

with which she followed, full of tears like Niobe, my poor
    father's body in the coffin—
    why she, yes even she—
150   O God, even an animal (that lacks the power of reason)
    would have mourned longer—she married my uncle,
    my father's brother, but no more like my father
    than I am like Hercules. Within a month,
    before the salt from her hypocritical mourning tears
155   had stopped inflaming her sore eyes,
    she married. O, what an evil haste, to hurry
    with such speed into an incestuous bed!
    It is not good, nor will it lead to anything good.
    But let my heart break, for I must keep silent.
        Enter HORATIO, MARCELLUS, *and* BARNARDO.

HORATIO
    Hail to my lord Hamlet!

HAMLET
160   I am glad to see that you are well.
    (*Recognizing him and expressing surprise*) Horatio!—
        or else my memory is bad.

HORATIO
    It's me, my lord, and always ready to be of service to you.

HAMLET
    Sir, you are my good friend, and I am yours.
    And what are you doing away from Wittenberg, Horatio?
165   (*Turning to Marcellus*) Marcellus.

MARCELLUS
    My good lord Hamlet!

HAMLET
    I am very glad to see you.
    (*To Barnardo*) Good evening, sir.
    (*To Horatio*) But tell me what brings you here from Wittenberg?

HORATIO
    My tendency to be lazy, my good lord.

HAMLET
170   I wouldn't allow your enemy to say that,
    nor shall you insult my hearing by forcing me
    to believe your own report
    against yourself. I know that you are not a shirker.

---

157 *incestuous* according to the moral theology of the time, marriage
with a brother's wife was incestuous.

But what is your affair in Elsinore?

175   We'll teach you to drink deep ere you depart.

HORATIO

My lord, I came to see your father's funeral.

HAMLET

I prithee do not mock me, fellow student.

I think it was to see my mother's wedding.

HORATIO

Indeed, my lord, it followed hard upon.

HAMLET

180   Thrift, thrift, Horatio. The funeral baked meats

Did coldly furnish forth the marriage tables.

Would I had met my dearest foe in heaven

Or ever I had seen that day, Horatio!

My father, methinks I see my father.

HORATIO

Where, my lord?

HAMLET

185   In my mind's eye, Horatio.

HORATIO

I saw him once. 'A was a goodly king.

HAMLET

'A was a man, take him for all in all,

I shall not look upon his like again.

HORATIO

My lord, I think I saw him yesternight.

HAMLET

190   Saw? Who?

HORATIO

My lord, the King your father.

HAMLET

                                    The King my father?

HORATIO

Season your admiration for a while

With an attent ear till I may deliver

Upon the witness of these gentlemen

This marvel to you.

HAMLET

195   For God's love let me hear!

But what are you doing in Elsinore?
175 We'll teach you to drink to excess before you go.

HORATIO
My lord, I came to attend your father's funeral.

HAMLET
Please don't make fun of me, fellow student.
I think you came to attend my mother's wedding.

HORATIO
Indeed, my lord, it took place just afterwards.

HAMLET
180 To save money, to save money, Horatio. The baked meats for the funeral reception
provided a cold buffet for the marriage feast.
I wish I had encountered my worst enemy in heaven
before I had seen that day, Horatio!
My father, it seems to me that I see my father.

HORATIO
Where, my lord?

HAMLET
185 In my imagination, Horatio.

HORATIO
I saw him once. He was a splendid king.

HAMLET
He was a man, the perfection of all manly qualities.
I won't ever see anyone like him again.

HORATIO
My lord, I think I saw him last night.

HAMLET
190 Saw? Who?

HORATIO
My lord, the King your father.

HAMLET
The King my father?

HORATIO
Control your amazement for a while
and listen closely while I tell you
what these gentlemen can vouch for,
a strange and wonderful thing.

HAMLET
195 For the love of God, tell me!

HORATIO
Two nights together had these gentlemen,
Marcellus and Barnardo, on their watch
In the dead waste and middle of the night
Been thus encountered. A figure like your father,
200   Armèd at point exactly, cap-a-pe,
Appears before them, and with solemn march
Goes slow and stately by them. Thrice he walked
By their oppressed and fear-surprisèd eyes,
Within his truncheon's length, whilst they, distilled
205   Almost to jelly with the act of fear,
Stand dumb and speak not to him. This to me
In dreadful secrecy impart they did,
And I with them the third night kept the watch,
Where, as they had delivered, both in time,
210   Form of the thing, each word made true and good,
The apparition comes. I knew your father.
These hands are not more like.

HAMLET
                                    But where was this?

MARCELLUS
My lord, upon the platform where we watched.

HAMLET
Did you not speak to it?

HORATIO
                            My lord, I did;
215   But answer made it none. Yet once methought
It lifted up it head and did address
Itself to motion like as it would speak:
But even then the morning cock crew loud,
And at the sound it shrunk in haste away
And vanished from our sight.

HAMLET
220   'Tis very strange.

HORATIO
As I do live, my honored lord, 'tis true,
And we did think it writ down in our duty
To let you know of it.

HORATIO
　For two nights in a row, these gentlemen,
　Marcellus and Barnardo, while on guard duty
　in the very middle of the night
　had been confronted thus : a figure like your father,
200　armed completely from head to foot,
　appears in front of them and marches solemnly
　by them, in a slow and deliberate way. He walks three times
　in front of their shocked and terrified eyes,
　as close to them as the length of his swagger stick, while they, turned
205　almost to jelly by fear,
　stand silent and do not speak to him. They told me about this,
　and pledged me to secrecy.
　And I stood guard with them on the third night.
　Just as they had described it, the ghost came, at the time
210　and in the shape that proved their story exactly true.
　I knew your father.
　(*Holding up his hands*) These hands are as similar to each other
　　as that apparition was to him.

HAMLET
　But where did this happen?

MARCELLUS
　My lord, upon the platform where we stood guard.

HAMLET
　Didn't you speak to it?

HORATIO
　My lord, I did.
215　But it did not answer me, although at one point I thought
　it lifted up its head and began
　to make a gesture as if it wanted to speak.
　But just then the morning cock crowed loudly,
　and at the sound it backed hastily away
　and disappeared from our sight.

HAMLET
220　It's very mysterious.

HORATIO
　As sure as I'm alive, my honored lord, it's true.
　And we thought it was clearly our duty
　to tell you about it.

HAMLET
Indeed, indeed, sirs, but this troubles me.
Hold you the watch tonight?

ALL
                                    We do, my lord.

HAMLET
Armed, say you?

ALL
Armed, my lord.

HAMLET
From top to toe?

ALL
                          My lord, from head to foot.

HAMLET
Then saw you not his face.

HORATIO
O, yes, my lord. He wore his beaver up.

HAMLET
What, looked he frowningly?

HORATIO
A countenance more in sorrow than in anger.

HAMLET
Pale or red?

HORATIO
Nay, very pale.

HAMLET
                          And fixed his eyes upon you?

HORATIO
Most constantly.

HAMLET
                          I would I had been there.

HORATIO
It would have much amazed you.

HAMLET
Very like, very like. Stayed it long?

HORATIO
While one with moderate haste might tell a hundred.

BOTH
Longer, longer.

HAMLET
Oh yes, indeed, gentlemen, but this worries me.
Will you be on guard duty tonight?

ALL
225   We will, my lord.

HAMLET
He was armed, you say?

ALL
Yes, armed, my lord.

HAMLET
From head to toe?

ALL
My lord, from head to foot.

HAMLET
Then you didn't see his face.

HORATIO
230   O yes, my lord. He wore the visor of his helmet up.

HAMLET
What was his expression? Was he frowning?

HORATIO
His face was more sorrowful than angry.

HAMLET
Was it pale or flushed?

HORATIO
No, very pale.

HAMLET
And did he keep his eyes fixed upon you?

HORATIO
Without wavering.

HAMLET
235   I wish I had been there.

HORATIO
It would really have amazed you.

HAMLET
Probably, most probably. Did it stay long?

HORATIO
As long as it would take to count, not too quickly, to a hundred.

MARCELLUS and BARNARDO
Longer than that, longer.

HORATIO
  Not when I saw't.
HAMLET
240   His beard was grizzled, no?
HORATIO
  It was as I have seen it in his life,
  A sable silvered.
HAMLET
                I will watch tonight.
  Perchance 'twill walk again.
HORATIO
                  I warr'nt it will.
HAMLET
  If it assume my noble father's person,
245 I'll speak to it though hell itself should gape
  And bid me hold my peace.* I pray you all,
  If you have hitherto concealed this sight,
  Let it be tenable in your silence still,
  And whatsomever else shall hap tonight,
250 Give it an understanding but no tongue;
  I will requite your loves. So fare you well.
  Upon the platform 'twixt eleven and twelve
  I'll visit you.
ALL
            Our duty to your honor.
HAMLET
  Your loves, as mine to you. Farewell.
              Exeunt [all but HAMLET].
255 My father's spirit—in arms? All is not well.
  I doubt some foul play. Would the night were come!
  Till then sit still, my soul. Foul deeds will rise,
  Though all the earth o'erwhelm them, to men's eyes.
              Exit.

[*Scene iii: A room.*] *Enter* LAERTES *and* OPHELIA, *his sister.*

LAERTES
  My necessaries are embarked. Farewell.
  And, sister, as the winds give benefit

---

  246 *peace* Hamlet considers the possibility that the spirit may be a
trick of the devil, an evil spirit sent to tempt him.

HORATIO
Not the time I saw it.

HAMLET
240   His beard was partly gray, wasn't it?

HORATIO
It looked the way I saw it when he was alive,
black with white hairs mingled in it.

HAMLET
I will stand guard tonight.
Maybe it will walk again.

HORATIO
I assure you, it will.

HAMLET
If it takes on the appearance of my noble father,
245   I'll speak to it, even if hell itself opens before me
and orders me to keep quiet. I entreat all of you,
if till now you've kept this sight secret,
continue to be silent.
And whatever else happens tonight,
250   I ask you to try to comprehend it but not talk about it.
I will repay your friendship. So goodbye.
I'll come to visit you on the guard platform between eleven
    and twelve.

ALL
Your grace can count on our duty.

HAMLET
I would rather have your affection, just as you have mine.
    Farewell.
        Exit HORATIO, MARCELLUS, *and* BARNARDO.
255   My father's ghost—in armor? All is not well.
I suspect there's been foul play. I wish night would come!
Till then, sit quietly, my soul. Evil deeds will always be exposed,
even if the whole earth covers them from man's sight.
    Exit HAMLET.

Act I, Scene iii: A Room in the Castle. Enter LAERTES *and*
OPHELIA.

LAERTES
My baggage is on shipboard. Farewell.
And sister, when there are favorable winds

And convoy is assistant, do not sleep,
But let me hear from you.

OPHELIA

                              Do you doubt that?

LAERTES

5   For Hamlet, and the trifling of his favor,
Hold it a fashion and a toy in blood,
A violet in the youth of primy nature,
Forward, not permanent, sweet, not lasting,
The perfume and suppliance of a minute,
No more.

OPHELIA

                    No more but so?

LAERTES

10   Think it no more.
For nature crescent does not grow alone
In thews and bulk, but as this temple waxes,
The inward service of the mind and soul
Grows wide withal. Perhaps he loves you now,
15   And now no soil nor cautel doth besmirch
The virtue of his will; but you must fear,
His greatness weighed, his will is not his own.
For he himself is subject to his birth.
He may not, as unvalued persons do,
20   Carve for himself; for on his choice depends
The safety and health of this whole state;
And therefore must his choice be circumscribed
Unto the voice and yielding of that body
Whereof he is the head. Then if he says he loves you,
25   It fits your wisdom so far to believe it
As he in his particular act and place
May give his saying deed, which is no further
Than the main voice of Denmark goes withal.
Then weigh what loss your honor may sustain
30   If with too credent ear you list his songs,
Or lose your heart, or your chaste treasure open
To his unmastered importunity.
Fear it, Ophelia, fear it, my dear sister,

and the means of communication are available, don't just sleep
but let me hear from you.

OPHELIA
How can you doubt that?

LAERTES
5   As for Hamlet and his flirtation with you,
think of it as a normal and playful passion,
like a violet in the early spring of life,
premature but not permanent, pleasant but not lasting,
the perfume and the diversion that fills up a moment—
nothing else.

OPHELIA
Nothing more than that?

LAERTES
10   Don't think that it can be anything more.
Since human growth is not just
a matter of muscles and size, but as the body develops,
the powers of the mind and spirit
grow along with it. Maybe he loves you now,
15   and maybe now no blemish nor deceit stains
the purity of his desire for you. But you must be cautious,
for if you consider his high rank, he can't simply do as he likes:
his future is determined by his noble birth.
He can't, like people of lower rank,
20   indulge his own wishes, since on his choice depends
the safety and well-being of this whole country.
And therefore his choice must be limited
by the approval and consent of the country
of which he is the head. So that if he says he loves you,
25   you will be smart to trust him only
if he can do what his position
allows, and that is to say only
when he acts in accord with the general approval of Denmark.
Then consider what damage your honor may suffer
30   if you believe his love songs,
or give him your love, or open up your treasured chastity
to his unrestrained demand.
Be careful, Ophelia, be careful, my dear sister,

And keep you in the rear of your affection,
35   Out of the shot and danger of desire.
The chariest maid is prodigal enough
If she unmask her beauty to the moon.
Virtue itself scapes not calumnious strokes.
The canker galls the infants of the spring
40   Too oft before their buttons be disclosed,
And in the morn and liquid dew of youth
Contagious blastments are most imminent.
Be wary then; best safety lies in fear;
Youth to itself rebels, though none else near.

OPHELIA
45   I shall the effect of this good lesson keep
As watchman to my heart. But, good my brother,
Do not, as some ungracious pastors do,
Show me the steep and thorny way to heaven,
Whiles, like a puffed and reckless libertine,
50   Himself the primrose path of dalliance treads
And recks not his own rede.
            Enter POLONIUS.

LAERTES
                    O, fear me not.
I stay too long. But here my father comes.
A double blessing is a double grace;
Occasion smiles upon a second leave.

POLONIUS
55   Yet here, Laertes? Aboard, aboard, for shame!
The wind sits in the shoulder of your sail,
And you are stayed for. There—my blessing with thee,
And these few precepts in thy memory
Look thou character. Give thy thoughts no tongue,
60   Nor any unproportioned thought his act.
Be thou familiar, but by no means vulgar.
Those friends thou hast, and their adoption tried,
Grapple them unto thy soul with hoops of steel,
But do not dull thy palm with entertainment
65   Of each new-hatched, unfledged courage. Beware

and hold yourself back from what your emotions might otherwise
    lead you to:
35   stay out of range of the dangerous artillery of desire.
The most reserved girl is liable to be thought immodest,
even if she shows her beauty only to the moon.
Virtue itself cannot avoid slanderous charges.
The cankerworm injures the young plants of the spring,
40   very often before their buds have even opened;
and so in the morning and fresh dew-time of youth
poisonous and withering blights are most threatening.
Be careful then; your best safety is in your fear.
Youth is liable to rebel on its own, even if no one else is near
    to encourage it.

OPHELIA
45   I shall keep the meaning of this good lesson
as a guard to my heart. But, my good brother,
don't act like some ungodly preachers
and show me the steep and thorny road to heaven,
while like a bloated and careless sinner
50   you yourself take the flowery road of pleasure
and ignore your own advice.
        Enter POLONIUS.

LAERTES
O, don't worry about me.
I've stayed too long. But here comes my father.
Two blessings from him give me twice as much grace;
chance graciously provides me with a second farewell.

POLONIUS
55   Still here, Laertes? Get going, go on, shame on you!
The wind puffs out the sail of your ship,
and they're waiting for you. There (*embracing Laertes*),
    let my blessing go with you,
and be sure to inscribe these few moral rules in your memory.
Keep your thoughts to yourself,
60   and do not translate any wild thought into action.
Be sociable, but by no means friendly with everybody.
Once you have friends and their friendship has been proved,
attach yourself to them with the strength of steel barrel-hoops,
but don't let your hand become insensitive by welcoming
65   each new and immature young buck. Avoid

Of entrance to a quarrel; but being in,
Bear't that th' opposèd may beware of thee.
Give every man thine ear, but few thy voice;
Take each man's censure, but reserve thy judgment.
70 Costly thy habit as thy purse can buy,
But not expressed in fancy; rich, not gaudy,
For the apparel oft proclaims the man,
And they in France of the best rank and station
Are of a most select and generous, chief in that.
75 Neither a borrower nor a lender be,
For loan oft loses both itself and friend,
And borrowing dulleth edge of husbandry.
This above all, to thine own self be true,
And it must follow, as the night the day,
80 Thou canst not then be false to any man.
Farewell. My blessing season this in thee!

LAERTES
Most humbly do I take my leave, my lord.

POLONIUS
The time invites you. Go, your servants tend.

LAERTES
Farewell, Ophelia, and remember well
What I have said to you.

OPHELIA
85   'Tis in my memory locked,
And you yourself shall keep the key of it.

LAERTES
Farewell.

        Exit LAERTES.

POLONIUS
What is't, Ophelia, he hath said to you?

OPHELIA
So please you, something touching the Lord Hamlet.

POLONIUS
90 Marry,* well bethought.
'Tis told me he hath very oft of late
Given private time to you, and you yourself
Have of your audience been most free and bounteous.

---

90 *Marry* originally the name of the Virgin Mary, the word was used as
a mild oath or introductory expression, meaning "indeed" or "to be sure."

getting into a quarrel, but once you're involved,
behave yourself so that your opponent will be afraid of you.
Listen to everyone, but give advice to few.
Pay attention to each man's opinion, but keep your judgment
    to yourself.
70 Let your clothing be as expensive as you can afford,
but avoid fancy dress. Let it be expensive, not loud,
since a man is often judged by his clothing,
and those of the highest class and position in France
show their nobility and gentility principally by dress.
75 Don't borrow or lend,
for lending is often the way to lose both your money and your
    friend,
and borrowing makes it easy to be a spendthrift.
This above all things: be true to yourself,
and it must follow, just as night comes after day,
80 that you can't then be false to any man.
Farewell. I hope my blessing preserves this good advice for you!

LAERTES
With your permission, I will be going now, my lord.

POLONIUS
The time is right. Go ahead, your servants are waiting.

LAERTES
Farewell, Ophelia, be sure to remember well
what I have said to you.

OPHELIA
85 It's locked in my memory,
and you yourself shall keep the key to it.

LAERTES
Farewell.
        Exit LAERTES.

POLONIUS
What is it, Ophelia, that he said to you?

OPHELIA
If you wish to know, something about Lord Hamlet.

POLONIUS
90 Indeed, I'm glad he mentioned it.
I've been told by my spies that he has lately very often
seen you in private, and that you yourself
have been free and generous in letting him see you.

If it be so—as so 'tis put on me,
95 And that in way of caution—I must tell you
You do not understand yourself so clearly
As it behooves my daughter and your honor.
What is between you? Give me up the truth.

OPHELIA
He hath, my lord, of late made many tenders*
100 Of his affection to me.

POLONIUS
Affection pooh! You speak like a green girl,
Unsifted in such perilous circumstance.
Do you believe his tenders, as you call them?

OPHELIA
I do not know, my lord, what I should think.

POLONIUS
105 Marry, I will teach you. Think yourself a baby
That you have ta'en these tenders for true pay
Which are not sterling. Tender yourself more dearly,
Or (not to crack the wind of the poor phrase)
Tend'ring it thus you'll tender me a fool.

OPHELIA
110 My lord, he hath importuned me with love
In honorable fashion.

POLONIUS
Ay, fashion you may call it. Go to, go to.

OPHELIA
And hath given countenance to his speech, my lord,
With almost all the holy vows of heaven.

POLONIUS
115 Ay, springes to catch woodcocks. I do know,
When the blood burns, how prodigal the soul
Lends the tongue vows. These blazes, daughter,
Giving more light than heat, extinct in both,
Even in their promise, as it is a-making,
120 You must not take for fire. From this time
Be something scanter of your maiden presence.

---

99 *tenders* as Ophelia uses it, the word means offers, but in what follows Polonius plays with other meanings when he speaks of tenders as chips
or counters, in the sense we still have in the phrase "legal tender." In lines

If that's so—as indeed I have been told about it
95   as something to be careful of—I have to inform you
that you don't understand as clearly
as you should what your position is as my daughter and as an
    honorable girl.
What is there between you? Let me have the truth.

OPHELIA
He has, my lord, lately made many offers
100   of his love to me.

POLONIUS
"Love," bah! You talk like a naive girl,
untested in such dangerous affairs.
Do you believe his "offers," as you call them?

OPHELIA
I do not know, my lord, what I should think.

POLONIUS
105   Indeed, I'll teach you. Think of yourself as a baby
for accepting as real money these "offers"
which are not genuine. Think more highly of yourself,
or (without riding the comparison till it's winded)
if you present yourself that way you'll present me with a
    foolish baby.

OPHELIA
110   My lord, he has entreated me with his love
in an honorable manner.

POLONIUS
Oh yes, "manner" is what you should call it. Oh, come now,
    come now.

OPHELIA
And he has supported his vows, my lord,
by swearing to heaven in almost every way possible that he is
    telling the truth.

POLONIUS
115   Yes, traps to catch dumb birds. I know
that when passion is hot, the soul lavishly
supplies promises for the tongue to speak. Daughter, these fiery
    words
give more light than heat, and both those effects die out
just as soon as they appear.
120   You mustn't mistake them for real passion. From now on
be less ready to grant Hamlet a meeting.

---

107 and 109, he plays with "tender," so that "you'll tender me a fool" may
have three meanings: make me look foolish, show me that you are a fool,
present me with a fool (i.e., an illegitimate child).

Set your entreatments at a higher rate
Than a command to parley. For Lord Hamlet,
Believe so much in him that he is young,
125 And with a larger tether may he walk
Than may be given you. In few, Ophelia,
Do not believe his vows, for they are brokers,
Not of that dye which their investments show,
But mere implorators of unholy suits,
130 Breathing like sanctified and pious bawds,
The better to beguile. This is for all:
I would not, in plain terms, from this time forth
Have you so slander any moment leisure
As to give words or talk with the Lord Hamlet.
135 Look to't, I charge you. Come your ways.

OPHELIA
I shall obey, my lord.
Exeunt.

[*Scene iv: A guard platform.*] *Enter* HAMLET, HORATIO, *and* MAR-
CELLUS.

HAMLET
The air bites shrewdly; it is very cold.

HORATIO
It is a nipping and an eager air.

HAMLET
What hour now?

HORATIO
I think it lacks of twelve.

MARCELLUS
No, it is struck.

HORATIO
5 Indeed? I heard it not. It then draws near the season
Wherein the spirit held his wont to walk.
A flourish of trumpets, and two pieces go off.
What does this mean, my lord?

Place a higher value on your conversations,
and don't talk just because he asks you. As for Lord Hamlet,
believe only this about him : that he is a young man,
125   and has more freedom
than you can have. In short, Ophelia,
don't believe his promises, for they are like bawds,
not really what their gaudy clothes proclaim them,
but out-and-out solicitors of sinful desires,
130   pretending to be holy and blessed persons
in order to fool you better. This is my final word.
To speak plainly, I don't want you from now on
to risk disgrace during your leisure time
by flirting or talking with Lord Hamlet.
135   Be sure of that, I order you. Come along.

OPHELIA
I shall obey, my lord.
    Exit OPHELIA *and* POLONIUS.

Act I, Scene iv: A guard platform of the castle. Enter HAMLET,
HORATIO, *and* MARCELLUS.

HAMLET
The air bites sharply ; it is very cold.

HORATIO
It is a nipping and brisk air.

HAMLET
What time is it now ?

HORATIO
I think it's almost twelve.

MARCELLUS
No, it has already struck twelve.

HORATIO
5   Really ? I didn't hear it. Then it's getting near the time
when the ghost is accustomed to walk.
    *A flourish of trumpets from within the castle and two
       cannon blasts are heard.*
What does this mean, my lord ?

HAMLET
    The King doth wake tonight and takes his rouse,
    Keeps wassail, and the swagg'ring upspring reels,
10   And as he drains his draughts of Rhenish down
    The kettledrum and trumpet thus bray out
    The triumph of his pledge.

HORATIO
                    Is it a custom?

HAMLET
    Ay, marry, is't,
    But to my mind, though I am native here
15   And to the manner born, it is a custom
    More honored in the breach than the observance.
    This heavy-headed revel east and west
    Makes us traduced and taxed of other nations.
    They clepe us drunkards and with swinish phrase
20   Soil our addition, and indeed it takes
    From our achievements, though performed at height,
    The pith and marrow of our attribute.
    So oft it chances in particular men
    That for some vicious mole of nature in them,
25   As in their birth, wherein they are not guilty,
    (Since nature cannot choose his origin)
    By the o'ergrowth of some complexion,
    Oft breaking down the pales and forts of reason,
    Or by some habit that too much o'erleavens
30   The form of plausive manners, that (these men,
    Carrying, I say, the stamp of one defect,
    Being nature's livery, or fortune's star)
    Their virtues else, be they as pure as grace,
    As infinite as man may undergo,
35   Shall in the general censure take corruption
    From that particular fault. The dram of evil
    Doth all the noble substance often dout,
    To his own scandal.

        Enter GHOST.

HORATIO
              Look, my lord, it comes.

HAMLET

The King is having a late party tonight, carousing,
drinking, reeling through a wild dance,
10   and as he empties his mug of Rhine wine
the kettledrum and trumpet bray out
and accompany his triumphant toast.

HORATIO

Is that customary?

HAMLET

Yes, indeed it is,
but as far as I'm concerned, even though I was born here
15   and am expected to continue the custom, it is a tradition
more honorably broken than observed.
This drunken partying causes nations to the east and west
to blame and censure us.
They call us drunkards and by naming us swine
20   stain our titles of honor; and indeed
our accomplishments (however well we perform them) are
robbed
of the essence which should give us a good reputation.
Thus it often happens to individual men
that because of some natural blemish in them,
25   which they acquire at birth and for which they are not to blame
(since we can't select our parents),
some characteristic becomes overdeveloped
and often breaks down the barriers of rational control.
Or some habit infects
30   their good manners. These men,
I tell you, have the mark of one imperfection,
whether given by nature at birth or determined by their bad
fortune.
So that, whatever other virtues they may have, even if they're as
pure as God's grace can make them,
or as close to infinite in their goodness as a man can manage,
35   those other good qualities shall in other men's eyes be corrupted
by that particular infection. The little drop of evil
thereby often undoes all of a man's good qualities,
so that he is completely disgraced.
    Enter the GHOST.

HORATIO

Look, my lord, here it comes.

HAMLET
Angels and ministers of grace defend us!
40 Be thou a spirit of health or goblin damned,
Bring with thee airs from heaven or blasts from hell,
Be thy intents wicked or charitable,
Thou com'st in such a questionable shape
That I will speak to thee. I'll call thee Hamlet,
45 King, father, royal Dane. O, answer me!
Let me not burst in ignorance, but tell
Why thy canonized bones, hearsèd in death,
Have burst their cerements, why the sepulcher
Wherein we saw thee quietly interred
50 Hath oped his ponderous and marble jaws
To cast thee up again. What may this mean
That thou, dead corse, again in complete steel,
Revisits thus the glimpses of the moon,
Making night hideous, and we fools of nature*
55 So horridly to shake our disposition
With thoughts beyond the reaches of our souls?
Say, why is this? Wherefore? What should we do?
        Ghost beckons Hamlet.
HORATIO
It beckons you to go away with it,
As if it some impartment did desire
To you alone.
MARCELLUS
60 Look with what courteous action
It waves you to a more removèd ground.
But do not go with it.
HORATIO
                    No, by no means.
HAMLET
It will not speak. Then I will follow it.
HORATIO
Do not, my lord.
HAMLET
                    Why, what should be the fear?
65 I do not set my life at a pin's fee,
And for my soul, what can it do to that,

---

54 *fools of nature* a fool of nature normally meant an idiot, but **Hamlet** uses the term to include everyone who is merely "natural" and therefore baffled by the supernatural.

HAMLET
Angels and messengers of God's grace defend us!
40 Whether you are a good spirit or a goblin from hell,
whether you bring healthy air from heaven or harmful winds
    from hell,
whether your intentions are evil or good,
you come in such a strange shape
that I must speak to you. I'll call you Hamlet,
45 King, father, royal Dane. O, answer me!
Don't let me burst with ignorance, but tell me
why your properly buried bones, confined in the grave,
have broken out of their shrouds? Why has the tomb
where we saw you quietly buried
50 opened its heavy marble jaws
to spew you out again? What can it mean
that you, a dead body, once more in full armor
comes out again in the moonlight,
making the night hideous and turning us into fools,
55 horribly disturbing our minds
with thoughts of events beyond our understanding?
Tell us, why is this happening? What is the reason? What
    should we do?
          GHOST *motions for* HAMLET *to follow.*
HORATIO
It waves at you to go away with it,
as if it wanted to deliver some message
to you alone.
MARCELLUS
60 Look at the polite gesture with which
it asks you to go to a more remote place.
But don't go with it.
HORATIO
No, by no means.
HAMLET
It won't speak here. Then I will follow it.
HORATIO
Do not, my lord.
HAMLET
Why, what is there to fear?
65 I don't value my life at a pin's worth.
As for my soul, what can it do to hurt that,

Being a thing immortal as itself?
It waves me forth again. I'll follow it.

HORATIO
What if it tempt you toward the flood, my lord,
70   Or to the dreadful summit of the cliff
That beetles o'er his base into the sea,
And there assume some other horrible form,
Which might deprive your sovereignty of reason
And draw you into madness? Think of it.
75   The very place puts toys of desperation,
Without more motive, into every brain
That looks so many fathoms to the sea
And hears it roar beneath.

HAMLET
                              It waves me still.
Go on; I'll follow thee.

MARCELLUS
You shall not go, my lord.

HAMLET
80   Hold off your hands!

HORATIO
Be ruled. You shall not go.

HAMLET
                              My fate cries out
And makes each petty artere in this body
As hardy as the Nemean lion's* nerve.
Still am I called! Unhand me, gentlemen.
85   By heaven, I'll make a ghost of him that lets me!
I say, away! Go on. I'll follow thee.
                    Exit GHOST, *and* HAMLET.

HORATIO
He waxes desperate with imagination.

MARCELLUS
Let's follow. 'Tis not fit thus to obey him.

HORATIO
    Have after! To what issue will this come?

MARCELLUS
90   Something is rotten in the state of Denmark.

---

83 *Nemean lion* one of the twelve labors of Hercules was the killing of this beast, which no weapon could harm. Hercules choked it to death.

since the soul is as immortal as the ghost?
It motions for me to go forward again. I'll follow it.

HORATIO
Suppose it leads you near the water, my lord,
70 or to the fearful top of the cliff
that hangs threateningly over its base into the sea,
and there it takes on another frightening shape
which might destroy your power of reason
and drive you mad? Think of it.
75 The place itself inspires suicidal fantasies
in everyone
who looks from such a great height down to the sea
and hears it roaring beneath.

HAMLET
It still motions for me to come.
(*To Ghost*) Go on; I'll follow you.

MARCELLUS (*holding him back*)
You shall not go, my lord.

HAMLET
80 Take your hands off me!

HORATIO
Listen to us. You shall not go.

HAMLET
My destiny calls out
and makes each small ligament in this body of mine
as strong as the sinews of the Nemean lion.
It still calls me! Let me go, gentlemen.
85 By heaven, I'll kill whoever prevents me!
I say, get away from me. (*To Ghost*) Go on; I'll follow you.
        Exit GHOST *and* HAMLET.

HORATIO
He's getting desperate with these fantasies.

MARCELLUS
Let's follow him. It isn't right to obey him in this.

HORATIO
Let's go after him! What is going to happen?

MARCELLUS
90 Something is rotten in this country of Denmark.

HORATIO
　Heaven will direct it.
MARCELLUS
　　　　　　Nay, let's follow him.
　　　Exeunt.

[*Scene v: The battlements.*] *Enter* GHOST *and* HAMLET.

HAMLET
　Whither wilt thou lead me? Speak; I'll go no further.
GHOST
　Mark me.
HAMLET
　　　　I will.
GHOST
　　　　　My hour is almost come,
　When I to sulf'rous and tormenting flames
　Must render up myself.
HAMLET
　　　　　　Alas, poor ghost.
GHOST
5　Pity me not, but lend thy serious hearing
　To what I shall unfold.
HAMLET
　　　　　　Speak. I am bound to hear.
GHOST
　So art thou to revenge, when thou shalt hear.
HAMLET
　What?
GHOST
　I am thy father's spirit,
10　Doomed for a certain term to walk the night,
　And for the day confined to fast in fires,
　Till the foul crimes done in my days of nature
　Are burnt and purged away. But that I am forbid
　To tell the secrets of my prison house,
15　I could a tale unfold whose lightest word
　Would harrow up thy soul, freeze thy young blood,
　Make thy two eyes like stars start from their spheres,

HORATIO
God will determine the outcome.
MARCELLUS
Come on, let's follow him.
    Exit HORATIO *and* MARCELLUS.

Act I, Scene v: Another part of the guard platform. Enter GHOST
and HAMLET.

HAMLET
Where are you leading me? Speak; I won't go any further.
GHOST
Listen to me carefully.
HAMLET
I will.
GHOST
The time is almost here
when I must give myself up
to the suffocating and torturing fires (of Purgatory).
HAMLET
I am sorry, poor ghost.
GHOST
5   Don't pity me, but listen carefully
to what I am going to reveal.
HAMLET
Speak. I am obligated to listen.
GHOST
As you are to avenge me, when you shall hear.
HAMLET
What?
GHOST
I am your father's ghost,
10   doomed to walk at night for a set term,
and during the day to do penance in fire
until the terrible crimes committed when I was alive
are burned away and I am purified. I am not allowed
to disclose the secrets of my prison; otherwise
15   I could tell you a story whose most trivial detail
would rip up your soul, freeze your young blood,
make your two eyes pop from their sockets like stars wrenched
    from their orbits,

Thy knotted and combinèd locks to part,
And each particular hair to stand on end
20   Like quills upon the fearful porpentine.
But this eternal blazon must not be
To ears of flesh and blood. List, list, O, list!
If thou didst ever thy dear father love——

HAMLET
O God!

GHOST
25   Revenge his foul and most unnatural murder.

HAMLET
Murder?

GHOST
Murder most foul, as in the best it is,
But this most foul, strange, and unnatural.

HAMLET
Haste me to know't, that I, with wings as swift
30   As meditation or the thoughts of love,
May sweep to my revenge.

GHOST
                    I find thee apt,
And duller shouldst thou be than the fat weed
That roots itself in ease on Lethe wharf,*
Wouldst thou not stir in this. Now, Hamlet, hear.
35   'Tis given out that, sleeping in my orchard,
A serpent stung me. So the whole ear of Denmark
Is by a forgèd process of my death
Rankly abused. But know, thou noble youth,
The serpent that did sting thy father's life
Now wears his crown.

HAMLET
                    O my prophetic soul!
40   My uncle?

GHOST
Ay, that incestuous, that adulterate beast,
With witchcraft of his wits, with traitorous gifts—
O wicked wit and gifts, that have the power

---

33 *Lethe wharf*   the bank of the river of forgetfulness in Hades.

make your tangled and braided hair come loose
and cause each individual hair to stand on end
20   like the quills on a frightened porcupine.
But this revelation about the hereafter is not allowed
to human ears. Listen, listen, O listen!
If you ever loved your dear father—

HAMLET
    O God!

GHOST
25   Revenge his revolting and most unnatural murder.

HAMLET
    Was it murder?

GHOST
    Revolting murder, as it is even at its best,
    but this was totally revolting, strange, and unnatural.

HAMLET
    Tell me quickly who did it, so that I may fly as swiftly
30   as thought or as the desires of love
    and swoop down in my revenge.

GHOST
    I find that you're ready,
    and you would be more sluggish than the thick weed
    that lazily roots itself on the banks of Lethe
    if you weren't aroused by this. Now, Hamlet, listen.
35   It is reported that while I was sleeping in my garden,
    a snake bit me. Thus the whole nation of Denmark
    by a false report of my death
    is grossly deceived. But know the truth, you noble young man,
    the snake that killed your father
    now wears his crown.

HAMLET
40   O my soul prophesied that!
    My uncle?

GHOST
    Yes, that incestuous, that adulterous animal,
    with the evil magic of his intelligence, aided by gifts that served
      his treachery—
    O evil intelligence and gifts that are so powerfully

45 So to seduce!—won to his shameful lust
    The will of my most seeming-virtuous queen.
    O Hamlet, what a falling-off was there,
    From me, whose love was of that dignity
    That it went hand in hand even with the vow
50 I made to her in marriage, and to decline
    Upon a wretch whose natural gifts were poor
    To those of mine.
    But virtue, as it never will be moved,
    Though lewdness court it in a shape of heaven,
55 So lust, though to a radiant angel linked,
    Will sate itself in a celestial bed
    And prey on garbage.
    But soft, methinks I scent the morning air;
    Brief let me be. Sleeping within my orchard,
60 My custom always of the afternoon,
    Upon my secure hour thy uncle stole
    With juice of cursed hebona* in a vial,
    And in the porches of my ears did pour
    The leperous distillment, whose effect
65 Holds such an enmity with blood of man
    That swift as quicksilver it courses through
    The natural gates and alleys of the body,
    And with a sudden vigor it doth posset
    And curd, like eager droppings into milk,
70 The thin and wholesome blood. So did it mine,
    And a most instant tetter barked about
    Most lazarlike with vile and loathsome crust
    All my smooth body.
    Thus was I, sleeping, by a brother's hand
75 Of life, of crown, of queen at once dispatched,
    Cut off even in the blossoms of my sin,
    Unhouseled, disappointed, unaneled,
    No reck'ning made, but sent to my account
    With all my imperfections on my head.
80 O, horrible! O, horrible! Most horrible!
    If thou hast nature in thee, bear it not.

---

62 *hebona* literally, "ebony," but Shakespeare apparently equates it
with "henbane," a poison.

45   seductive!—he persuaded my queen to give in to his shameful
          lust,
       she who seemed so virtuous.
       O Hamlet, what a decline from goodness that was in her,
       to betray me, whose love was so worthy
       that it was completely true to the promise
50   I made her when we married, and then to degrade herself
       with a wretch whose physical attractions were poor
       next to mine.
       But just as virtue will never be persuaded to sin,
       even if lust looks angelic when it woos,
55   so lust, even if joined to a beautiful angel,
       will grow tired in a heavenly bed of love
       and soon want to feed on garbage.
       But wait a moment, I think I smell the morning air;
       let me be brief. While sleeping in my garden,
60   as I used to every afternoon,
       your uncle crept up on me during that unsuspecting time
       with a little glass filled with the juice of cursed hebona,
       and into my ear poured
       the leprous drug, whose effects
65   are so harmful to human blood.
       Swift as mercury it runs through
       the natural passages of the body,
       and with an immediate strength it coagulates
       and curdles, like drops of vinegar in milk,
70   the healthy and flowing blood. That's what it did to mine,
       and a leprous scab suddenly formed
       a hard covering with a horrible and disgusting crust
       all over my smooth body.
       So, while sleeping, I was deprived by a brother's hand
75   all at once of my life, my crown, and my queen,
       and cut off when I was full of sin,
       without the sacrament of communion, not prepared by
          confession, not anointed with the last rites.
       No account made of my sins, I was sent to judgment
       with all of them on my head.
80   O, horrible! O, horrible! Most horrible!
       If you have natural feelings in you, don't stand for it.

Let not the royal bed of Denmark be
A couch for luxury and damnèd incest.
But howsomever thou pursues this act,
85   Taint not thy mind, nor let thy soul contrive
Against thy mother aught. Leave her to heaven
And to those thorns that in her bosom lodge
To prick and sting her. Fare thee well at once.
The glowworm shows the matin to be near
90   And 'gins to pale his uneffectual fire.
Adieu, adieu, adieu. Remember me.
    Exit.

HAMLET
O all you host of heaven! O earth! What else?
And shall I couple hell? O fie! Hold, hold, my heart,
And you, my sinews, grow not instant old,
95   But bear me stiffly up. Remember thee?
Ay, thou poor ghost, whiles memory holds a seat
In this distracted globe. Remember thee?
Yea, from the table of my memory
I'll wipe away all trivial fond records,
100   All saws of books, all forms, all pressures past
That youth and observation copied there,
And thy commandment all alone shall live
Within the book and volume of my brain,
Unmixed with baser matter. Yes, by heaven!
105   O most pernicious woman!
O villain, villain, smiling, damnèd villain!
My tables*—meet it is I set it down
That one may smile, and smile, and be a villain.
At least I am sure it may be so in Denmark.
    [*Writes.*]
110   So, uncle, there you are. Now to my word:
It is "Adieu, adieu, remember me."
I have sworn't.

HORATIO and MARCELLUS [*Within*]
My lord, my lord!
    Enter HORATIO *and* MARCELLUS.

---

107   *tables*   a small writing tablet or memorandum book.

Don't let the royal marriage bed of Denmark be
a resting-place for lust and unholy incest.
But however you manage this act of revenge,
85   don't poison your own mind, and don't allow yourself to plot
anything against your mother. Let heaven punish her
and let her punish herself with that thorny guilt that lives in
    her breast
and pricks and stings her. Quickly now, goodbye.
The glowworm shows that morning is near
90   by beginning to put out his cold light.
Farewell, farewell, farewell. Remember me.
     Exit GHOST.

HAMLET
O all you angels in heaven! O earth! What else can I swear by?
And shall I include hell? O damn it! Be still, be still, my heart.
And you, my body, don't get old suddenly
95   but hold me straight up. Remember you?
Oh yes, you poor ghost, as long as my memory works
in this distracted head. Remember you?
Yes, from the notebooks of my memory
I'll erase any trivial and foolish remembrances,
100   all wise sayings from books, all images, all impressions from
    the past
that youthful experience has written there,
and only your commandment shall live
in the book of my brain,
not mixed with less important things. Yes, by heaven!
105   O most treacherous woman!
O villain, villain, smiling villain who belongs in hell!
My notebook, I should write it down
that one may smile, and smile, and still be a villain.
At least I'm sure it can happen in Denmark.
     (*Writes in a pocket notebook*)
110   So, uncle, there you are. Now, as to my promise:
it is, "Farewell, farewell, remember me."
I've sworn to do it.

HORATIO and MARCELLUS (*calling from offstage*)
My lord, my lord!
     Enter HORATIO *and* MARCELLUS.

MARCELLUS
                    Lord Hamlet!
HORATIO
                              Heavens secure him!
HAMLET
    So be it!
MARCELLUS
115   Illo, ho, ho, ho, my lord!
HAMLET
    Hillo, ho, ho, boy! Come, bird, come.*
MARCELLUS
    How is't, my noble lord?
HORATIO
                         What news, my lord?
HAMLET
    O, wonderful!
HORATIO
    Good my lord, tell it.
HAMLET
                    No, you will reveal it.
HORATIO
    Not I, my lord, by heaven.
MARCELLUS
120   Nor I, my lord.
HAMLET
    How say you then? Would heart of man once think it?
    But you'll be secret?
BOTH
                    Ay, by heaven, my lord.
HAMLET
    There's never a villain dwelling in all Denmark
    But he's an arrant knave.
HORATIO
125   There needs no ghost, my lord, come from the grave
    To tell us this.
HAMLET
                Why, right, you are in the right;
    And so, without more circumstance at all,
    I hold it fit that we shake hands and part:
    You, as your business and desire shall point you,

---

116 *Come, bird, cóme*   Hamlet answers Marcellus with the cry used by falconers to call their hawks.

MARCELLUS (*looking for Hamlet*)
Lord Hamlet!
HORATIO
Heaven keep him safe!
HAMLET
I hope it will!
MARCELLUS
115   Hey, hey, where are you, my lord?
HAMLET
Hey, hey you, boy! Come bird, come.
MARCELLUS
Are you all right, my noble lord?
HORATIO
What happened, my lord?
HAMLET
O, something remarkable!
HORATIO
My good lord, tell us about it.
HAMLET
No, you'll reveal the secret.
HORATIO
Not I, my lord, I swear by heaven.
MARCELLUS
120   Neither will I, my lord.
HAMLET
What can I tell you then? Did anyone ever think that it could be?
But will you keep it secret?
BOTH
Oh yes, we swear by heaven, my lord.
HAMLET
There isn't a villain living in all of Denmark
who isn't an absolute crook.
HORATIO
125   We don't need a ghost come from the grave, my lord,
to tell us this.
HAMLET
Of course, you're right.
And so, without any more fooling around at all,
I think it's right that we shake hands and depart.
You go wherever you have a mind or a need to go,

130 For every man hath business and desire
Such as it is, and for my own poor part,
Look you, I'll go pray.
HORATIO
These are but wild and whirling words, my lord.
HAMLET
I am sorry they offend you, heartily;
Yes, faith, heartily.
HORATIO
135   There's no offense, my lord.
HAMLET
Yes, by Saint Patrick,* but there is, Horatio,
And much offense too. Touching this vision here,
It is an honest ghost, that let me tell you.
For your desire to know what is between us,
140 O'ermaster't as you may. And now, good friends,
As you are friends, scholars, and soldiers,
Give me one poor request.
HORATIO
What is't, my lord? We will.
HAMLET
Never make known what you have seen tonight.
BOTH
My lord, we will not.
HAMLET
                    Nay, but swear't.
HORATIO
145   In faith,
My lord, not I.
MARCELLUS
                Nor I, my lord—in faith.
HAMLET
Upon my sword.
MARCELLUS
                We have sworn, my lord, already.
HAMLET
Indeed, upon my sword, indeed.
        GHOST *cries under the stage.*
GHOST
Swear.

---

136 *Saint Patrick*   supposed to be the keeper of Purgatory, from where
the Ghost has come. He was also the patron saint of confusion and mistakes.

130 since every man has something to do and something he needs,
whatever it is and as for little old me—
listen, I'll go pray.

HORATIO
These are nothing but crazy and confused words, my lord.

HAMLET
I'm sorry they insult you, really sorry.
Yes, by God, really.

HORATIO
135 There's no insult in them, my lord.

HAMLET
Yes, by St. Patrick, but there is, Horatio,
and a great insult too. As for this ghost here,
it is a reliable ghost, let me assure you of that.
As for your curiosity about what we said to each other,
140 control it as best you can. And now, good friends,
since you are my friends, and soldiers, and scholars,
grant me one small favor.

HORATIO
Whatever it is, my lord, we'll do it.

HAMLET
Never tell anyone what you've seen tonight.

BOTH
My lord, we will not.

HAMLET
No, you must swear it.

HORATIO
145 By my faith,
my lord, I won't.

MARCELLUS
Nor I, my lord—by my faith.

HAMLET (*holding up the hilt of his sword to form a cross*)
Swear upon my sword.

MARCELLUS
We've already sworn, my lord.

HAMLET
I want you actually to swear upon my sword—you must.

GHOST (*crying out fom under the stage*)
Swear.

HAMLET

150   Ha, ha, boy, say'st thou so? Art thou there, truepenny?
          Come on. You hear this fellow in the cellarage.
          Consent to swear.

HORATIO
                         Propose the oath, my lord.

HAMLET
          Never to speak of this that you have seen.
          Swear by my sword.

GHOST [*Beneath*]

155   Swear.

HAMLET
          Hic et ubique? Then we'll shift our ground;
          Come hither, gentlemen,
          And lay your hands again upon my sword.
          Swear by my sword

160   Never to speak of this that you have heard.

GHOST [*Beneath*]
          Swear by his sword.

HAMLET
          Well said, old mole! Canst work i' th' earth so fast?
          A worthy pioner! Once more remove, good friends.

HORATIO
          O day and night, but this is wondrous strange!

HAMLET

165   And therefore as a stranger give it welcome.
          There are more things in heaven and earth, Horatio,
          Than are dreamt of in your philosophy.
          But come:
          Here as before, never, so help you mercy,

170   How strange or odd so'er I bear myself
          (As I perchance hereafter shall think meet
          To put an antic disposition on),
          That you, at such times seeing me, never shall
          With arms encumb'red thus, or this headshake,

175   Or by pronouncing of some doubtful phrase,
          As "Well, well, we know," or "We could, an if we would,"

HAMLET
150   Aha, ha, old boy, you say so too? Are you there,
           you good old sport?
       Come on. You hear this guy in the basement:
       agree to swear.

HORATIO
       Tell us what to swear, my lord.

HAMLET
       That you will never talk about what you have seen here.
       Swear by my sword.

GHOST *(beneath the stage)*
155   Swear.

HAMLET
       Are you here and everywhere? Then we'll move.
       Come over here, gentlemen,
       and put your hands on my sword again.
       Swear by my sword
160   that you will never speak about what you have heard.

GHOST *(beneath the stage)*
       Swear by his sword.

HAMLET
       That's the ticket, old mole! Can you move around so fast
           underground?
       A great digger! Let's move once again, good friends.

HORATIO
       I swear by day and night that this is incredibly strange!

HAMLET
165   And therefore give it the courteous reception due a stranger.
       There are more things in heaven and earth, Horatio,
       than ordinary science can guess.
       But look:
       as I was saying before, never, so help you God,
170   no matter how strange or oddly I behave
       (since I may later think it proper
       to act in a grotesque manner),
       when you see me doing that, don't ever
       fold your arms this way or shake your head,
           (making appropriate gestures to accompany his speech)
175   or use some skeptical expression
       such as, "Well, well, we know what this is," or "We could explain,
           if we wanted to,"

Or "If we list to speak," or "There be, an if they might,"
Or such ambiguous giving out, to note
That you know aught of me—this do swear,
180   So grace and mercy at your most need help you.
GHOST [*Beneath*]
Swear.
            [*They swear.*]
HAMLET
Rest, rest, perturbèd spirit. So, gentlemen,
With all my love I do commend me to you,
And what so poor a man as Hamlet is
185   May do t' express his love and friending to you,
God willing, shall not lack. Let us go in together,
And still your fingers on your lips, I pray.
The time is out of joint. O cursèd spite,
That ever I was born to set it right!
190   Nay, come, let's go together.
            Exeunt.

[*Act II, Scene i: A room.*] *Enter old* POLONIUS, *with his man*
REYNALDO.

POLONIUS
Give him this money and these notes, Reynaldo.
REYNALDO
I will, my lord.
POLONIUS
You shall do marvell's wisely, good Reynaldo,
Before you visit him, to make inquire
Of his behavior.
REYNALDO
5   My lord, I did intend it.
POLONIUS
Marry, well said, very well said. Look you sir,
Inquire me first what Danskers are in Paris,
And how, and who, what means, and where they keep,
What company, at what expense; and finding

or "If we cared to talk," or "There are those who might,"
or by such indirect claims of knowledge give a sign
that you know what is up with me. Swear this,
180   as you hope to have grace and mercy from God when you most
need them.
GHOST *(beneath the stage)*
Swear.
    Horatio and Marcellus swear.
HAMLET *(to Ghost)*
Rest, rest, troubled spirit. *(To Horatio and Marcellus)*
So, gentlemen,
with all my love I wish you well,
and whatever a poor man like Hamlet
185   can do to show his love and friendship to you,
God willing, shall not go undone. Let's go inside together,
and keep quiet about this always, please.
The times are twisted and distorted. O what a dreadful fate,
that I was ever born to set them right!
190   No, don't stand on ceremony, come in together with me.
    Exit HAMLET, HORATIO, *and* MARCELLUS.

Act II, Scene i: A room in the castle. Enter POLONIUS, *with his servant,* REYNALDO.

POLONIUS
Give him this money and these messages, Reynaldo.
REYNALDO
I will, my lord.
POLONIUS
It will be very clever of you, good Reynaldo,
before you visit him, to make inquiries
about his behavior.
REYNALDO
5   My lord, that is what I planned to do.
POLONIUS
Indeed, that's right, very good. Listen here, sir,
first find out which Danes are in Paris,
and how they live there, who they are, what their income is, and
which places they frequent,
who their friends are, what they spend. And if you find out

10 By this encompassment and drift of question
That they do know my son, come you more nearer
Than your particular demands will touch it.
Take you as 'twere some distant knowledge of him,
As thus, "I know his father and his friends,
15 And in part him." Do you mark this, Reynaldo?

REYNALDO
Ay, very well, my lord.

POLONIUS
"And in part him, but," you may say, "not well,
But if't be he I mean, he's very wild,
Addicted so and so." And there put on him
20 What forgeries you please; marry, none so rank
As may dishonor him—take heed of that—
But, sir, such wanton, wild, and usual slips
As are companions noted and most known
To youth and liberty.

REYNALDO
                            As gaming, my lord.

POLONIUS
25 Ay, or drinking, fencing, swearing, quarreling,
Drabbing. You may go so far.

REYNALDO
My lord, that would dishonor him.

POLONIUS
Faith, no, as you may season it in the charge.
You must not put another scandal on him,
30 That he is open to incontinency.
That's not my meaning. But breathe his faults so quaintly
That they may seem the taints of liberty,
The flash and outbreak of a fiery mind,
A savageness in unreclaimèd blood,
Of general assault.

REYNALDO
35   But, my good lord——

10   in this roundabout way of talking and in the general drift of
      the conversation
that they know my son, become more intimate with them
than direct questioning would allow.
Pretend that you have some distant acquaintance with him;
for example, "I know his father and his friends,

15   and him a little bit." Do you understand this, Reynaldo?

REYNALDO
Yes, very well, my lord.

POLONIUS
"And him a little bit, but," you might say, "not very well,
but if he's the one I'm thinking of, he's very wild,
full of such and such bad habits." And at that point accuse him

20   of whatever invented faults you like: of course, none so bad
that they will disgrace him—take care in that—
but, sir, such unrestrained, wild, and normal faults
as are well known and observed to go along
with being young and free.

REYNALDO
Like gambling, my lord.

POLONIUS
25   Yes, or drinking, duelling, cursing, brawling,
whoring—you can go as far as that.

REYNALDO
My lord, that would disgrace him.

POLONIUS
Goodness, no, since you can qualify these things as you describe
      them.
You mustn't accuse him of another kind of disgrace,

30   that he is always licentious.
That's not what I mean. But describe his faults so delicately
that they look like sins which are the results of freedom,
the sudden energy of an active mind,
a wildness in the untamed blood
common to all young men.

REYNALDO
35   But, my good lord—

POLONIUS
Wherefore should you do this?
REYNALDO
                                    Ay, my lord,
I would know that.
POLONIUS
                              Marry, sir, here's my drift,
And I believe it is a fetch of warrant.
You laying these slight sullies on my son
40   As 'twere a thing a little soiled i' th' working,
Mark you,
Your party in converse, him you would sound,
Having ever seen in the prenominate crimes
The youth you breathe of guilty, be assured
45   He closes with you in this consequence:
"Good sir," or so, or "friend," or "gentleman"—
According to the phrase or the addition
Of man and country—
REYNALDO
                              Very good, my lord.
POLONIUS
And then, sir, does 'a this— 'a does—
50   What was I about to say? By the mass, I was about to say
something! Where did I leave?
REYNALDO
At "closes in the consequence," at "friend or so," and
"gentleman."
POLONIUS
At "closes in the consequence"—Ay, marry!
55   He closes thus: "I know the gentleman;
I saw him yesterday, or t'other day,
Or then, or then, with such or such, and, as you say,
There was 'a gaming, there o'ertook in's rouse,
There falling out at tennis"; or perchance,
60   "I saw him enter such a house of sale,"
Videlicet, a brothel, or so forth.
See you now—
Your bait of falsehood take this carp of truth,

POLONIUS
Why should you do this?
REYNALDO
Yes, my lord,
I want to know that.
POLONIUS
All right, sir, here's what I mean,
and I think it is a justifiable trick.
When you accuse my son of having these small blemishes
40   (in the same way that an article may become a little shopworn)—
listen closely—
the person you're talking to, the one you want information from,
if he at any time has seen the young man commit any of the
    aforementioned crimes
you say he's guilty of, you can be sure
45   that he will agree with you this way:
"Good sir," or something like that, or "friend," or "gentleman"—
according to the salutation or the title of address customary
for him and his country—
REYNALDO
Very good, my lord.
POLONIUS
And then, sir, he does this—he does—
50   What was I going to say? By God, I was going
    to say
something! Where did I stop?
REYNALDO
At "agrees with you this way," at "friend or something like
    that," and
"gentleman."
POLONIUS
At "agrees with you this way"—Oh, yes indeed!
55   He agrees with you this way: "I know the gentleman;
I saw him yesterday, or the other day,
or then, or then, with so and so. And just as you say,
there he was gambling, there he was drunk,
there he was quarreling over a tennis match," or perhaps,
60   "I saw him go into this house where it's for sale,"
namely, a house of prostitution, or so forth.
Now look—
with your bait of lies you've caught a fish of truth,

And thus do we of wisdom and of reach,
65   With windlasses and with assays of bias,
By indirections find directions out.
So, by my former lecture and advice,
Shall you my son. You have me, have you not?

REYNALDO
My lord, I have.

POLONIUS
God bye ye, fare ye well.

REYNALDO
70   Good my lord.

POLONIUS
Observe his inclination in yourself.

REYNALDO
I shall, my lord.

POLONIUS
And let him ply his music.

REYNALDO
Well, my lord.

POLONIUS
Farewell.
          Exit REYNALDO. *Enter* OPHELIA.
          How now, Ophelia, what's the matter?

OPHELIA
75   O my lord, my lord, I have been so affrighted!

POLONIUS
With what, i' th' name of God?

OPHELIA
My lord, as I was sewing in my closet,
Lord Hamlet, with his doublet all unbraced,
No hat upon his head, his stockings fouled,
80   Ungartered, and down-gyvèd to his ankle,
Pale as his shirt, his knees knocking each other,
And with a look so piteous in purport,
As if he had been loosèd out of hell
To speak of horrors—he comes before me.

65 and that's the way those of us who have wisdom and ability
use roundabout methods and oblique approaches,
by devious methods we find out the way things are going,
and if you take the advice and warning I have just given you,
so shall you, my son. You understand me, don't you?

REYNALDO
My lord, I do.

POLONIUS
God be with you, farewell.

REYNALDO
70 Thank you, my good lord.

POLONIUS
Use yourself as an example to judge what his interests are.

REYNALDO
I shall, my lord.

POLONIUS
And let him go on with what he's doing.

REYNALDO
Very good, my lord.

POLONIUS
Goodbye.
        Exit REYNALDO.
        Enter OPHELIA.
Hello, Ophelia, what's the matter?

OPHELIA
75 O my lord, my lord, I have been so frightened!

POLONIUS
By what, in God's name?

OPHELIA
My lord, as I was sewing in my room,
Lord Hamlet, with his jacket entirely open;
without a hat; his stockings dirty,
80 without garters, and hanging around his ankles like fetters;
looking as pale as his white shirt; with his knees knocking
        against each other;
and with such a pitiful expression on his face,
as if he had been turned out of hell
to tell of its torments—he comes and stands in front of me.

POLONIUS
Mad for thy love?
OPHELIA
85   My lord, I do not know,
But truly I do fear it.
POLONIUS
                        What said he?
OPHELIA
He took me by the wrist and held me hard;
Then goes he to the length of all his arm,
And with his other hand thus o'er his brow
90   He falls to such perusal of my face
As 'a would draw it. Long stayed he so.
At last, a little shaking of mine arm,
And thrice his head thus waving up and down,
He raised a sigh so piteous and profound
95   As it did seem to shatter all his bulk
And end his being. That done, he lets me go,
And, with his head over his shoulder turned,
He seemed to find his way without his eyes,
For out o' doors he went without their helps,
100   And to the last bended their light on me.
POLONIUS
Come, go with me. I will go seek the King.
This is the very ecstasy of love,
Whose violent property fordoes itself
And leads the will to desperate undertakings
105   As oft as any passions under heaven
That does afflict our natures. I am sorry.
What, have you given him any hard words of late?
OPHELIA
No, my good lord; but as you did command,
I did repel his letters and denied
His access to me.
POLONIUS
110   That hath made him mad.
I am sorry that with better heed and judgment
I had not quoted him. I feared he did but trifle
And meant to wrack thee; but beshrew my jealousy.

POLONIUS
Insane with love for you?

OPHELIA
85   My lord, I don't know,
but I'm really afraid that's it.

POLONIUS
What did he say?

OPHELIA
He grabbed my wrist and held it hard.
Then he fixed me at arm's length;
and shading his brow with his other hand this way,
90   he began to stare at my face
as if he were going to draw it. He stayed in that position a
long time.
Finally, he shook my arm a little;
and nodding his head this way three times,
he let out such a pathetic and deep sigh
95   that it seemed to shatter his whole body,
as if he were dying. When that was over, he let me go;
and turning his head over his shoulder toward me as he walked,
he seemed to find his way out of the room without looking,
for he went through the door without the help of his eyes.
100 And to the last moment he kept his eyes on me.

POLONIUS
Come, come along with me. I will look for the King.
This is the true madness of love,
whose violent nature destroys itself
and leads the mind to desperate projects.
105 Love does this as often as any of those earthly passions
that afflict our natures. I am sorry.
What, have you spoken harshly to him lately?

OPHELIA
No, my good lord. I only did what you ordered:
I refused to receive his letters and did not let
him see me.

POLONIUS
110 That has made him insane.
I am sorry that I did not observe him with closer attention and
better judgment.
I was afraid he was only flirting
and was out to seduce you, but curse my suspicions.

By heaven, it is as proper to our age
115 To cast beyond ourselves in our opinions
As it is common for the younger sort
To lack discretion. Come, go we to the King.
This must be known, which, being kept close, might move
More grief to hide than hate to utter love.
120 Come.
                Exeunt.

[*Scene ii: The castle.*] *Flourish. Enter* KING *and* QUEEN, ROSEN-
CRANTZ, *and* GUILDENSTERN [*with others*].

KING
Welcome, dear Rosencrantz and Guildenstern.
Moreover that we much did long to see you,
The need we have to use you did provoke
Our hasty sending. Something have you heard
5   Of Hamlet's transformation: so call it,
Sith nor th' exterior nor the inward man
Resembles that it was. What it should be,
More than his father's death, that thus hath put him
So much from th' understanding of himself,
10   I cannot dream of. I entreat you both
That, being of so young days brought up with him,
And sith so neighbored to his youth and havior,
That you vouchsafe your rest here in our court
Some little time, so by your companies
15   To draw him on to pleasures, and to gather
So much as from occasion you may glean,
Whether aught to us unknown afflicts him thus,
That opened lies within our remedy.
QUEEN
Good gentlemen, he hath much talked of you,
20   And sure I am, two men there is not living
To whom he more adheres. If it will please you
To show us so much gentry and good will
As to expend your time with us awhile
For the supply and profit of our hope,

By heaven, it is as natural for men of my age
115   to be excessively cautious in our opinions
as it is common for younger men
to be reckless. Come, let's go to the King.
This must be made known. If it were kept secret it might cause
more trouble than the displeasure we shall incur by revealing
        that Hamlet loves you.
120   Come on.
            Exit POLONIUS *and* OPHELIA.

Act II, Scene ii: The castle. A flourish of trumpets. Enter KING,
QUEEN, ROSENCRANTZ, GUILDERSTERN, *and other courtiers.*

KING
Welcome, my dear Rosencrantz and Guildenstern.
In addition to wanting very much to see you for your own sake,
the need I have to put you to work caused
me to send for you so suddenly. You have heard something
5   about Hamlet's complete change. It should be called that,
since neither the outer nor the inner man
is like what it was before. What it can be
besides his father's death that has in this way caused him
so much to lose his self control,
10   I cannot imagine. I ask you both,
you who were brought up with him from early youth,
and are therefore so familiar with his youthful behavior,
to agree to remain here in my court
for a while. And thus by your companionship
15   lead him to enjoy himself, and try to learn
as much as you can from what happens
whether there is anything unknown to me that makes him ill
        in this way,
which if it is revealed, I may cure.
    QUEEN
Good gentlemen, he has spoken a great deal about you,
20   and I'm sure there are not two other men living
to whom he is more attached. If it will please you
to be courteous and friendly enough
to spend your time here with us a while
to support and advance our plan,

25   Your visitation shall receive such thanks
      As fits a king's remembrance.
ROSENCRANTZ
                              Both your Majesties
      Might, by the sovereign power you have of us,
      Put your dread pleasures more into command
      Than to entreaty.
GUILDENSTERN
                              But we both obey,
30   And here give up ourselves in the full bent
      To lay our service freely at your feet,
      To be commanded.
KING
      Thanks, Rosencrantz and gentle Guildenstern.
QUEEN
      Thanks, Guildenstern and gentle Rosencrantz.
35   And I beseech you instantly to visit
      My too much changèd son. Go, some of you,
      And bring these gentlemen where Hamlet is.
GUILDENSTERN
      Heavens make our presence and our practices
      Pleasant and helpful to him!
QUEEN
                              Ay, amen!
      Exeunt ROSENCRANTZ *and* GUILDENSTERN [*with some At-
      tendants*]. *Enter* POLONIUS.
POLONIUS
40   Th' ambassadors from Norway, my good lord,
      Are joyfully returned.
KING
      Thou still hast been the father of good news.
POLONIUS
      Have I, my lord? Assure you, my good liege,
      I hold my duty, as I hold my soul,
45   Both to my God and to my gracious king;
      And I do think, or else this brain of mine
      Hunts not the trail of policy so sure
      As it hath used to do, that I have found
      The very cause of Hamlet's lunacy.

25   your visit shall be rewarded with gratitude
worthy of a king.
ROSENCRANTZ
Both your highnesses
could use the supreme power you have over us
to convert your dreaded wishes into a command
rather than a request.
GUILDENSTERN
But we will both obey you,
30   and here surrender ourselves entirely
and put ourselves freely at your disposal
to receive orders.
KING
Thank you, Rosencrantz and courteous Guildenstern.
QUEEN
Thank you, Guildenstern and courteous Rosencrantz.
35   And I urge you to go right away and see
my far too completely transformed son. (*To attendants*) Go,
some of you here,
and bring these gentlemen to Hamlet.
GUILDENSTERN
May heaven make our company and our efforts
pleasant and helpful to him!
QUEEN
Oh yes, I hope so!
      Exit ROSENCRANTZ *and* GUILDENSTERN *with some*
         attendants.
      Enter POLONIUS.
POLONIUS
40   The ambassadors from Norway, my good lord,
have returned with good news.
KING
You have always been the bearer of good news.
POLONIUS
Have I, my lord? I assure you, my dear sovereign,
I consider it my duty as well as my spiritual responsibility
45   to serve both my God and my gracious king.
And I think, or else I am
not so good at managing affairs
as I once was, that I have found
the true cause of Hamlet's insanity.

KING

50   O, speak of that! That do I long to hear.

POLONIUS

Give first admittance to th' ambassadors.

My news shall be the fruit to that great feast.

KING

Thyself do grace to them and bring them in.

Exit POLONIUS.

He tells me, my dear Gertrude, he hath found

55   The head and source of all your son's distemper.

QUEEN

I doubt it is no other but the main,

His father's death and our o'erhasty marriage.

KING

Well, we shall sift him.

Enter POLONIUS, VOLTEMAND, *and* CORNELIUS.

Welcome, my good friends.

Say, Voltemand, what from our brother Norway?

VOLTEMAND

60   Most fair return of greetings and desires.

Upon our first, he sent out to suppress

His nephew's levies, which to him appeared

To be a preparation 'gainst the Polack;

But better looked into, he truly found

65   It was against your Highness, whereat grieved,

That so his sickness, age, and impotence

Was falsely borne in hand, sends out arrests

On Fortinbras; which he, in brief, obeys,

Receives rebuke from Norway, and in fine,

70   Makes vow before his uncle never more

To give th' assay of arms against your Majesty.

Whereon old Norway, overcome with joy,

Gives him threescore thousand crowns* in annual fee

And his commission to employ those soldiers,

75   So levied as before, against the Polack,

With an entreaty, herein further shown,

[*Gives a paper.*]

That it might please you to give quiet pass

---

73 *crowns* gold or silver coins of the time. If we consider its modern
equivalent to be five English shillings, sixty thousand crowns would be about

KING

50   O, tell me about it! That's what I want to know.

POLONIUS

  Let the ambassadors be admitted first.
  My news shall be like the dessert to that great feast.

KING

  Welcome them yourself with proper courtesies, and bring
     them in.
     Exit POLONIUS.
  He tells me, my dear Gertrude, that he's found
55   the root cause and source of all your son's mental disturbance.

QUEEN

  I suspect it is none other than the main cause,
  his father's death and our far too sudden marriage.

KING

  Well, we shall question him closely.
     Enter POLONIUS, VOLTEMAND, *and* CORNELIUS.
  Welcome, my good friends.
  Tell us, Voltemand, what is the news from our ally, the king of
     Norway?

VOLTEMAND

60   He returns your greetings and good wishes with great courtesy.
  After our first conference with him, he ordered
  his nephew's recruitments ended. They had looked to him
  like preparations to fight against the Poles;
  but investigated more carefully, they were, he found,
65   directed against your Highness. Offended
  that his sickness, old age, and physical weakness
  had caused him to be taken such advantage of, he orders
  Fortinbras to stop his activities. Fortinbras quickly obeys,
  accepts the king of Norway's censure, and in the end
70   swears in front of his uncle that he will never again
  try to fight against your Majesty.
  The old king is so happy with this
  that he gives him sixty thousand crowns as an annual gift
  and orders him to use the soldiers
75   he has already raised against the Poles,
  sending you a request which is described further here (*handing*
     Claudius a paper).
  He asks you to allow them safe-conduct

$40,000. But the sum Fortinbras receives is clearly much larger than that in terms of Elizabethan purchasing power.

Through your dominions for this enterprise,
On such regards of safety and allowance
As therein are set down.

KING

80   It likes us well;
And at our more considered time we'll read,
Answer, and think upon this business.
Meantime, we thank you for your well-took labor.
Go to your rest; at night we'll feast together.
Most welcome home!

            Exeunt AMBASSADORS.

POLONIUS

85   This business is well ended.
My liege and madam, to expostulate
What majesty should be, what duty is,
Why day is day, night night, and time is time,
Were nothing but to waste night, day, and time.

90   Therefore, since brevity is the soul of wit,
And tediousness the limbs and outward flourishes,
I will be brief. Your noble son is mad.
Mad call I it, for, to define true madness,
What is't but to be nothing else but mad?
But let that go.

QUEEN

95   More matter, with less art.

POLONIUS

Madam, I swear I use no art at all.
That he's mad; 'tis true: 'tis true 'tis pity,
And pity 'tis 'tis true—a foolish figure.
But farewell it, for I will use no art.

100   Mad let us grant him then; and now remains
That we find out the cause of this effect,
Or rather say, the cause of this defect,
For this effect defective comes by cause.
Thus it remains, and the remainder thus.

105   Perpend.
I have a daughter: have, while she is mine,
Who in her duty and obedience, mark,

through your kingdom in this expedition,
according to the safeguards and provisions
that are set down there.

KING

80   This pleases me very much.
When I have time to consider it carefully, I'll read it,
think about this business, and answer the request.
In the meantime, I thank you for your efficient work.
Go and enjoy your rest; tonight we'll celebrate together.
I am glad to welcome you home!
  Exit VOLTEMAND *and* CORNELIUS.

POLONIUS

85   This matter is neatly concluded.
My sovereign and madam, to argue about
what kingship should be, what duty is,
why day is day, night is night, and time is time—
that would be nothing but a waste of night, day, and time.
90   Therefore, since to be brief is the essence of wisdom,
and to be long-winded the external and merely decorative
  part of it,
I will be brief. Your noble son is insane.
Insane is what I call it; for to describe actual insanity,
what is it but to be nothing but insane?
But forget about that.

QUEEN

95   Give us more facts and less verbal cleverness.

POLONIUS

Madam, I swear I am not being clever at all.
That he's insane, it's true. It can truly be called a shame,
and it's a shame it's true—a foolish figure of speech.
But goodbye to it, for I won't play with words any more.
100   Let's agree that he's insane. What is left
is for us to find out the cause of this effect,
or instead let us say, the cause of this defect;
for this result is not merely accidental but has a cause.
Therefore, this is what's left to say, and what's left is
  therefore this.
105   Consider carefully.
I have a daughter. That is, I have her while she is unmarried,
and she out of her duty and obedience to me—note carefully—

Hath given me this. Now gather, and surmise.
    [Reads the letter].
"To the celestial, and my soul's idol, the most beautified
110   Ophelia"—
That's an ill phrase, a vile phrase; "beautified" is a vile phrase.
But you shall hear. Thus:
"In her excellent white bosom, these, &c."

QUEEN
Came this from Hamlet to her?

POLONIUS
115   Good madam, stay awhile. I will be faithful.
      "Doubt thou the stars are fire,
        Doubt that the sun doth move;
     Doubt truth to be a liar,
        But never doubt I love.
120   O dear Ophelia, I am ill at these numbers. I have not art to
reckon my groans; but that I love thee best, O most best, believe
it. Adieu.
     Thine evermore, most dear lady, whilst this machine is to him,
     HAMLET."
125   This in obedience hath my daughter shown me,
And more above hath his solicitings,
As they fell out by time, by means, and place,
All given to mine ear.

KING
                  But how hath she
Received his love?

POLONIUS
                  What do you think of me?
KING
130   As of a man faithful and honorable.

POLONIUS
I would fain prove so. But what might you think,
When I had seen this hot love on the wing
(As I perceived it, I must tell you that,
Before my daughter told me), what might you,
135   Or my dear Majesty your Queen here, think,

has given me this (*holding up a letter*). Now listen, and guess.
(*Reading the letter*) "To the heavenly, the idol my soul
    worships, the most beautified
110   Ophelia"—
That's an awkward word, an ugly word; "beautified" is an ugly
    word.
(*The King and Queen look impatient.*) But I will read the rest
    to you. Here it is:
"In her magnificent white bosom, these, and so on."

QUEEN
And is this what Hamlet sent to her?

POLONIUS
115   Good madam, wait a bit. I'll read it exactly as it is.
"Doubt that the stars are made of fire,
doubt that the sun moves in the sky of blue,
suspect truth itself and call it a liar,
but never doubt that I love you.
120   O my dear Ophelia, I am a terrible poet. I have no talent
for summing up my pains in poetry; but please believe, dearest
    one, that I love you more than anyone else.
Goodbye.
Yours forever, dearest lady, while I still possess this bodily
    frame,
HAMLET."
125   My daughter in obedience has shown this to me;
and, moreover, his other attentions to her,
when, how, and where they happened—
she has told me all.

KING
But how has she
reacted to his love?

POLONIUS
What do you think I am?

KING
130   A faithful and honorable servant.

POLONIUS
I would gladly prove it. But what would you think,
if when I had seen this passionate love in operation
(as I noticed it, I must tell you,
before my daughter told me), what would you think,
135   or my dear Majesty, your Queen here,

If I had played the desk or table book,
Or given my heart a winking, mute and dumb,
Or looked upon this love with idle sight?
What might you think? No, I went round to work
140   And my young mistress thus I did bespeak:
"Lord Hamlet is a prince, out of thy star.
This must not be." And then I prescripts gave her,
That she should lock herself from his resort,
Admit no messengers, receive no tokens.
145   Which done, she took the fruits of my advice,
And he, repellèd, a short tale to make,
Fell into a sadness, then into a fast,
Thence to a watch, thence into a weakness,
Thence to a lightness, and, by this declension,
150   Into the madness wherein now he raves,
And all we mourn for.

KING
                                        Do you think 'tis this?
QUEEN
    It may be, very like.
POLONIUS
    Hath there been such a time, I would fain know that,
    That I have positively said " 'Tis so,"
    When it proved otherwise?
KING
155   Not that I know.
POLONIUS [*pointing to his head and shoulder*]
    Take this from this, if this be otherwise.
    If circumstances lead me, I will find
    Where truth is hid, though it were hid indeed
    Within the center.
KING
                                        How may we try it further?
POLONIUS
160   You know sometimes he walks four hours together
    Here in the lobby.
QUEEN
                                        So he does indeed.

if I had remained silent like a desk or a closed notebook,
or given my heart a signal to remain silent,
or seen this love and pretended not to understand?
What would you think of me? No, I went right to work,
140   and I spoke to my young lady thus:
"Lord Hamlet is a prince, far above you in rank.
This love must not be." And then I gave her instructions
that she should keep herself in her room away from his company,
let in no messengers, and accept no presents from him.
145   When she had heard me, she carried out my orders.
And, to keep the story short, he was rejected
and became depressed, then stopped eating,
then couldn't sleep, then became weak,
and then lightheaded. And by this kind of a decline,
150   he became insane the way he is now,
so that we all grieve for him.

KING (*to the Queen*)
Do you think this is the way it happened?

QUEEN
It sounds very plausible.

POLONIUS
I would like to know, has there ever been a time
when I have said with confidence, "This is so,"
and it proved not to be so?

KING
155   Not that I know.

POLONIUS (*pointing to his head and shoulder*)
Cut this off from this, if things are different.
If there are clues to follow, I will find
where truth is hidden, even if it's hidden right
in the center of the earth.

KING
How can we test this further?

POLONIUS
160   You know that sometimes he walks four hours at a time
here in the hall.

QUEEN
Yes, he does that.

POLONIUS

At such a time I'll loose my daughter to him.
Be you and I behind an arras* then.
Mark the encounter. If he love her not,
165 And be not from his reason fall'n thereon,
Let me be no assistant for a state
But keep a farm and carters.

KING

We will try it.

Enter HAMLET *reading on a book.*

QUEEN

But look where sadly the poor wretch comes reading.

POLONIUS

Away, I do beseech you both, away.

Exit KING *and* QUEEN.

170 I'll board him presently. O, give me leave.
How does my good Lord Hamlet?

HAMLET

Well, God-a-mercy.

POLONIUS

Do you know me, my lord?

HAMLET

Excellent, excellent well. You are a fishmonger.

POLONIUS

175 Not I, my lord.

HAMLET

Then I would you were so honest a man.

POLONIUS

Honest, my lord?

HAMLET

Ay, sir. To be honest, as this world goes, is to be one man picked
out of ten thousand.

POLONIUS

That's very true, my lord.

180

HAMLET

For if the sun breed maggots in a dead dog, being a God kissing
carrion —— Have you a daughter?

POLONIUS

I have, my lord.

---

163 *arras* a hanging placed around the walls of a room to keep out
dampness and cold. It was often far enough from the wall so that a person
could be concealed behind it.

POLONIUS
On such an occasion, I'll set my daughter free to meet him.
You and I will be behind a wall-hanging then.
Watch their meeting closely. If he doesn't love her
165   and hasn't gone crazy because of it,
you can fire me as court counsellor,
and I'll run a farm and a horse and wagon.
KING
I'll put it to the test.
        Enter HAMLET, *reading a book.*
QUEEN
But look over there, here comes the poor fellow seriously
reading a book.
POLONIUS
Go away, I urge both of you, go.
        Exit KING *and* QUEEN.
170   (*To the audience*) I'll approach him, right now. (*To Hamlet*) O,
I beg your pardon.
How are you, my good Lord Hamlet?
HAMLET
I'm all right, thank God.
POLONIUS
Do you know who I am, my lord?
HAMLET
Certainly, certainly. You are a fish seller.
POLONIUS
175   Not I, my lord.
HAMLET
Then I wish you were as honest as one.
POLONIUS
Honest, my lord?
HAMLET
Yes sir. To be honest in this kind of world is to be one man
out of ten thousand.
POLONIUS
180   That's very true, my lord.
HAMLET
Since if the heat of the sun breeds maggots in a dead dog, the
sun is a god who kisses
dead flesh—Do you have a daughter?
POLONIUS
I have, my lord.

HAMLET

185   Let her not walk i' th' sun.* Conception is a blessing, but as
your daughter may conceive, friend, look to't.

POLONIUS [*aside*]

How say you by that? Still harping on my daughter. Yet he
knew me not at first. 'A said I was a fishmonger. 'A is far gone,
far gone. And truly in my youth I suffered much extremity for
love, very near this. I'll speak to him again.—What do you read,
190   my lord?

HAMLET

Words, words, words.

POLONIUS

What is the matter, my lord?

HAMLET

Between who?*

POLONIUS

I mean the matter that you read, my lord.

HAMLET

195   Slanders, sir; for the satirical rogue says here that old men have
gray beards, that their faces are wrinkled, their eyes purging
thick amber and plumtree gum, and that they have a plentiful
lack of wit, together with most weak hams. All which, sir, though
I most powerfully and potently believe, yet I hold it not honesty
200   to have it thus set down; for you yourself, sir, should be old as
I am if, like a crab, you could go backward.

POLONIUS [*aside*]

Though this be madness, yet there is method in't. Will you walk
out of the air, my lord?

HAMLET

Into my grave.

---

184 *sun*   that is, in the sunshine of his sexual attentions, with a pun on
"son." In what follows, Hamlet is also punning on the word "conception,"
which means understanding, and conceiving a child.

HAMLET
Don't let her walk in the sun. Conceiving is a good thing, but
185   your daughter may "conceive" in a very different way. My friend,
take care.

POLONIUS (*to the audience*)
What does he mean by that? Still obsessed with my daughter.
Yet he
didn't know who I was at first. He said I was a fish seller. He is
far gone,
far gone. And certainly when I was young I was driven crazy by
love, very much like this. I'll speak to him again.—What are
you reading,
190   my lord?

HAMLET
Words, words, words.

POLONIUS
What is the matter, my lord?

HAMLET
Is there something the matter?

POLONIUS
I mean, what is your reading matter?

HAMLET
195   Lies, sir; for this mocking rascal says here that old men have
gray beards, that their faces are wrinkled, that their eyes
discharge
thick liquid and sticky gum, and that they have terrifically
empty heads; and to add to all that, very skinny thighs. All of
this, sir,
I believe is absolutely and inescapably true, but I don't consider
it decent
200   to write it out like this. After all, you yourself, sir, would be
as old as
I am if you could age backwards, like a crab.

POLONIUS (*to the audience*)
Even though this is crazy yet it has a point. Would you care to
come
indoors, my lord?

HAMLET
Into my grave.

---

193 *Between who?* Hamlet pretends to misunderstand "matter," as if
it meant the basis of a dispute or quarrel.

POLONIUS

205   Indeed, that's out of the air. [*Aside*] How pregnant sometimes
his replies are! A happiness that often madness hits on, which
reason and sanity could not so prosperously be delivered of. I
will leave him and suddenly contrive the means of meeting between him and my daughter.—My lord, I will take my leave

210   of you.

HAMLET

You cannot take from me anything that I will more willingly
part withal—except my life, except my life, except my life.
            Enter GUILDENSTERN *and* ROSENCRANTZ.

POLONIUS

Fare you well, my lord.

HAMLET

These tedious old fools!

POLONIUS

215   You go to seek the Lord Hamlet? There he is.

ROSENCRANTZ

To Polonius

God save you, sir!
            Exit POLONIUS.

GUILDENSTERN

My honored lord!

ROSENCRANTZ

My most dear lord!

HAMLET

My excellent good friends! How dost thou, Guildenstern? Ah,

220   Rosencrantz! Good lads, how do you both?

ROSENCRANTZ

As the indifferent children of the earth.

GUILDENSTERN

Happy in that we are not overhappy.
On Fortune's cap we are not the very button.

HAMLET

Nor the soles of her shoe?

ROSENCRANTZ

225   Neither, my lord.

HAMLET

Then you live about her waist, or in the middle of her favors?

POLONIUS
205   Oh yes, that is indoors. (*To the audience*) How full of meaning
his answers sometimes are. There is an aptness of expression
    that insane persons often come up with, which
sane and reasonable people can't invent so successfully. I
will leave him and immediately find a way of arranging a
    meeting
between him and my daughter.—My lord, I will take my leave
210   of you.
HAMLET
You can't take anything else from me that I will give up more
    willingly—
except for my life, except for my life, except for my life.
        Enter GUILDENSTERN *and* ROSENCRANTZ.
POLONIUS
Farewell, my lord (*moving away from Hamlet*).
HAMLET
These boring old fools!
POLONIUS (*to Rosencrantz and Guildenstern*)
215   Are you looking for Lord Hamlet? There he is.
ROSENCRANTZ (*to Polonius*)
Thank you very much, sir!
        Exit POLONIUS.
GUILDENSTERN
My honored lord!
ROSENCRANTZ
My dearest lord!
HAMLET
My dear good friends! How are you, Guildenstern? Oh,
220   Rosencrantz! Good old boys, how are you both?
ROSENCRANTZ
Neither better nor worse than anyone else.
GUILDENSTERN
We're happy because we haven't been too lucky.
We're not the feather in Fortune's cap.
HAMLET
But you're not under her feet?
ROSENCRANTZ
225   No, not that bad, my lord.
HAMLET
Then you live around her stomach, or right in the middle of her
    lucky lap?

GUILDENSTERN
Faith, her privates we.

HAMLET
In the secret parts of Fortune? O, most true!
She is a strumpet. What news?

ROSENCRANTZ
230   None, my lord, but that the world's grown honest.

HAMLET
Then is doomsday near. But your news is not true. Let me question more in particular. What have you, my good friends, deserved at the hands of Fortune that she sends you to prison hither?

GUILDENSTERN
235   Prison, my lord?

HAMLET
Denmark's a prison.

ROSENCRANTZ
Then is the world one.

HAMLET
A goodly one, in which there are many confines, wards, and dungeons, Denmark being one o' th' worst.

ROSENCRANTZ
240   We think not so, my lord.

HAMLET
Why, then 'tis none to you, for there is nothing either good or bad but thinking makes it so. To me it is a prison.

ROSENCRANTZ
Why then your ambition makes it one. 'Tis too narrow for your mind.

HAMLET
245   O God, I could be bounded in a nutshell and count myself a king of infinite space, were it not that I have bad dreams.

GUILDENSTERN
Which dreams indeed are ambition, for the very substance of the ambitious is merely the shadow of a dream.

HAMLET
A dream itself is but a shadow.

GUILDENSTERN
By God, we're in her private parts, we're her intimate friends.

HAMLET
In the private parts of Fortune? O, how true!
She's a whore. What else is new?

ROSENCRANTZ
230   Nothing, my lord, except that the world's turned honest.

HAMLET
Then the end of the world is near. But your report is not true. Let me ask
you more specific questions. What have you, my good friends,
done to Fortune that she sends you here to prison?

GUILDENSTERN
235   Prison, my lord?

HAMLET
Denmark's a prison.

ROSENCRANTZ
Then the whole world is one.

HAMLET
A roomy one, in which there are many detention areas, cells, and
jails, Denmark being one of the worst.

ROSENCRANTZ
240   We don't think so, my lord.

HAMLET
Why, then, as far as you're concerned, it isn't, since nothing is either good or
bad unless you think it is. To me it is a prison.

ROSENCRANTZ
Why, then, your ambition makes it one to you. It's too small for your
desires.

HAMLET
245   O, God, I could live in a nutshell and think of myself as a
king of infinite spaces, except that I am troubled by bad dreams.

GUILDENSTERN
Those dreams are in fact ambition, since the reality itself that
ambitious people pursue is nothing but a phantom out of their
dreams.

HAMLET
A dream itself is nothing but a phantom.

ROSENCRANTZ
250   Truly, and I hold ambition of so airy and light a quality that it
is but a shadow's shadow.

HAMLET
Then are our beggars bodies, and our monarchs and outstretched
heroes the beggars' shadows. Shall we to th' court? For, by my
fay, I cannot reason.

BOTH
255   We'll wait upon you.

HAMLET
No such matter. I will not sort you with the rest of my servants,
for, to speak to you like an honest man, I am most dreadfully
attended. But in the beaten way of friendship, what make you at
Elsinore?

ROSENCRANTZ
260   To visit you, my lord; no other occasion.

HAMLET
Beggar that I am, I am even poor in thanks, but I thank you;
and sure, dear friends, my thanks are too dear a halfpenny.
Were you not sent for? Is it your own inclining? Is it a free visitation? Come, come, deal justly with me. Come, come; nay, speak.

GUILDENSTERN
265   What should we say, my lord?

HAMLET
Why anything—but to th' purpose. You were sent for, and there
is a kind of confession in your looks, which your modesties have
not craft enough to color. I know the good King and Queen
have sent for you.

ROSENCRANTZ
270   To what end, my lord?

ROSENCRANTZ

250   Right, and I say that ambition is so light and insubstantial a
            thing that it
        is nothing but a phantom of a phantom.

HAMLET

        If that's the case, then only tramps have actual bodies, and kings
            and heroes who seek glory
        are merely shadows of the tramps. Shall we go in to the court?
            For, by
        God, I'm no good at arguing.

BOTH

255   We'll accompany you.

HAMLET

        I won't hear of it. I won't put you in a class with the rest of
            my servants;
        for to tell you the truth, I am served badly.
        But to speak to you as old friends, what are you doing here in
            Elsinore?

ROSENCRANTZ

260   We've come to visit you, my lord; we have no other purpose.

HAMLET

        I am so poor that I don't even have thanks to reward you with,
            but I do thank you.
        And you can be certain, old chums, that my thanks aren't worth
            a nickel.
        Weren't you asked to come? Is it your own inclination that
            brought you here? Did you come on your own?
        Come on, come on, be straight with me. Come on, come on;
            now look, tell me.

GUILDENSTERN

265   What do you want us to say, my lord?

HAMLET

        Whatever you like—as long as it's the truth. You were sent for,
            and you
        give yourselves away by your looks, which your protests
        aren't clever enough to hide. I know that the good King and
            Queen
        have asked you to come.

ROSENCRANTZ

270   What for, my lord?

HAMLET

That you must teach me. But let me conjure you by the rights
of our fellowship, by the consonancy of our youth, by the obligation of our ever-preserved love, and by what more dear a better
proposer can charge you withal, be even and direct with me,
275   whether you were sent for or no.

ROSENCRANTZ [*Aside to Guildenstern*]

What say you?

HAMLET [*aside*]

Nay then, I have an eye of you.—If you love me, hold not off.

GUILDENSTERN

My lord, we were sent for.

HAMLET

I will tell you why; so shall my anticipation prevent your dis-
280   covery, and your secrecy to the King and Queen molt no feather.
I have of late, but wherefore I know not, lost all my mirth,
forgone all custom of exercises; and indeed, it goes so heavily
with my disposition that this goodly frame, the earth, seems to
me a sterile promontory; this most excellent canopy, the air,
285   look you, this brave o'erhanging firmament, this majestical roof
fretted with golden fire: why, it appeareth nothing to me but a
foul and pestilent congregation of vapors. What a piece of work
is a man, how noble in reason, how infinite in faculties, in form
and moving how express and admirable, in action how like an
290   angel, in apprehension how like a god: the beauty of the world,
the paragon of animals; and yet to me, what is this quintessence
of dust? Man delights not me; nor woman neither, though by
your smiling you seem to say so.

ROSENCRANTZ

My lord, there was no such stuff in my thoughts.

HAMLET
I want you to tell me that. But let me ask you, for
old time's sake, because we are all young, and for the sake
of the responsibility we have toward each other as old friends,
   and for whatever else may be important that a better
talker could urge you with, level with me
275   and tell me whether or not you were sent for.

ROSENCRANTZ (*privately to Guildenstern*)
What do you think we should tell him?

HAMLET (*to the audience*)
All right, then, I know what you're up to.—If you're my friends,
don't put me on.

GUILDENSTERN
My lord, we were sent for.

HAMLET
I'll tell you why; that way my guessing your secret shall keep you
280   from revealing it, and your promise to the King and Queen shall
   not be broken in the least.
I have lately, although I don't know why, lost my sense of humor
and given up all my usual activities. And the truth is that I am so
downcast that this beautiful structure, the earth, looks like
a barren cliff of land; this magnificent tent, the air above—
285   look at it, this splendid heaven hanging over us, this awe-
   inspiring roof
adorned with the golden fire of the sun—why the whole thing
   looks to me like nothing but a
dirty and poisonous collection of gases. What a masterpiece
is a man, so noble in his power of reason, so unlimited in his
   other powers, in his shape
and his movements so admirably well-framed, so angelic in his
   actions,
290   so god-like in his understanding. Man is the most beautiful
   creature in the world,
the noblest of the animal creation; and yet to me, what is he
   except the concentrated essence
of mere dirt? Man gives me no pleasure; nor does woman,
   although
your grins seem to hint at something off-color like that.

ROSENCRANTZ
My lord, I was thinking no such thing.

HAMLET
295   Why did ye laugh then, when I said "Man delights not me"?

ROSENCRANTZ
To think, my lord, if you delight not in man, what lenten* entertainment the players shall receive from you. We coted them on the way, and hither are they coming to offer you service.

HAMLET
He that plays the king shall be welcome; his Majesty shall
300   have tribute of me; the adventurous knight shall use his foil and target; the lover shall not sigh gratis; the humorous man* shall end his part in peace; the clown shall make those laugh whose lungs are tickle o' th' sere; and the lady shall say her mind freely, or the blank verse shall halt for't. What players are they?

ROSENCRANTZ
305   Even those you were wont to take such delight in, the tragedians of the city.

HAMLET
How chances it they travel? Their residence, both in reputation and profit, was better both ways.

ROSENCRANTZ
I think their inhibition comes by the means of the late innova-
310   tion.*

HAMLET
Do they hold the same estimation they did when I was in the city? Are they so followed?

ROSENCRANTZ
No indeed, are they not.

HAMLET
How comes it? Do they grow rusty?

ROSENCRANTZ
315   Nay, their endeavor keeps in the wonted pace, but there is, sir, an eyrie of children, little eyases, that cry out on the top of question and are most tyrannically clapped for't. These are now the fashion, and so berattle the common stages (so they call

---

296 *lenten*   that is, during the forty days before Easter, abstinence from meat and periodic fasting were the rule, and the word therefore means meager or sparse.

301 *humorous man*   a type of character prominent in the comedies of the time (e.g., Ben Jonson's *Every Man in His Humor,* 1598). The eccentric, "humorous" personality was dominated by certain traits produced by

HAMLET

295   Why did you laugh, then, when I said "Man gives me no
          pleasure"?

ROSENCRANTZ

      I was just wondering, my lord, that if you get no pleasure from
          man, what sort of miserable

      reception the acting company will get from you. We overtook
          them

      on our way here, and they're coming to offer to entertain you.

HAMLET

      The actor that plays the king shall be welcome; his Majesty shall

300   get tribute money from me. The knight in search of adventure
          will be able to use his sword and

      shield; the lover will not sigh for nothing; the eccentric man will
          finish playing his part and be reconciled with his enemies. The
          clown will make those laugh who

      are ready to laugh at the drop of a hat; and the leading lady will
          be allowed to speak her mind freely,

      even if the poetry comes off lamely. Which acting company is it?

ROSENCRANTZ

305   The same group you used to enjoy so much, the tragic actors
      from the city.

HAMLET

      Why are they on the road? They had a better reputation
      and made more money when they played in their own theater.

ROSENCRANTZ

      I think they are prohibited from that by the recent new

310   regulations.

HAMLET

      Are they still as successful as they were when I was in the
      city? Do they still have as many admirers?

ROSENCRANTZ

      Not at all, they don't.

HAMLET

      How did that happen? Have they grown stale?

ROSENCRANTZ

315   No, they're as good as they ever were, but there is, sir,
      a nest of child-actors, little baby hawks who cry with shrill voices
      as they recite the dialogue and are outrageously applauded for
          that. These kids are

      now the rage, and people ridicule the common playhouses (that's
          what they call

---

an excess of one of the "humors."

      310 *late innovation*   may refer to a government order of 1600 restrict-
ing the number of playhouses in London to two and the number of per-
formances to two a week. Or it may allude to the new popularity of companies of child actors (see lines 315-34).

them) that many wearing rapiers are afraid of goosequills and
320 dare scarce come thither.

HAMLET
What, are they children? Who maintains 'em? How are they
escoted? Will they pursue the quality no longer than they can
sing? Will they not say afterwards, if they should grow themselves to common players (as it is most like, if their means are
325 no better), their writers do them wrong to make them exclaim
against their own succession?

ROSENCRANTZ
Faith, there has been much to-do on both sides, and the nation
holds it no sin to tarre them to controversy. There was, for a
while, no money bid for argument unless the poet and the player
330 went to cuffs in the question.

HAMLET
Is't possible?

GUILDENSTERN
O, there has been much throwing about of brains.

HAMLET
Do the boys carry it away?

ROSENCRANTZ
Ay, that they do, my lord—Hercules and his load too.*

HAMLET
335 It is not very strange, for my uncle is King of Denmark, and
those that would make mouths at him while my father lived
give twenty, forty, fifty, a hundred ducats apiece for his picture
in little. 'Sblood, there is something in this more than natural,
if philosophy could find it out.
A flourish.

GUILDENSTERN
340 There are the players.

HAMLET
Gentlemen, you are welcome to Elsinore. Your hands, come
then. Th' appurtenance of welcome is fashion and ceremony.

---

334 *Hercules and his load too* one of the twelve labors of Hercules
was holding up the world for Atlas; the child actors are carrying off both
Hercules and the world. This may be an allusion to Shakespeare's own

them), so that many men of fashion are afraid that satirists will make fun of them if they
320   dare come to the ordinary public theaters.

HAMLET

Don't tell me that these actors are all children? Who runs these children's companies? Who
supports them? Will they be members of the acting profession only until their voices
change? Won't they say afterwards, if they grow up
to be ordinary actors in the public theaters (as is bound to happen, if they have nothing else
325   with which to support themselves), that their playwrights injure them by making them criticize
their own future?

ROSENCRANTZ

By God, there's been a lot of fuss on both sides, and people
don't see anything wrong in egging them on to quarrel. For a
time, you couldn't sell a play unless it had a writer and an actor
330   fighting about this very question.

HAMLET

Is that a fact?

GUILDENSTERN

O, a lot of heads have been knocked around.

HAMLET

Are the boy actors winning?

ROSENCRANTZ

Oh yes, they certainly are—they're giving even the Globe theater some stiff competition.

HAMLET

335   That's no big mystery, for my uncle is King of Denmark, and
the same people who made fun of him when my father was alive
now pay twenty, forty, fifty, a hundred dollars apiece for his
miniature portrait. Christ, there's something unnatural in this,
if only psychology could discover what causes it.
    A flourish of trumpets.

GUILDENSTERN

340   There are the actors.

HAMLET (*to Rosencrantz and Guildenstern*)

Gentlemen, welcome to Elsinore. Shake hands, come on in
then. Welcome should be accompanied by proper and formal
greeting.

Globe playhouse, which is said to have had for its sign a picture of Hercules supporting the globe.

Let me comply with you in this garb, lest my extent to the
players (which I tell you must show fairly outwards) should
345   more appear like entertainment than yours. You are welcome.
But my uncle-father and aunt-mother are deceived.

GUILDENSTERN
In what, my dear lord?

HAMLET
I am but mad north-northwest: when the wind is southerly I
know a hawk from a handsaw.*

Enter POLONIUS.

POLONIUS
350   Well be with you, gentlemen.

HAMLET
Hark you, Guildenstern, and you too; at each ear a hearer. That
great baby you see there is not yet out of his swaddling clouts.

ROSENCRANTZ
Happily he is the second time come to them, for they say an old
man is twice a child.

HAMLET
355   I will prophesy he comes to tell me of the players. Mark it.—
You say right, sir; a Monday morning, 'twas then indeed.

POLONIUS
My lord, I have news to tell you.

HAMLET
My lord, I have news to tell you. When Roscius* was an actor in
Rome——

POLONIUS
360   The actors are come hither, my lord.

HAMLET
Buzz, buzz.

POLONIUS
Upon my honor——

HAMLET
Then came each actor on his ass——

POLONIUS
The best actors in the world, either for tragedy, comedy, history,

---

349 *hawk from a handsaw*   hawk can refer to the bird but also to a
kind of ax; handsaw is a carpenter's tool, but is also a pun on hernshaw,
or heron, a bird often hunted by hawks. Rosencrantz and Guildenstern
are the hawks; Hamlet is the heron, their prey. In the same way, "mad

Let me be courteous with you in this way ; otherwise my
behavior to the
actors (which I can tell you must be publicly courteous) would
345   appear more friendly than my attitude has been to you. You are
welcome.
But my uncle-father and aunt-mother are wrong.

GUILDENSTERN
About what, my dear lord?

HAMLET
I am crazy only part of the time ; when the wind blows from
the south I
can tell the difference between the hunter and his prey.
Enter POLONIUS.

POLONIUS
350   Good day to you, gentlemen.

HAMLET
Listen, Guildenstern, (*to Rosencrantz*) and you too : one on
either side of me. That
big old boy you see there is not yet out of his baby clothes.

ROSENCRANTZ
Maybe this is the second time he's worn them, for they say an old
man becomes like a child again.

HAMLET
355   I predict he's come to tell me about the actors. Watch this.
(*Speaking so Polonius can hear*) You're right, sir ; it was on
Monday morning, that's when it was.

POLONIUS
My lord, I have news for you.

HAMLET
My lord, I have news for you. When Roscius was an actor in
Rome—

POLONIUS
360   The actors have arrived, my lord.

HAMLET
Blah, blah.

POLONIUS
I tell you, upon my word—

HAMLET
If that's how they got here, then each actor came on his donkey—

POLONIUS
They are the best actors in the world, equally good at tragedy,
comedy, history,

---

north-northwest" means that he is insane only on one point of the compass;
that is, only when he wants to be.

358 *Roscius* the most famous Roman comic actor (died 62 B.C.).
Hamlet hits at the staleness of Polonius' news.

365   pastoral, pastoral-comical, historical-pastoral, tragical-historical, tragical-comical-historical-pastoral; scene individable, or poem unlimited.* Seneca* cannot be too heavy, nor Plautus* too light. For the law of writ and the liberty, these are the only men.

HAMLET
O Jeptha* judge of Israel, what a treasure hadst thou!

POLONIUS
370   What a treasure had he, my lord?

HAMLET
Why,

    "One fair daughter, and no more,
      The which he lovèd passing well."

POLONIUS [*aside*]
Still on my daughter.

HAMLET
375   Am I not i' th' right, old Jeptha?

POLONIUS
If you call me Jeptha, my lord, I have a daughter that I love passing well.

HAMLET
Nay, that follows not.

POLONIUS
What follows then, my lord?

HAMLET
380   Why,

    "As by lot, God wot,"
and then, you know,

    "It came to pass, as most like it was."
The first row of the pious chanson will show you more, for look
385   where my abridgment comes.

    Enter the PLAYERS.

You are welcome, masters, welcome, all. I am glad to see thee well. Welcome, good friends. O, old friend, why, thy face is valanced since I saw thee last. Com'st thou to beard me in Denmark? What, my young lady and mistress?* By'r Lady, your

---

367 *poem unlimited* some classical literary critics of the time thought that plays should observe unity of place; that is, that all the events in them should happen in one place. "Poem unlimited" refers to plays which disregarded that rule and others, like the unity of time, which insisted that all events happen within one day.

367 *Seneca* Roman Stoic philosopher and playwright (died 65 A.D.), who was considered a model of the tragic dramatist.

365   pastoral, pastoral-comical, historical-pastoral, tragical-historical,
tragical-comical-historical-pastoral; plays observing the unity
      of place, or plays
which hop all over the place. Seneca in their hands is never
      boring, nor Plautus too silly.
For playing both strictly according to what's written and also for
improvising, these are the only actors worth watching.

HAMLET
O Jepthah, judge of Israel, what a treasure you had!

POLONIUS
370   What sort of treasure did he have, my lord?

HAMLET
Why,
      "One beautiful daughter, and that's all,
      whom he loved above all things."

POLONIUS *(to the audience)*
He's still thinking about my daughter.

HAMLET
375   Don't you think I'm right, old Jepthah?

POLONIUS
If you call me Jepthah, my lord, then I must acknowledge a
      daughter that I love
above all things.

HAMLET
No, that doesn't follow.

POLONIUS
What follows, then, my lord?

HAMLET
380   Why,
      "As if by chance, God knows,"
and then you know how it goes,
      "It happened, as it was bound to happen."
The first stanza of the holy ballad will tell you more, since
385   here comes my interruption.
         Enter the Actors.
Welcome, masters, welcome to you all. *(To the Leading Actor)* I
      am glad to see you looking so
well. *(To all)* Welcome, my good friends. *(To individual actors)*
      O, my old pal, what's this? Your face has
acquired a fringe of beard since I saw you last. Have you come
      to Denmark to beard me (i.e., to insult me)?
Who is this? My young lady and madam herself? By our Lady,
      your

---

367 *Plautus* Roman playwright (c. 254-184 B.C.), a model of the comic dramatist.

369 *Jeptha* Hamlet refers to a 16th-century ballad about Jepthah, a judge of Israel who sacrificed his daughter (see Judges 11:34-39). In what follows, he quotes several lines of the ballad.

389 *mistress* Hamlet is kidding the boy actor who played the women's roles.

390   ladyship is nearer to heaven than when I saw you last by the altitude of a chopine. Pray God your voice, like a piece of uncurrent gold, be not cracked within the ring.* Masters, you are all welcome. We'll e'en to't like French falconers, fly at anything we see. We'll have a speech straight. Come, give us a taste
395   of your quality. Come, a passionate speech.

PLAYER
What speech, my good lord?

HAMLET
I heard thee speak me a speech once, but it was never acted, or if it was, not above once, for the play, I remember, pleased not the million; 'twas caviary to the general, but it was (as I re-
400   ceived it, and others, whose judgments in such matters cried in the top of mine) an excellent play, well digested in the scenes, set down with as much modesty as cunning. I remember one said there were no sallets in the lines to make the matter savory; nor no matter in the phrase that might indict the author of
405   affectation, but called it an honest method, as wholesome as sweet, and by very much more handsome than fine. One speech in't I chiefly loved. 'Twas Aeneas' tale to Dido, and thereabout of it especially when he speaks of Priam's* slaughter. If it live in your memory, begin at this line—let me see, let me see:
410   "The rugged Pyrrhus, like th' Hyrcanian beast*———"

---

392 *cracked within the ring*   that is, broken or changed, so that the boy can no longer play women's parts. A gold coin was unacceptable as currency ("uncurrent") if it was cracked from the edge through the ring surrounding the stamped head of the sovereign.

408 *Priam's*   in the second book of Vergil's *Aeneid*, the Trojan hero, Aeneas, tells Dido, the Queen of Carthage, the story of the fall of Troy. Priam, the king of Troy, is killed during the conquest of the city by Pyrrhus, son of Achilles.

410 *Hyrcanian beast*   Hyrcania, in the Caucasus region in southern Russia, was known for its tigers.

390 ladyship is a little taller than when I saw you last by the
height of a platform shoe. I hope to God your boy's voice, like a
two-bit slug, hasn't changed and lost its high (and genuine)
ring. Masters, you are
all welcome. Let's get to it, just like French falconers, have a
hit at any-
thing we see. Let's hear you recite a speech right away. Come on,
let's have a sample
395 of your talent. Come on, an emotional speech.

LEADING ACTOR
Any particular speech, my good lord?

HAMLET
You recited a speech for me once, but it was never done on
stage, or
if it were, not more than once; for the play, as I recall, did not
please
the crowd. It was like caviar to the common people (i.e., too
special for ordinary taste). But it was (as far as I
400 was concerned, and others, whose judgments in such things
carried
more weight than mine) an excellent play, the scenes well
arranged,
written with a nice balance between the simple and the artful. I
recall that somebody
said there were no spicy jokes in the lines to make the plot
savory;
and he said there was nothing in the language that might convict
the author of being
405 pretentious. But he said it was a proper way to write, as
instructive as
it was pleasing, and much more properly called beautiful than
gaudy. There was one speech
in it that I loved best of all. It was Aeneas telling his story to
Dido, and
especially the part in it when he describes the murder of Priam.
If you can still
remember it, begin at this line—let me see, how does it go?
410 "The rugged Pyrrhus, like the Hyrcanian tiger—"

'Tis not so; it begins with Pyrrhus:
    "The rugged Pyrrhus, he whose sable arms,
    Black as his purpose, did the night resemble
    When he lay couchéd in th' ominous horse,
415   Hath now this dread and black complexion smeared
    With heraldry more dismal. Head to foot
    Now is he total gules, horridly tricked
    With blood of fathers, mothers, daughter, sons,
    Baked and impasted with the parching streets,
420   That lend a tyrannous and a damnèd light
    To their lord's murder. Roasted in wrath and fire,
    And thus o'ersizèd with coagulate gore,
    With eyes like carbuncles, the hellish Pyrrhus
    Old grandsire Priam seeks."
425 So, proceed you.

POLONIUS
Fore God, my lord, well spoken, with good accent and good
discretion.

PLAYER
                    "Anon he finds him,
    Striking too short at Greeks. His antique sword,
430   Rebellious to his arm, lies where it falls,
    Repugnant to command. Unequal matched,
    Pyrrhus at Priam drives, in rage strikes wide,
    But with the whiff and wind of his fell sword
    Th' unnervèd father falls. Then senseless Ilium,
435   Seeming to feel this blow, with flaming top
    Stoops to his base, and with a hideous crash
    Takes prisoner Pyrrhus' ear. For lo, his sword,
    Which was declining on the milky head
    Of reverend Priam, seemed i' th' air to stick.
440   So as a painted tyrant Pyrrhus stood,
    And like a neutral to his will and matter
    Did nothing.
    But as we often see, against some storm,
    A silence in the heavens, the rack stand still,
445   The bold winds speechless, and the orb below
    As hush as death, anon the dreadful thunder

That's not the way it goes; it begins with Pyrrhus:
"The rugged Pyrrhus, whose black weapons
were as black as his intentions, looked like the night
when he was hiding in the threatening Trojan horse.
415 He has now smeared this frightening black color
with a more ill-omened insignia. Now he is from head to foot
all red, horribly adorned
with the blood of fathers, mothers, daughters, sons;
caked and encrusted by the heat from the burning streets,
420 which provide a fierce and hellish light
for their lord's murder. Flaming with anger and heat,
smeared with dried blood,
and with eyes burning like jewels, the devilish Pyrrhus
looks for old grandfather Priam."
425 Now, you go on with it.

POLONIUS
By God, my lord, that was well spoken, with a fine articulation
and with good
control.

LEADING ACTOR
"Soon he finds him,
trying vainly to fight the Greeks. His old sword,
430 too heavy for his hand, stays down when he tries to lift it,
resisting his command. Much more than a match for him,
Pyrrhus swings at Priam, strikes wide in his anger,
but with the whizzing breeze of his cruel sword
knocks the exhausted father down. Then the battlements of
senseless Troy,
435 as if they felt this blow, collapse in flames;
and this awful crash
makes Pyrrhus stop and listen. For now, his sword
was coming down on the white head
of old Priam, but it seemed to get stuck in mid-air.
440 So Pyrrhus stood still like a tyrant in a picture,
uncertain about his purpose and his task,
and he did nothing.
But in the same way that we often see just before a storm
a stillness in the sky, the clouds standing still,
445 the loud winds mute, and the earth below
as quiet as the grave, and then suddenly the frightening thunder

Doth rend the region, so after Pyrrhus' pause,
A rousèd vengeance sets him new awork,
And never did the Cyclops'* hammers fall
450   On Mars's armor, forged for proof eterne,
With less remorse than Pyrrhus' bleeding sword
Now falls on Priam.
Out, out, thou strumpet Fortune! All you gods,
In general synod take away her power,
455   Break all the spokes and fellies from her wheel,
And bowl the round nave down the hill of heaven,
As low as to the fiends."

POLONIUS
This is too long.

HAMLET
It shall to the barber's, with your beard.—Prithee say on. He's
460   for a jig or a tale of bawdry, or he sleeps. Say on; come to
Hecuba.*

PLAYER
"But who (ah woe!) had seen the mobled queen——"

HAMLET
"The mobled queen"?

POLONIUS
That's good, "Mobled queen" is good.

PLAYER
465   "Run barefoot up and down, threat'ning the flames
With bisson rheum; a clout upon that head
Where late the diadem stood, and for a robe,
About her lank and all o'erteemèd loins,
A blanket in the alarm of fear caught up—
470   Who this had seen, with tongue in venom steeped
'Gainst Fortune's state would treason have pronounced.
But if the gods themselves did see her then,
When she saw Pyrrhus make malicious sport
In mincing with his sword her husband's limbs,
475   The instant burst of clamor that she made
(Unless things mortal move them not at all)
Would have made milch the burning eyes of heaven
And passion in the gods."

---

449 *Cyclops* in Greek and Roman mythology, giants who worked in
Vulcan's forge and made armor for the gods. Mars is the god of war.

splits the air; so after Pyrrhus' pause,
a freshly awakened revenge puts him to work aga:.
And the Cyclops' hammers never pounded
450   Mars's armor as they forged it for eternal endurance
with less pity than Pyrrhus' bloody sword
now comes down on Priam.
Out with you, out, Fortune, you whore! All you gods,
in full council take away her power,
455   smash all the spokes and rims of her wheel,
and roll the round hub down the hill of heaven
all the way down to hell."

POLONIUS
This goes on too long.

HAMLET
We'll send it to the barber's, to be clipped with your beard.—
Please go on. He wants
460   either a song and dance or a dirty joke, or else he falls asleep
Go on; come to
the part about Hecuba.

LEADING ACTOR
"But if anyone (how terrible!) had seen the muffled queen—"

HAMLET
"The muffled queen"?

POLONIUS
That's a good phrase. "Muffled queen" is good.

LEADING ACTOR
"running barefoot up and down, trying to put out the flames
with her blinding tears; a rag upon that head
which used to wear the crown; and for a dress
she wore around her thin body, worn out with bearing many
    children,
a blanket snatched up in her fright and alarm—
470   if anyone had seen this he would have, with great hatred,
rebelled against Fortune's control of human affairs.
Had even the gods themselves observed her then,
when she watched Pyrrhus playing his evil game
of chopping up her husband's limbs with his sword,
475   her sudden explosion of grief
(unless human events don't affect the gods at all)
would have made the fiery eyes of heaven milky with their tears
and created grief even in the gods."

---

461 *Hecuba* Priam's wife (see note for line 408).

POLONIUS

480   Look, whe'r he has not turned his color, and has tears in's eyes.
Prithee no more.

HAMLET

'Tis well. I'll have thee speak out the rest of this soon. Good my
lord, will you see the players well bestowed? Do you hear? Let
them be well used, for they are the abstract and brief chronicles
of the time. After your death you were better have a bad epitaph
485   than their ill report while you live.

POLONIUS

My lord, I will use them according to their desert.

HAMLET

God's bodkin, man, much better! Use every man after his desert,
and who shall scape whipping? Use them after your own honor
and dignity. The less they deserve, the more merit is in your
490   bounty. Take them in.

POLONIUS

Come, sirs.

HAMLET

Follow him, friends. We'll hear a play tomorrow. [*Aside to
Player*] Dost thou hear me, old friend? Can you play *The Murder
of Gonzago*?

PLAYER

495   Ay, my lord.

HAMLET

We'll ha't tomorrow night. You could for a need study a speech
of some dozen or sixteen lines which I would set down and
insert in't, could you not?

PLAYER

Ay, my lord.

HAMLET

500   Very well. Follow that lord, and look you mock him not. My

POLONIUS
Notice, he has turned pale and has tears in his eyes.
480   Please, no more of this.

HAMLET
It's just as well to end here. I would like you to recite the rest
    of this soon. (*To Polonius*) My good
lord, will you see to it that the actors are properly entertained?
    Do you hear me? Let
them be well treated, since they function as a summary and short
    history
of our time. You're better off with an uncomplimentary epitaph
    after your death
485   than with their unflattering report of you while you're alive.

POLONIUS
My lord, I will treat them according to their worth.

HAMLET
By God's little body, man, treat them much better than that!
    Treat every man according to his worth
and who shall go unpunished? Treat them in relation to your
    own honor
and importance. The less they deserve, the more credit you get
490   for your generosity. Accompany them inside.

POLONIUS
Come with me, gentlemen.

HAMLET
Follow him, friends. I want you to put on a play tomorrow.
    (*To the Leading Actor*) Are you listening, old friend? Can you
    put on *The Murder*
    of Gonzago?

LEADING ACTOR
495   Yes, my lord.

HAMLET
Let's have it tomorrow night. You could, if necessary, memorize
    a speech
of about a dozen or sixteen lines which I would write and
put into the play, couldn't you?

LEADING ACTOR
Yes, my lord.

HAMLET
500   Very good. Go inside with that lord, and be sure you don't make
    fun of him. (*To the actors*) My

good friends, I'll leave you till night. You are welcome to Elsinore.
                    Exeunt POLONIUS *and* PLAYERS.
ROSENCRANTZ
    Good my lord.
                    Exeunt ROSENCRANTZ *and* GUILDENSTERN.
HAMLET
    Ay, so, God bye to you.—Now I am alone.
505   O, what a rogue and peasant slave am I!
    Is it not monstrous that this player here,
    But in a fiction, in a dream of passion,
    Could force his soul so to his own conceit
    That from her working all his visage wanned,
510   Tears in his eyes, distraction in his aspect,
    A broken voice, and his whole function suiting
    With forms to his conceit? And all for nothing!
    For Hecuba!
    What's Hecuba to him, or he to Hecuba,
515   That he should weep for her? What would he do
    Had he the motive and the cue for passion
    That I have? He would drown the stage with tears
    And cleave the general ear with horrid speech,
    Make mad the guilty and appall the free,
520   Confound the ignorant, and amaze indeed
    The very faculties of eyes and ears.
    Yet I,
    A dull and muddy-mettled rascal, peak
    Like John-a-dreams, unpregnant of my cause,
525   And can say nothing. No, not for a king,
    Upon whose property and most dear life
    A damned defeat was made. Am I a coward?
    Who calls me villain? Breaks my pate across?
    Plucks off my beard and blows it in my face?
530   Tweaks me by the nose? Gives me the lie i' th' throat
    As deep as to the lungs? Who does me this?
    Ha, 'swounds, I should take it, for it cannot be
    But I am pigeon-livered* and lack gall
    To make oppression bitter, or ere this
535   I should ha' fatted all the region kites
    With this slave's offal. Bloody, bawdy villain!

---

533 *pigeon-livered* popular belief held that doves or pigeons were mild
and gentle because their livers produced no gall.

good friends, goodbye until tonight. Welcome to Elsinore.
Exit POLONIUS *and the Actors.*

ROSENCRANTZ
My good lord, goodbye.
Exit ROSENCRANTZ *and* GUILDENSTERN.

HAMLET
Yes, all right, goodbye to you.—Now I am alone.

505 O what a swindler and miserable flunky I am!
Isn't it grotesque that this actor here,
in nothing but a made-up situation, with imaginary emotions,
could force himself to feel the part?
So that his imagination made his face grow all pale,

510 brought tears to his eyes, gave himself a desperate look,
a faltering voice, and matched the actions of his body
to expressions that suited his conception of the part? And all of
this for nothing!
For Hecuba!
What does Hecuba mean to him, or he to Hecuba,

515 that he should cry about her? What would he do
if he had the motive and cue for passion
that I have? He would drown the stage with tears
and deafen the audience with horrifying words,
drive guilty spectators insane and appall the innocent,

520 shatter the ignorant, and even astound
the very senses of sight and hearing.
And yet I,
a slow and weak-kneed faker, mope around
like a day-dreamer, unmoved to action by my situation

525 and unable to say a thing. No, not even for a king
whose own person and precious life
were destroyed so devilishly. Am I a coward?
Who calls me a scoundrel? Cracks me on the skull?
Plucks off my beard and blows it in my face?

530 Pinches my nose? Accuses me of being a liar
through and through? Who dares do this to me?
Oh, by Christ's wounds, I would put up with it, for I must
be chicken-hearted and without enough nerve
to resent injustice, or long before this

535 I would have fed this bastard's guts
to the scavenging hawks that fly overhead. Murdering, lustful
villain!

Remorseless, treacherous, lecherous, kindless villain!
O, vengeance!
Why, what an ass am I! This is most brave,
540 That I, the son of a dear father murdered,
Prompted to my revenge by heaven and hell,
Must, like a whore, unpack my heart with words
And fall a-cursing like a very drab,
A scullion! Fie upon't, foh! About, my brains.
545 Hum——
I have heard that guilty creatures sitting at a play
Have by the very cunning of the scene
Been struck so to the soul that presently
They have proclaimed their malefactions.
550 For murder, though it have no tongue, will speak
With most miraculous organ. I'll have these players
Play something like the murder of my father
Before mine uncle. I'll observe his looks,
I'll tent him to the quick. If 'a do blench,
555 I know my course. The spirit that I have seen
May be a devil, and the devil hath power
T' assume a pleasing shape, yea, and perhaps
Out of my weakness and my melancholy,
As he is very potent with such spirits,
560 Abuses me to damn me. I'll have grounds
More relative than this. The play's the thing
Wherein I'll catch the conscience of the King.
            Exit.

[*Act III, Scene i: The castle.*] *Enter* KING, QUEEN, POLONIUS,
ROSENCRANTZ, GUILDENSTERN, LORDS.   ·

KING
And can you by no drift of conference
Get from him why he puts on this confusion,
Grating so harshly all his days of quiet
With turbulent and dangerous lunacy?

Pitiless, deceitful, lecherous, unnatural villain!
O, revenge!
Why, what a jackass I am! This is really fine,
540   that I, the son of a beloved father who's been murdered
and who is urged to seek revenge by heaven and hell,
have to relieve my feelings with words, like a whore,
and start cursing like a real prostitute,
a kitchen maid. To hell with it, phew! Get to work, think.
545   Let's see. . . .
I've heard that guilty persons watching a play
have been so moved by the convincing reality of the scene
that they have then and there
confessed their crimes.
550   For murder, even if it cannot actually speak, will find
some miraculous way to reveal itself. I'll have these actors
put on something like the murder of my father
in front of my uncle. I'll watch his expressions,
I'll probe him to the heart. If he pales,
555   I know what to do. The ghost that I've seen
may be a devil, and the devil has the ability
to take an attractive form; oh yes, and maybe
he exploits my exhaustion and my depression,
since he is very powerful when you're in such moods,
560   and fools me in order to send me to hell. I'll have more conclusive
     proof
than this. The play's the thing
with which I'll trap the guilty conscience of the King.
     Exit HAMLET.

Act III, Scene i: The castle. Enter KING, QUEEN, POLONIUS,
OPHELIA, ROSENCRANTZ, GUILDENSTERN, *and several
Lords.*

KING
And can't you manage the conversation some way
to trick him into revealing the reason why he fakes this
     craziness,
upsetting so badly what should be for him a time of peace and
     quiet
with noisy and dangerous insanity?

ROSENCRANTZ

5   He does confess he feels himself distracted,
      But from what cause 'a will by no means speak.

GUILDENSTERN

      Nor do we find him forward to be sounded,
      But with a crafty madness keeps aloof
      When we would bring him on to some confession
      of his true state.

QUEEN

10   Did he receive you well?

ROSENCRANTZ

      Most like a gentleman.

GUILDENSTERN

      But with much forcing of his disposition.

ROSENCRANTZ

      Niggard of question, but of our demands
      Most free in his reply.

QUEEN

                    Did you assay him

15   To any pastime?

ROSENCRANTZ

      Madam, it so fell out that certain players
      We o'er-raught on the way; of these we told him,
      And there did seem in him a kind of joy
      To hear of it. They are here about the court,

20   And, as I think, they have already order
      This night to play before him.

POLONIUS

                    'Tis most true,
      And he beseeched me to entreat your Majesties
      To hear and see the matter.

KING

      With all my heart, and it doth much content me

25   To hear him so inclined.
      Good gentlemen, give him a further edge
      And drive his purpose into these delights.

ROSENCRANTZ

      We shall, my lord.

          Exeunt ROSENCRANTZ *and* GUILDENSTERN.

ROSENCRANTZ
5   He does admit that he feels he's losing his grip,
but he absolutely refuses to say what's causing it.

GUILDENSTERN
And we don't find that he's willing to be questioned,
but hides himself behind a shrewd craziness
when we try to get him to tell us what
is really going on with him.

QUEEN
10   Did he welcome you in a friendly way?

ROSENCRANTZ
In a very polite way.

GUILDENSTERN
But he had to force himself to be polite.

ROSENCRANTZ
He didn't have much to say on his own but was
very ready to answer our questions.

QUEEN
Did you try to tempt him
15   to any entertainment?

ROSENCRANTZ
Madam, it happened that on the way here we met
a company of actors; we told Hamlet about them,
and he seemed rather happy in a way
to hear the news. They are staying here in the court,
20   and I think they already have their orders
to put on a play for him tonight.

POLONIUS
That's exactly right,
and he asked me to request that your Majesties
come and see the play.

KING
I'd love to, and it makes me very happy
25   to hear that he's interested in the theater.
Good gentlemen, give him more encouragement
and help him to amuse himself with these pleasures.

ROSENCRANTZ
We shall, my lord.
       Exit ROSENCRANTZ *and* GUILDENSTERN.

KING

                        Sweet Gertrude, leave us too,
For we have closely sent for Hamlet hither,
30   That he, as 'twere by accident, may here
Affront Ophelia.
Her father and myself (lawful espials)
Will so bestow ourselves that, seeing unseen,
We may of their encounter frankly judge
35   And gather by him, as he is behaved,
If't be th' affliction of his love or no
That thus he suffers for.

QUEEN

                       I shall obey you.
And for your part, Ophelia, I do wish
That your good beauties be the happy cause
40   Of Hamlet's wildness. So shall I hope your virtues
Will bring him to his wonted way again,
To both your honors.

OPHELIA

                  Madam, I wish it may.
    [*Exit* QUEEN.]

POLONIUS

Ophelia, walk you here.—Gracious, so please you,
We will bestow ourselves. [*To Ophelia*] Read on this book,
45   That show of such an exercise may color
Your loneliness. We are oft to blame in this,
'Tis too much proved, that with devotion's visage
And pious action we do sugar o'er
The devil himself.

KING [*aside*]

                  O, 'tis too true.
50   How smart a lash that speech doth give my conscience!
The harlot's cheek, beautied with plast'ring art,
Is not more ugly to the thing that helps it
Than is my deed to my most painted word.
O heavy burden!

KING
> Dearest Gertrude, please leave too,
> since I have secretly sent for Hamlet to come here,
30   so that he may, as if by accident,
> meet Ophelia.
> Her father and I (as lawfully appointed spies)
> will hide ourselves so that, out of sight but able to see,
> we may freely judge from their meeting,
35   and determine from watching him and his behavior
> whether or not it is his love sickness
> that causes his insanity.

QUEEN
> I'll do as you say.
> And as for you, Ophelia, I really hope
> that your innocent charms are the fortunate cause
40   of Hamlet's wildness. In that way, I hope your goodness
> will restore him to his normal self,
> which will be a credit to both of you.

OPHELIA
> Madam, I hope it turns out that way.
>   *Exit* QUEEN.

POLONIUS
> Ophelia, walk here.—Your gracious Majesty, if it pleases you,
> we will hide ourselves. (*To Ophelia*) Read this book.
45   A display of devotion like this will make
> your being alone look plausible. People often sin in this way
> (as is too well known), so that by putting on a devout face
> and faking holy actions we sugar over
> the devil himself.

KING (*to the audience*)
> O, that's too true.
50   What a painful whiplash that speech gives my conscience!
> The whore's face, beautified with make-up,
> is not more ugly compared to the paint and powder that disguises
>   it,
> than is my crime compared to the fancy words that conceal it.
> O what a heavy burden!

POLONIUS

55   I hear him coming. Let's withdraw, my lord.
     [*Exeunt* KING *and* POLONIUS.]
     Enter HAMLET.

HAMLET

     To be, or not to be: that is the question:
     Whether 'tis nobler in the mind to suffer
     The slings and arrows of outrageous fortune,
     Or to take arms against a sea of troubles,
60   And by opposing end them. To die, to sleep—
     No more—and by a sleep to say we end
     The heartache, and the thousand natural shocks
     That flesh is heir to! 'Tis a consummation
     Devoutly to be wished. To die, to sleep—
65   To sleep—perchance to dream: ay, there's the rub,
     For in that sleep of death what dreams may come
     When we have shuffled off this mortal coil,
     Must give us pause. There's the respect
     That makes calamity of so long life:
70   For who would bear the whips and scorns of time,
     Th' oppressor's wrong, the proud man's contumely,
     The pangs of despised love, the law's delay,
     The insolence of office, and the spurns
     That patient merit of th' unworthy takes,
75   When he himself might his quietus make
     With a bare bodkin? Who would fardels bear,
     To grunt and sweat under a weary life,
     But that the dread of something after death,
     The undiscovered country, from whose bourn
80   No traveler returns, puzzles the will,
     And makes us rather bear those ills we have,
     Than fly to others that we know not of?
     Thus conscience does make cowards of us all,
     And thus the native hue of resolution
85   Is sicklied o'er with the pale cast of thought,
     And enterprises of great pitch and moment,
     With this regard their currents turn awry,

POLONIUS

55   I hear Hamlet coming. Let's hide, my lord.
         Exit KING *and* POLONIUS.
         Enter HAMLET.

HAMLET

    To be, or not to be; that is what really matters.
    Is it nobler to accept passively
    the trials and tribulations that unjust fate sends,
    or to resist an ocean of troubles,
60   and, by our own effort, defeat them? To die, to fall asleep—
    perhaps that's all there is to it—and by that sleep suppose
      we put an end to
    the heartache and the thousands of pains and worries
    that are part of being human! That's an end
    we could all look forward to. To die, to sleep—
65   to sleep—maybe to dream: yes, that's the catch.
    For in that sleep of death the nightmares that may come
    when we have freed ourselves from the turmoil of this mortal life
    must make us hesitate. There's the thought
    that makes a disaster out of living to a ripe old age.
70   After all, who wants to put up with the lashes and insults of
      this world,
    the tyrant's injustice and contempt of arrogant men,
    the pains of rejected love, the law's frustrating slowness,
    insults from our superiors, and the snubs
    that deserving and hopeful people have to take from powerful
      inferiors,
75   when he could end the whole process by killing himself
    with a bare dagger? Who would want to carry the load,
    to grunt and sweat under the burden of an exhausting life,
    except that the fear of what may happen to us after death—
    that undiscovered country, that territory from which
80   no explorer has ever come back—makes us confused and hesitant,
    and forces us to go on with the troubles we have,
    rather than rush into new and unknown ones?
    So, too much thinking turns us all into cowards,
    and the bright and healthy color of our intentions
85   turns pale and weak as we brood about them.
    And important and ambitious projects
    thus get sidetracked,

And lose the name of action.—Soft you now,
The fair Ophelia!—Nymph, in thy orisons
Be all my sins remembered.

OPHELIA

90   Good my lord,
How does your honor for this many a day?

HAMLET
I humbly thank you; well, well, well.

OPHELIA
My lord, I have remembrances of yours
That I have longèd long to redeliver.
I pray you now, receive them.

HAMLET

95   No, not I,
I never gave you aught.

OPHELIA
My honored lord, you know right well you did,
And with them words of so sweet breath composed
As made these things more rich. Their perfume lost,
100   Take these again, for to the noble mind
Rich gifts wax poor when givers prove unkind.
There, my lord.

HAMLET
Ha, ha! Are you honest?

OPHELIA
My lord?

HAMLET
105   Are you fair?

OPHELIA
What means your lordship?

HAMLET
That if you be honest and fair, your honesty should admit no
discourse to your beauty.

OPHELIA
Could beauty, my lord, have better commerce than with hon-
110   esty?

and remain nothing but big plans.—But wait a minute now,
here's the beautiful Ophelia! Maiden, as you say your prayers,
ask God to forgive all my sins.

OPHELIA

90   My good lord,
how have you been these many days that I
haven't seen you?

HAMLET

Thank you for asking; fine, fine, fine.

OPHELIA

My lord, I have gifts of yours
that I've wanted for a long time to return to you.
Please, take them back.

HAMLET

95   No, not from me—
I never gave you anything.

OPHELIA

My honored lord, you know very well that you did,
and as you gave them you said such sweet things
that the gifts were made even richer. Since that sweetness is
gone,
100   take them back again; for to someone with a noble mind
expensive presents are made cheap when the givers turn out to be
cruel.
There, my lord. (*Gives him the presents*)

HAMLET

Ha, ha! Are you chaste?

OPHELIA

What do you mean, my lord?

HAMLET

105   Are you beautiful?

OPHELIA

What does your lordship mean?

HAMLET

That if you're chaste and beautiful, your chastity shouldn't
allow itself
to converse with your beauty.

OPHELIA

Could beauty, my lord, do anything better than to converse with
110   modesty?

HAMLET

Ay, truly; for the power of beauty will sooner transform honesty from what it is to a bawd than the force of honesty can translate beauty into his likeness. This was sometime a paradox, but now the time gives it proof. I did love you once.

OPHELIA

115   Indeed, my lord, you made me believe so.

HAMLET

You should not have believed me, for virtue cannot so inoculate our old stock but we shall relish of it. I loved you not.

OPHELIA

I was the more deceived.

HAMLET

Get thee to a nunnery. Why wouldst thou be a breeder of sin-
120   ners? I am myself indifferent honest, but yet I could accuse me of such things that it were better my mother had not borne me: I am very proud, revengeful, ambitious, with more offenses at my beck than I have thoughts to put them in, imagination to give them shape, or time to act them in. What should such fellows
125   as I do crawling between earth and heaven? We are arrant knaves all; believe none of us. Go thy ways to a nunnery. Where's your father?

OPHELIA

At home, my lord.

HAMLET

Let the doors be shut upon him, that he may play the fool
130   nowhere but in's own house. Farewell.

OPHELIA

O help him, you sweet heavens!

HAMLET

If thou dost marry, I'll give thee this plague for thy dowry: be thou as chaste as ice, as pure as snow, thou shalt not escape calumny. Get thee to a nunnery. Go, farewell. Or if thou wilt

HAMLET

Yes, certainly; for beauty's power will change chastity

from what it is into a pimp long before the force of chastity can transform

beauty into something chaste. This used to be a saying nobody believed, but

the way things are now proves that it's true. I loved you once.

OPHELIA

115   Oh yes, my lord, you persuaded me to believe you.

HAMLET

You shouldn't have believed me, for goodness can't be grafted on to

our old sinful nature without some taste of sin remaining. I didn't love you.

OPHELIA

I was even more fooled then.

HAMLET

Get yourself to a convent. Why do you want to give birth to

120   sinners? I myself am moderately virtuous, but I could accuse myself

of such crimes that it would be better if my mother had never given birth to me;

I am very proud, revengeful, ambitious, and capable of more crimes

than I have words with which to describe them, imagination to plan them, or time to commit them. Why are people

125   like me allowed to sneak around here between earth and sky? We are all outright

crooks; don't believe any of us. Get on your way to a convent. Where's your father?

OPHELIA

He's at home, my lord.

HAMLET

Shut the doors and lock him in, so that he can act like a fool

130   only in his own house. Goodbye.

OPHELIA

O help him, dear God!

HAMLET

If you get married, I'll give you this disease as your dowry:

whether you are as virginal as ice, as pure as snow, you won't avoid

135   needs marry, marry a fool, for wise men know well enough what
monsters* you make of them. To a nunnery, go, and quickly
too. Farewell.

OPHELIA
Heavenly powers, restore him!

HAMLET
I have heard of your paintings, well enough. God hath given you
140   one face, and you make yourselves another. You jig and amble,
and you lisp; you nickname God's creatures and make your
wantonness your ignorance. Go to, I'll no more on't; it hath
made me mad. I say we will have no moe marriage. Those that
are married already—all but one*—shall live. The rest shall keep
145   as they are. To a nunnery, go.
        Exit.

OPHELIA
O what a noble mind is here o'erthrown!
The courtier's, soldier's, scholar's, eye, tongue, sword,
Th' expectancy and rose of the fair state,
The glass of fashion, and the mold of form,
150   Th' observed of all observers, quite, quite down!
And I, of ladies most deject and wretched,
That sucked the honey of his musicked vows,
Now see that noble and most sovereign reason
Like sweet bells jangled, out of tune and harsh,
155   That unmatched form and feature of blown youth
Blasted with ecstasy. O, woe is me
T' have seen what I have seen, see what I see!
        Enter KING *and* POLONIUS.

_____

136 *monsters* alludes to the notion that the husbands of unfaithful
wives grew horns. Any allusion to horns, even of the vaguest sort, was

slanderous gossip. Get yourself to a convent. Go ahead, goodbye.
   Or if you must
135   get married, marry a fool, for smart men know very well what
   sort of monstrous deceived husbands you turn them into. To a
   convent, go on, and quickly
   too. Goodbye.

OPHELIA
   O powers of heaven, make him sane again!

HAMLET
   I've been told about your deceiving make-up, oh yes, I know.
   God has given you
140   one face, and you prepare another one for yourselves. You wiggle
   and slink around,
   and you speak with an affected air; you call everyone by silly
   names and mask your
   lecherous behavior by claiming childish innocence. Oh no, I won't
   put up with it; it has
   made me crazy. I say that there will be no more marriages.
   As for those who are
   already married, all except one shall be allowed to live. Everyone
   else shall stay
145   unmarried. To a convent, go on.
   Exit HAMLET.

OPHELIA
   O what a great mind has been destroyed here!
   An eloquent courtier, a brave soldier, a wise scholar,
   the hope and the ornament of his country,
   the standard for fashionable dress and the model of excellent
   behavior,
150   the one on whom all eyes are focussed, totally, totally gone!
   And I, the saddest and most miserable of women,
   who loved to hear his sweet and eloquent promises,
   now I see his fine and powerful intellect
   like lovely church bells badly played, out of tune and grating to
   the ear,
155   I see that unrivalled model and standard of blooming youth
   destroyed by madness. O how miserable I am
   to have seen this and to see it now!
   Enter KING *and* POLONIUS.

---

therefore a joke on cuckoldry.
144 *all but one*   a reference to Claudius.

KING
Love? His affections do not that way tend,
Nor what he spake, though it lacked form a little,
160   Was not like madness. There's something in his soul
O'er which his melancholy sits on brood,
And I do doubt the hatch and the disclose
Will be some danger; which for to prevent,
I have in quick determination
165   Thus set it down: he shall with speed to England
For the demand of our neglected tribute.
Haply the seas, and countries different,
With variable objects, shall expel
This something-settled matter in his heart,
170   Whereon his brains still beating puts him thus
From fashion of himself. What think you on't?
POLONIUS
It shall do well. But yet do I believe
The origin and commencement of his grief
Sprung from neglected love. How now, Ophelia?
175   You need not tell us what Lord Hamlet said;
We heard it all. My lord, do as you please,
But if you hold it fit, after the play,
Let his queen mother all alone entreat him
To show his grief. Let her be round with him,
180   And I'll be placed, so please you, in the ear
Of all their conference. If she find him not,
To England send him, or confine him where
Your wisdom best shall think.
KING
                    It shall be so.
Madness in great ones must not unwatched go.
        Exeunt.

[*Scene ii: The castle.*] *Enter* HAMLET *and three of the* PLAYERS.

HAMLET
Speak the speech, I pray you, as I pronounced it to you, trip-
pingly on the tongue. But if you mouth it, as many of our players
do, I had as lief the town crier spoke my lines. Nor do not saw

KING
Was that because of love? I don't think he's inclined that way,
nor was what he said, although it was a little confused,
160   like insane talk. There's something on his mind
that his depression makes him brood about,
and I am afraid that when it is delivered and revealed,
it will be dangerous for me. And in order to prevent that
I have suddenly decided
165   what to do: he will quickly be sent to England
to collect the overdue tribute money they owe us.
Maybe the ocean voyage and the sight of other countries
and different things will get rid of
this nearly obsessive concern of his,
170   which is constantly on his mind and thereby makes him
so different from his usual self. What do you think of this plan?
POLONIUS
It will work very well. But I still think
the source and the beginning of what is troubling him
came from unrequited love. What's the matter, Ophelia?
175   You don't have to tell us what Lord Hamlet said;
we heard it all. (*To Claudius*) My lord, do what you want;
but if you agree, I think that after the play is over,
his mother, the queen, should talk to him alone and ask him
to let her know his troubles. Tell her to be blunt with him,
180   and I'll station myself, if you agree, where I can overhear
all their conversation. If she doesn't learn the truth from him,
send him to England, or shut him up wherever
you in your wisdom think it best.
KING
That's what I'll do.
Insanity in powerful people must be carefully observed.
Exit KING, POLONIUS, *and* OPHELIA.

Act III, Scene ii: Inside the castle. Enter HAMLET *and three of
the Actors.*

HAMLET
Recite the speech, please, the way I read it to you,
distinctly and clearly. But if you ham it up, the way many actors
do, I would just as soon have the town crier recite my lines. And
don't wave

the air too much with your hand, thus, but use all gently, for in
the very torrent, tempest, and (as I may say) whirlwind of your
passion, you must acquire and beget a temperance that may give
it smoothness. O, it offends me to the soul to hear a robustious
periwig-pated fellow tear a passion to tatters, to very rags, to split
the ears of the groundlings,* who for the most part are capable
of nothing but inexplicable dumb shows and noise. I would have
such a fellow whipped for o'erdoing Termagant.* It out-herods
Herod.* Pray you avoid it.

PLAYER
I warrant your honor.

HAMLET
Be not too tame neither, but let your own discretion be your
tutor. Suit the action to the word, the word to the action, with
this special observance, that you o'erstep not the modesty of
nature. For anything so o'erdone is from the purpose of playing,
whose end, both at the first and now, was and is, to hold, as
'twere, the mirror up to nature; to show virtue her own feature,
scorn her own image, and the very age and body of the time his
form and pressure. Now, this overdone, or come tardy off,
though it makes the unskillful laugh, cannot but make the
judicious grieve, the censure of the which one must in your
allowance o'erweigh a whole theater of others. O, there be
players that I have seen play, and heard others praise, and that

---

9 *groundlings* those who paid the lowest admission price to the theater
and stood on the "ground" or in the pit of the playhouse, the area we now
call the "orchestra."

your hands around too much this way (*showing them the
exaggerated gestures*), but take everything nice and easy.
For in

5 the middle of the storm, hurricane, and (you'll pardon the
exaggeration) tornado of your
emotions, you have to achieve and communicate a restraint
that makes
your performance believable. O, it really makes me sick to hear
a boisterous
fellow with a wig on ripping an emotion apart—into absolute
shreds—to impress
the groundlings standing near the stage, most of whom can't
understand

10 anything but meaningless pantomimes and plenty of racket
onstage. I'd like to have
such a fellow beaten up for out-doing noisy Termagant. It's
worse than
King Herod. Please don't do it.

LEADING ACTOR
I assure your honor we won't.

HAMLET
Don't be too dull either, but let your own judgment be your

15 guide. Make your gestures suit the words and the words the
gestures,
keeping this special rule in mind, that you don't go beyond the
moderate boundaries
of what is natural. For anything exaggerated like that is
contrary to the purpose of acting;
whose point, from its beginnings to now, was and is, to reflect, as
we may say, the nature of things, to show goodness what it
should look like,

20 to expose that which is hateful, and to show the image and the
actual feeling of contemporary life.
Now if this is distorted, or is badly done,
it may make the ignorant laugh, but it can only
displease knowledgeable people, whose unfavorable judgment
must, in your
estimation, be more important than the praise of a whole theater
of others. O, there are
actors that I've seen act, and heard others praise, and praise

---

11 *Termagant*   the name given in medieval drama to a deity, supposedly
worshipped by the Moslems, who was violent and overbearing.

12 *Herod*   the Jewish king who sought to kill the infant Jesus was represented in medieval drama as an extravagant and blustering tyrant.

highly (not to speak it profanely), that neither having th' accent
of Christians, nor the gait of Christian, pagan, nor man, have
so strutted and bellowed that I have thought some of Nature's
journeymen had made men, and not made them well, they im-
30   itated humanity so abominably.

PLAYER
I hope we have reformed that indifferently with us, sir.

HAMLET
O, reform it altogether! And let those that play your clowns
speak no more than is set down for them, for there be of them
that will themselves laugh, to set on some quantity of barren
35   spectators to laugh too, though in the meantime some necessary
question of the play be then to be considered. That's villainous
and shows a most pitiful ambition in the fool that uses it. Go
make you ready.
    Exit PLAYERS.
    Enter POLONIUS, GUILDENSTERN, *and* ROSENCRANTZ.
How now, my lord? Will the King hear this piece of work?

POLONIUS
40   And the Queen too, and that presently.

HAMLET
Bid the players make haste.
    Exit POLONIUS.
Will you two help to hasten them?

ROSENCRANTZ
Ay, my lord.
    Exeunt they two.

HAMLET
What, ho, Horatio!
    Enter HORATIO.

HORATIO
45   Here, sweet lord, at your service.

highly (and I don't mean to be irreverent), that didn't sound at all like

civilized Christians, didn't walk like Christians, pagans, or any men,

but paraded up and down the stage shouting so loudly, that I thought as I watched them that some of Nature's

unskilled apprentices had made mankind, and made it pretty badly, since these actors

30   imitated human nature so terribly.

LEADING ACTOR
I hope we have managed more or less to avoid that difficulty, sir.

HAMLET
O, avoid it completely! And make sure that the actors who play the comic parts

say no more than their written lines, for there are some of them who make themselves laugh in order to encourage a few empty-headed

35   spectators to laugh too, even though in the meantime a crucial part of the play is about to begin. That's dreadful

and shows a pathetic desire to upstage the other actors in the fool who does it. Go now and

get ready for the play.
Exit the Actors.
Enter POLONIUS, GUILDENSTERN, *and* ROSEN-
CRANTZ.

What's up, my lord? Will the King come and watch this play?

POLONIUS
40   Yes, and so will the Queen, and very soon.

HAMLET
Tell the actors to hurry.
Exit POLONIUS.
Will you two also tell them to hurry?

ROSENCRANTZ
Yes, my lord.
Exit ROSENCRANTZ *and* GUILDENSTERN.

HAMLET
Hello there, Horatio!
Enter HORATIO.

HORATIO
45   Here I am, my dear lord, at your service.

HAMLET
  Horatio, thou art e'en as just a man
  As e'er my conversation coped withal.
HORATIO
  O, my dear lord——
HAMLET
                    Nay, do not think I flatter.
  For what advancement may I hope from thee,
50   That no revenue hast but thy good spirits
  To feed and clothe thee? Why should the poor be flattered?
  No, let the candied tongue lick absurd pomp,
  And crook the pregnant hinges of the knee
  Where thrift may follow fawning. Dost thou hear?
55   Since my dear soul was mistress of her choice
  And could of men distinguish her election,
  S'hath sealed thee for herself, for thou hast been
  As one, in suff'ring all, that suffers nothing,
  A man that Fortune's buffets and rewards
60   Hast ta'en with equal thanks; and blest are those
  Whose blood and judgment are so well commeddled
  That they are not a pipe for Fortune's finger
  To sound what stop she please. Give me that man
  That is not passion's slave, and I will wear him
65   In my heart's core, ay, in my heart of heart,
  As I do thee. Something too much of this—
  There is a play tonight before the King.
  One scene of it comes near the circumstance
  Which I have told thee, of my father's death.
70   I prithee, when thou seest that act afoot,
  Even with the very comment of thy soul
  Observe my uncle. If his occulted guilt
  Do not itself unkennel in one speech,
  It is a damnèd ghost that we have seen,
75   And my imaginations are as foul
  As Vulcan's stithy.* Give him heedful note,
  For I mine eyes will rivet to his face,
  And after we will both our judgments join
  In censure of his seeming.

---

76 *Vulcan's stithy* Vulcan is the god of fire, the metalworker and artisan of the gods, who presides over a large forge.

HAMLET
Horatio, you come as close to being what a man should be
as anyone I have ever met.
HORATIO
O, my dear lord—
HAMLET
No, I'm not flattering you.
After all, what kind of benefit could I hope to get from you,
50   who have no income except your good disposition
to feed and dress yourself with? Why should anyone flatter
the poor?
No, let the sugary, flattering tongue lick the hand of ridiculous,
ostentatious rich men,
and let the pliable hinges of the knee bend
wherever there is profit to be made from servility. Do you
understand?
55   Ever since my precious mind could choose
and was able to judge the qualities of men,
it has marked you out as someone to admire; for you have acted
like a man who endured all misfortunes and seemed to rise
entirely above them,
a man who has accepted Fortune's blows and rewards
60   with the same confident attitude. And happy are those people
in whom emotion and reason are so thoroughly mixed
that they're not merely a flute on which Fortune's finger
can play any note she pleases. Let me have that man
who isn't a slave to his emotions, and I will cherish him
65   deep in my heart, yes, in the very heart of my heart,
as I do you. But I'm talking too much about this—
listen, a play is to be put on tonight for the King.
One scene in it resembles the facts concerning
my father's death, which I've told you about.
70   I would like you, when you see that scene beginning,
to use your sharpest critical gaze
and watch my uncle. If his hidden guilt
doesn't reveal itself after one speech,
the ghost we have seen is the devil,
75   and my suspicions are as filthy
as Vulcan's forge. Watch him carefully,
for I will keep my eyes riveted on his face,
and later we'll compare our opinions
to reach a verdict on his false appearance of innocence.

HORATIO

Well, my lord.

80   If 'a steal aught the whilst this play is playing,
And scape detecting, I will pay the theft.

Enter Trumpets and Kettledrums, KING, QUEEN, POLONIUS,
OPHELIA, ROSENCRANTZ, GUILDENSTERN, *and other Lords
attendant with his Guard carrying torches. Danish March.
Sound a Flourish.*

HAMLET

They are coming to the play: I must be idle;
Get you a place.

KING

How fares our cousin Hamlet?

HAMLET

85   Excellent, i' faith, of the chameleon's dish,*
I eat the air, promise-crammed; you cannot feed capons so.

KING

I have nothing with this answer, Hamlet; these words are not
mine.

HAMLET

No, nor mine now. [*To* POLONIUS] My lord, you played once i'
90   th' university, you say?

POLONIUS

That did I, my lord, and was accounted a good actor.

HAMLET

What did you enact?

POLONIUS

I did enact Julius Caesar. I was killed i' th' Capitol;* Brutus
killed me.

HAMLET

95   It was a brute part of him to kill so capital a calf there. Be the
players ready?

ROSENCRANTZ

Ay, my lord. They stay upon your patience.

QUEEN

Come hither, my dear Hamlet, sit by me.

---

85 *chameleon's dish* Hamlet deliberately misinterprets the King's
"fares" to mean "what sort of food do you eat?" Chameleons were thought
to feed on air, and Hamlet claims ironically that he lives on the King's
promise that he will succeed to the throne.

HORATIO
Well, my lord,
80　if he steals anything while the play is being acted
and isn't caught, I will pay for it myself.
　　Enter musicians with trumpets and kettledrums. After
　　them, enter KING, QUEEN, POLONIUS, OPHELIA,
　　ROSENCRANTZ, GUILDENSTERN, *and other cour-*
　　tiers, including soldiers carrying torches. A Danish
　　march is played, and the trumpets sound a flourish.
HAMLET (*to Horatio*)
They are coming to see the play; I have to pretend to be crazy.
Find a place to watch from.
KING
How is my nephew, Hamlet?
HAMLET
85　Just fine, indeed I am, for I eat the chameleon's dish.
I feed on the air, chock-full of promises; you can't fatten capons
　　that way.
KING
I don't know what you're talking about, Hamlet; you're not
　　answering
my question.
HAMLET
No, it's not my question now anyway. (*To Polonius*) My lord,
　　weren't you once an actor when
90　you were in college?
POLONIUS
Yes, I was, my lord, and I was considered a good actor.
HAMLET
What part did you play?
POLONIUS
I played Julius Caesar. I was killed in the Capitol; Brutus
killed me.
HAMLET
95　It was a brutal role for him to kill such a perfect fool there.
　　Are the
actors ready to begin?
ROSENCRANTZ
Yes, my lord. They're waiting for you to be ready to watch.
QUEEN
Come here, my dear Hamlet, sit next to me.

---

93 *Capitol* the great temple of Jupiter in Rome, but generally taken
to be the Senate House. Hamlet puns in his reply: "capital/Capitol" (see
also "Brutus/brutal").

HAMLET
No, good mother. Here's metal more attractive.

POLONIUS [*to the King*]
100   O ho! Do you mark that?

HAMLET
Lady, shall I lie in your lap?
[*He lies at Ophelia's feet.*]

OPHELIA
No, my lord.

HAMLET
I mean, my head upon your lap?

OPHELIA
Ay, my lord.

HAMLET
105   Do you think I meant country matters?*

OPHELIA
I think nothing, my lord.

HAMLET
That's a fair thought to lie between maids' legs.

OPHELIA
What is, my lord?

HAMLET
Nothing.

OPHELIA
110   You are merry, my lord.

HAMLET
Who, I?

OPHELIA
Ay, my lord.

HAMLET
O God, your only jig-maker!* What should a man do but be
merry? For look you how cheerfully my mother looks, and my
115   father died within's two hours.

OPHELIA
Nay, 'tis twice two months, my lord.

HAMLET
So long? Nay then, let the devil wear black, for I'll have a suit
of sables.* O heavens! Die two months ago, and not forgotten

---

105 *country matters* rustic activities, with an obscene pun included.
113 *jig-maker* a jig was a comic performance given at the end of a
play or during an interval. A "jig-maker" is a comedian.

HAMLET
No, good mother. (*Looking at Ophelia*) Here's metal that draws
me magnetically to it.
POLONIUS (*to the King*)
100   Aha! Do you hear that?
HAMLET
Lady, shall I lie down in your lap? (*He lies down at Ophelia's
feet.*)
OPHELIA
No, my lord.
HAMLET
What I mean is, can I put my head on your lap?
OPHELIA
Yes, my lord.
HAMLET
105   Do you think I was talking about a roll in the hay?
OPHELIA
I think nothing at all, my lord.
HAMLET
To lie between girls' legs is a nice thought.
OPHELIA
What is, my lord?
HAMLET
Nothing.
OPHELIA
110   You're in a good mood, my lord.
HAMLET
Who, I?
OPHELIA
Yes, you my lord.
HAMLET
O God, that's me, your very best jig-maker! What else can a
person do but be
jolly? Take a good look at how happy my mother looks, and my
115   father died less than two hours ago.
OPHELIA
No, it was four months ago, my lord.
HAMLET
Was it so long ago as that? All right then, let the devil wear
mourning for I'll wear clothing
trimmed with sable. O by the heavens! The man died two months
ago and he's still not forgotten?

---

118 *sables* then as now extremely expensive fur, but Hamlet plays on
the other meaning of the word, "black."

120 yet? Then there's hope a great man's memory may outlive his life half a year. But, by'r Lady, 'a must build churches then, or else shall 'a suffer not thinking on, with the hobby-horse, whose epitaph is "For O, for O, the hobby-horse is forgot!"*

The trumpets sound. Dumb show follows:

Enter a KING *and a* QUEEN *very lovingly, the* QUEEN *embracing him, and he her. She kneels; and makes show of protestation unto him. He takes her up, and declines his head upon her neck. He lies him down upon a bank of flowers. She, seeing him asleep, leaves him. Anon come in another man: takes off his crown, kisses it, pours poison in the sleeper's ears, and leaves him. The* QUEEN *returns, finds the* KING *dead, makes passionate action. The poisoner, with some three or four, come in again, seem to condole with her. The dead body is carried away. The poisoner woos the* QUEEN *with gifts; she seems harsh awhile, but in the end accepts love.*

Exeunt.

OPHELIA
What means this, my lord?

HAMLET
Marry, this is miching mallecho; it means mischief.

OPHELIA
125   Belike this show imports the argument of the play.
Enter PROLOGUE.

HAMLET
We shall know by this fellow. The players cannot keep counsel; they'll tell all.

OPHELIA
Will 'a tell us what this show meant?

HAMLET
Ay, or any show that you will show him. Be not you ashamed
130   to show, he'll not shame to tell you what it means.

---

122   *hobby-horse is forgot*   the "hobby-horse" is a character dressed as a horse in traditional country sports and skits like the morris dance. The line

Then there is hope that a great man may be remembered
120   half a year after his death. But, by the Virgin Mary, he must
      pay for the building of churches then, or
      else he must put up with being forgotten like the hobbyhorse,
      whose
      epitaph is : "For O, for O, the hobbyhorse is forgot!"
            The trumpets sound. The actors stage the following pan-
            tomime:
            Enter KING *and* QUEEN, *openly affectionate, their arms*
            around one another. She kneels; by her gestures she dem-
            onstrates her faithful love for him. He lifts her to her
            feet and puts his head on her neck. He lies down on a
            flowery place. Seeing that he's asleep, she leaves the stage.
            Soon another man comes in. He takes off the King's
            crown, kisses it, pours poison in the sleeper's ear from a
            vial he carries, and leaves the stage. The QUEEN *re-*
            turns, finds the KING *dead, displays great grief in her*
            motions and expressions. The poisoner comes in again
            with three or four others and consoles the QUEEN. *The*
            dead body is carried off stage. The poisoner courts the
            QUEEN *by giving her gifts; she refuses him for a while*
            with disdainful looks, but in the end gives in.
            Exit the Actors.

OPHELIA
What does this mean, my lord?

HAMLET
Why, this is sneaking mischief; it means they're up to no good.

OPHELIA
125   It may be that this pantomime tells us what the play will be
      about.
            Enter an actor who plays the Prologue.

HAMLET
This fellow shall tell us. The actors can't keep a secret;
they'll reveal it all.

OPHELIA
Will he tell us what this pantomime meant?

HAMLET
Oh yes, or any show that you will show him. If you're not
      ashamed
130   to show it, he won't be ashamed to tell you what it means.

Hamlet quotes is from a popular ballad lamenting the suppression of such
sports in Shakespeare's day.

OPHELIA
You are naught, you are naught; I'll mark the play.

PROLOGUE
For us, and for our tragedy,
Here stooping to your clemency,
We beg your hearing patiently.
[*Exit.*]

HAMLET
135   Is this a prologue, or the posy of a ring?

OPHELIA
'Tis brief, my lord.

HAMLET
As woman's love.
Enter [two Players as] KING *and* QUEEN.

PLAYER KING
Full thirty times hath Phoebus' cart gone round
Neptune's salt wash and Tellus' orbèd ground,
140   And thirty dozen moons with borrowed sheen
About the world have times twelve thirties been,
Since love our hearts, and Hymen did our hands,
Unite commutual in most sacred bands.

PLAYER QUEEN
So many journeys may the sun and moon
145   Make us again count o'er ere love be done!
But woe is me, you are so sick of late,
So far from cheer and from your former state,
That I distrust you. Yet, though I distrust,
Discomfort you, my lord, it nothing must.
150   For women fear too much, even as they love,
And women's fear and love hold quantity,
In neither aught, or in extremity.
Now what my love is, proof hath made you know,
And as my love is sized, my fear is so.
155   Where love is great, the littlest doubts are fear;
Where little fears grow great, great love grows there.

OPHELIA
You are crude, you are too crude; I'll watch the play.

PROLOGUE
For us and for our tragic play,
we bow here and ask your mercy,
and we ask you to listen with patience.
Exit Prologue.

HAMLET
135   Is this an introduction, or the inscription inside a ring?

OPHELIA
It is short, my lord.

HAMLET
Like a woman's love.
Enter PLAYER KING *and* PLAYER QUEEN.

PLAYER KING
The sun god's chariot has made thirty complete circuits around
the god of the ocean's salt seas and the goddess of the earth's
sphere,
140   and three hundred and sixty moons with their reflected light
from the sun
have gone around the world three hundred and sixty times
since our hearts were joined by mutual love and our hands by the
god of marriage
in most holy bonds.

PLAYER QUEEN
May the sun and moon make us count as
145   many of their trips again before our love is over!
But how sad for me, you have been so sick recently,
so far from being happy and so different from the way you were,
that I am worried about you. Yet, even though I'm worried,
my lord, don't let it upset you in the least.
150   For women tend to worry too much, the same way they love,
and women's anxiety and love are in direct proportion to each
other,
nothing of both, or to an extreme in both.
Now, experience has taught you what my love is like,
and the dimension of my love is the same as that of my anxiety.
155   When love is great, the smallest worries are turned into anxiety;
when small worries turn into great ones, great love is to be
found there.

PLAYER KING
Faith, I must leave thee, love, and shortly too;
My operant powers their functions leave to do:
And thou shalt live in this fair world behind,
160   Honored, beloved, and haply one as kind
For husband shalt thou——

PLAYER QUEEN
                                    O, confound the rest!
Such love must needs be treason in my breast.
In second husband let me be accurst!
None wed the second but who killed the first.

HAMLET [*aside*]
165   That's wormwood.

PLAYER QUEEN
The instances that second marriage move
Are base respects of thrift, but none of love.
A second time I kill my husband dead
When second husband kisses me in bed.

PLAYER KING
170   I do believe you think what now you speak,
But what we do determine oft we break.
Purpose is but the slave to memory,
Of violent birth, but poor validity,
Which now like fruit unripe sticks on the tree,
175   But fall unshaken when they mellow be.
Most necessary 'tis that we forget
To pay ourselves what to ourselves is debt.
What to ourselves in passion we propose,
The passion ending, doth the purpose lose.
180   The violence of either grief or joy
Their own enactures with themselves destroy:
Where joy most revels, grief doth most lament;
Grief joys, joy grieves, on slender accident.
This world is not for aye, nor 'tis not strange
185   That even our loves should with our fortunes change,
For 'tis a question left us yet to prove,

PLAYER KING
By my faith, I must leave you, my love, and soon too;
my bodily powers are beginning to malfunction.
And you will stay behind in this lovely world,
160   honored, loved, and I hope you shall have
a husband who loves you as much——
PLAYER QUEEN
O, don't say any more!
Such love would be treason in my heart.
Let me be cursed if I marry a second husband!
No one marries a second husband without killing the first.
HAMLET (*to the audience*)
165   That's a bitter reminder.
PLAYER QUEEN
The motives that cause second marriages
are sordid financial considerations that have nothing to do with
      love.
I kill my husband a second time
when my second husband kisses me in bed.
PLAYER KING
170   I believe you're sincere in what you're saying now,
but we often fail to stick to our resolutions.
Good intentions have to be remembered in order to work;
they're made suddenly, but they don't have any lasting power.
Now they're like unripe fruit which stays on the tree,
175   but they fall without shaking when they're ripe.
It's only natural that we forget
to pay ourselves what we owe ourselves.
When we're excited, we say we'll do something,
but once the emotion subsides, we lose our inclination.
180   The intensity of either happiness or sadness means
that they destroy any plans for action once they burn themselves
      out.
Where happiness is the greatest, the sadness which follows will
      be the most grievous;
sadness turns to happiness, happiness to sadness, over the most
      trivial incident.
This world won't last forever, and it's not therefore strange
185   that even our loves should change according to our circum-
      stances;
since it's still uncertain

Whether love lead fortune, or else fortune love.
The great man down, you mark his favorite flies;
The poor advanced makes friends of enemies;
190   And hitherto doth love on fortune tend,
For who not needs shall never lack a friend;
And who in want a hollow friend doth try,
Directly seasons him his enemy.
But, orderly to end where I begun,
195   Our wills and fates do so contrary run
That our devices still are overthrown;
Our thoughts are ours, their ends none of our own.
So think thou wilt no second husband wed,
But die thy thoughts when thy first lord is dead.

PLAYER QUEEN
200   Nor earth to me give food, nor heaven light,
Sport and repose lock from me day and night,
To desperation turn my trust and hope,
An anchor's cheer in prison be my scope,
Each opposite that blanks the face of joy
205   Meet what I would have well, and it destroy:
Both here and hence pursue me lasting strife,
If, once a widow, ever I be wife!

HAMLET
If she should break it now!

PLAYER KING
'Tis deeply sworn. Sweet, leave me here awhile;
210   My spirits grow dull, and fain I would beguile
The tedious day with sleep.

PLAYER QUEEN
                Sleep rock thy brain,
    [He] sleeps.
And never come mischance between us twain!
    Exit.

whether love dominates chance, or chance controls love.
When an important man loses his power, notice how his best
    friend runs away ;
when the poor man gets money and power his enemies become
    his friends.

190 And up to now, being loved depends on the luck you've had,
for anyone who is secure and powerful and doesn't need friends
    is never without them ;
but anyone who's down on his luck and asks his false friend for
    help,
turns him at once into his enemy.
But, to come back properly to where I started,

195 our desires and fortunes run in such different directions
that our plans are always defeated.
Our intentions are our own, but their results are not what we
    planned.
So, you may think you won't marry a second husband,
but your resolutions will also perish when your first husband
    is dead.

PLAYER QUEEN
200 May the earth refuse to provide food for me, may the sun hide
    its light,
may I be cut off day and night from amusement and rest,
may my faith and hope be turned to despair,
may my aim in life be as limited as a hermit's diet in prison,
may the contrary event that makes the face of joy pale
205 confront whatever I want to turn out well and destroy it.
Both here on earth and in the life to come may I be pursued by
    endless trouble.
if I ever marry again after becoming a widow!

HAMLET
What will happen if she breaks her word now!

PLAYER KING
That's a solemn vow. Sweetheart, leave me alone here for a
    while.
210 I feel tired, and I would like to pass the time
on this dull day by sleeping.

PLAYER QUEEN
Let sleep soothe your tired mind (*Player King sleeps*),
and may bad luck never separate us.
      Exit PLAYER QUEEN.

HAMLET
Madam, how like you this play?

QUEEN
The lady doth protest too much, methinks.

HAMLET
215   O, but she'll keep her word.

KING
Have you heard the argument? Is there no offense in't?

HAMLET
No, no, they do but jest, poison in jest; no offense i' th' world.

KING
What do you call the play?

HAMLET
The Mousetrap. Marry, how? Tropically.* This play is the image
220   of a murder done in Vienna: Gonzago is the Duke's name; his
wife, Baptista. You shall see anon. 'Tis a knavish piece of work,
but what of that? Your Majesty, and we that have free souls, it
touches us not. Let the galled jade winch; our withers are un-
wrung.
    Enter LUCIANUS.
225   This is one Lucianus, nephew to the King.

OPHELIA
You are as good as a chorus, my lord.

HAMLET
I could interpret between you and your love, if I could see the
puppets dallying.

OPHELIA
You are keen, my lord, you are keen.

HAMLET
230   It would cost you a groaning to take off mine edge.

---

219 *Tropically* wordplay "Tropically/trap," and the word is in fact
spelled "trapically" in the 1604 edition of the play. "Tropically" is from
"trope," a figure of speech.

HAMLET

Madam, how do you like this play?

QUEEN

The lady makes too many declarations of her good intentions,
I think.

HAMLET

215   O, but she'll do what she says.

KING

Do you know what the plot is? Is there anything insulting to
my majesty in it?

HAMLET

No, no, they're only joking, poisoning in fun; no insult at all
in it.

KING

What is the name of the play?

HAMLET

The Mousetrap. Why, you may ask? It's a figure of speech. This
play is based
220   on a real murder committed in Vienna. Gonzago is the Duke's
name; his
wife is called Baptista. You will see the murder itself in a
moment. It's a nasty sort of business,
but what does it matter? Your Majesty, and those of us who
have clear consciences, it
doesn't bother us. Let the guilty ones, like the sore-backed horse,
wince in pain; our shoulders are not
aching from any burden of guilt.
Enter LUCIANUS.
225   This is a certain Lucianus, the King's nephew.

OPHELIA

You're just like a narrator, my lord.

HAMLET

I could speak the dialogue between you and your lover if I were
the puppet-master
and could catch you making love.

OPHELIA

You're sharp and bitter, my lord, you're sharp and bitter.

HAMLET

230   You would have to sigh and groan in bed (and in childbirth, too)
to make me dull.

OPHELIA
Still better, and worse.

HAMLET
So you mistake your husbands.—Begin, murderer. Leave thy damnable faces and begin. Come, the croaking raven doth bellow for revenge.

LUCIANUS
235   Thoughts black, hands apt, drugs fit, and time agreeing,
Confederate season, else no creature seeing,
Thou mixture rank, of midnight weeds* collected,
With Hecate's ban* thrice blasted, thrice infected,
Thy natural magic and dire property
240   On wholesome life usurps immediately.
Pours the poison in his ears.

HAMLET
'A poisons him i' th' garden for his estate. His name's Gonzago. The story is extant, and written in very choice Italian. You shall see anon how the murderer gets the love of Gonzago's wife.

OPHELIA
The King rises.

HAMLET
245   What, frighted with false fire?

QUEEN
How fares my lord?

POLONIUS
Give o'er the play.

KING
Give me some light. Away!

POLONIUS
Lights, lights, lights!
Exeunt all but HAMLET *and* HORATIO.

---

237 *midnight weeds* according to popular beliefs about magic, weeds collected at midnight were especially effective for casting spells.

OPHELIA

That's an even better answer, and also a worse one (i.e., a filthier one).

HAMLET

That's what you women think husbands promise: for better or for worse. (*To Lucianus*) Come on, get started, murderer. Stop making those

horrible faces and get started. Come on, let's have a line like "the croaking raven bellows like a bull

for revenge."

LUCIANUS

235   I have evil thoughts, ready hands, suitable drugs, and the time is right,

the darkness of night helps me, and nobody can see me. (*Holds up a vial of poison.*)

You foul and disgusting concoction, made from weeds collected at midnight,

withered and contaminated three times by the curse of that witch, Hecate,

your natural magic powers and your fearful qualities can

240   immediately destroy a healthy life. (*He pours the poison in the Player King's ear.*)

HAMLET

He poisons him in the garden to get his property. The King's name is Gonzago.

The story still exists, and is written in very fine Italian. You shall

soon see how the murderer wins the love of Gonzago's wife.

OPHELIA

The King is getting up.

HAMLET

245   What, is he frightened by blank cartridges?

QUEEN (*to Claudius*)

Are you feeling all right, my lord?

POLONIUS

Stop the play.

KING

Bring me some lights. Let's leave!

POLONIUS

Lights, lights, lights!

> *Attendants with torches come forward, and exit everyone except* HAMLET *and* HORATIO.

---

238 *Hecate's ban* Hecate was the Greek goddess of ghosts and magic, a protectress of enchanters and witches. She appears as a character in *Macbeth* (IV, i).

HAMLET

250   Why, let the strucken deer go weep,
          The hart ungallèd play:
          For some must watch, while some must sleep;
          Thus runs the world away.
       Would not this, sir, and a forest of feathers—if the rest of my
255   fortunes turn Turk with me—with two Provincial roses on my
       razed* shoes, get me a fellowship in a cry of players?

HORATIO

Half a share.

HAMLET

A whole one, I.
          For thou dost know, O Damon* dear,
260   This realm dismantled was
          Of Jove himself; and now reigns here
             A very, very—pajock.*

HORATIO

You might have rhymed.

HAMLET

O good Horatio, I'll take the ghost's word for a thousand pound.
265   Didst perceive?

HORATIO

Very well, my lord.

HAMLET

Upon the talk of poisoning?

HORATIO

I did very well note him.

HAMLET

          Ah ha! Come, some music! Come, the recorders!
270   For if the King like not the comedy,
          Why then, belike he likes it not, perdy.
       Come, some music!

          Enter ROSENCRANTZ *and* GUILDENSTERN.

GUILDENSTERN

Good my lord, vouchsafe me a word with you.

HAMLET

Sir, a whole history.

GUILDENSTERN

275   The King, sir——

---

256 *razed* Hamlet describes an Elizabethan actor's trimmings: "feath-
ers" — plumes worn by tragic actors, "Provincial roses" — ribbon rosettes
designed to look like roses (of Provençe), and "razed shoes" — shoes deco-
rated with slashes.

259 *Damon* in the well known story from Roman mythology, Damon

HAMLET (*singing*)
250   Why, let the wounded deer cry,
    but the unhurt deer play.
    For some must stay awake, while some must sleep;
    that's the way of the world.
    Wouldn't this performance, sir, and a ton of actor's plumes—
    if the rest of my
255   luck goes bad—along with two rosettes on my
    fancy shoes, earn me membership in a company of actors?
HORATIO
    Half a share of the profits.
HAMLET
    A whole one for me.
    (*Singing*) For you certainly know, O Damon dear,
260   this kingdom was deprived
    of Jove himself; and there now reigns here
    an absolute, absolute—peacock.
HORATIO
    You could have made those lines rhyme.
HAMLET
    O, good Horatio. I'll bet you a thousand pounds that the Ghost
    is right.
265   Did you see?
HORATIO
    Very clearly, my lord.
HAMLET
    When the dialogue was about poisoning?
HORATIO
    I observed the King very carefully.
HAMLET
    Aha! Come on, let's have some music! Come on, bring on the
    recorders!
270   (*Singing*) For if the King doesn't like the comedy,
    why, then, by God, it may be that he doesn't like it.
    Come on, let's have some music.
        Enter ROSENCRANTZ *and* GUILDENSTERN.
GUILDENSTERN
    My good lord, please let me have a word with you.
HAMLET
    Sir, not just one word, but a whole history.
GUILDENSTERN
275   The King, sir—

---

and Pythias were such devoted friends that Damon pledged his life as a
hostage for the condemned Pythias.
    262 *pajock* substitute for "ass," the word that would have rhymed.
According to the natural history of the time, the habits of the peacock
were repulsive.

HAMLET
Ay, sir, what of him?

GUILDENSTERN
Is in his retirement marvelous distemp'red.

HAMLET
With drink, sir?

GUILDENSTERN
No, my lord, with choler.

HAMLET
280   Your wisdom should show itself more richer to signify this to the
doctor, for me to put him to his purgation would perhaps plunge
him into more choler.*

GUILDENSTERN
Good my lord, put your discourse into some frame, and start not
so wildly from my affair.

HAMLET
285   I am tame, sir; pronounce.

GUILDENSTERN
The Queen, your mother, in most great affliction of spirit hath
sent me to you.

HAMLET
You are welcome.

GUILDENSTERN
Nay, good my lord, this courtesy is not of the right breed. If it
290   shall please you to make me a wholesome answer, I will do your
mother's commandment: if not, your pardon and my return shall
be the end of my business.

HAMLET
Sir, I cannot.

ROSENCRANTZ
What, my lord?

HAMLET
295   Make you a wholesome answer; my wit's diseased. But, sir, such
answer as I can make, you shall command, or rather, as you
say, my mother. Therefore no more, but to the matter. My
mother, you say——

---

282 *choler* Hamlet deliberately takes "choler" (anger) to mean that
the King is bilious, that is, suffering from an excess of bile, one of the four

HAMLET
Yes, sir, what about him?
GUILDENSTERN
—left the play because he was very upset.
HAMLET
From drinking too much, sir?
GUILDENSTERN
No, my lord, from anger.
HAMLET
280 It would be much wiser of you to tell this to the
doctor, since for me to prescribe a laxative for him would
perhaps make
him even more bilious.
GUILDENSTERN
My good lord, put your words into some logical order, and don't
jump away
so erratically from what I'm talking about.
HAMLET
285 I am now submissive, sir; speak.
GUILDENSTERN
The Queen, your mother, is deeply troubled and has
sent me to see you.
HAMLET
You're welcome here.
GUILDENSTERN
No, my good lord, this kind of politeness is not appropriate
here. If you
290 will please give me a reasonable answer, I will obey your
mother's command; if not, begging your pardon, I'll return and
tell her, and that shall
be the end of my errand.
HAMLET
Sir, I cannot.
ROSENCRANTZ
Cannot what, my lord?
HAMLET
295 I can't give you a reasonable answer; my mind is disturbed.
But, sir, whatever
response I can manage, you shall receive; or rather, as you
say, my mother shall. Therefore no more excuses, but let's get
to the issue. My
mother you say—

---

fluids of the human body, according to the physiological theory of the time:
blood, phlegm, choler (or bile), and black bile.

ROSENCRANTZ

300   Then thus she says: your behavior hath struck her into amazement and admiration.

HAMLET

O wonderful son, that can so stonish a mother! But is there no
sequel at the heels of this mother's admiration? Impart.

ROSENCRANTZ

She desires to speak with you in her closet ere you go to bed.

HAMLET

We shall obey, were she ten times our mother. Have you any
305   further trade with us?

ROSENCRANTZ

My lord, you once did love me.

HAMLET

And do still, by these pickers and stealers.*

ROSENCRANTZ

Good my lord, what is your cause of distemper? You do surely
bar the door upon your own liberty, if you deny your griefs to
310   your friend.

HAMLET

Sir, I lack advancement.

ROSENCRANTZ

How can that be, when you have the voice of the King himself
for your succession in Denmark?
          Enter the PLAYERS *with recorders.*

HAMLET

Ay, sir, but "while the grass grows"—the proverb* is some-
315   thing musty. O, the recorders. Let me see one. To withdraw with
you—why do you go about to recover the wind of me as if you
would drive me into a toil?

GUILDENSTERN

O my lord, if my duty be too bold, my love is too unmannerly.

HAMLET

I do not well understand that. Will you play upon this pipe?

---

307   *stealers*   the catechism of the Church of England says that we must
keep our hands from "picking and stealing."

ROSENCRANTZ

Then this is what she says : your actions have stunned her with
300   bewilderment and wonder.

HAMLET

O what a wonderful son I am that can astound a mother! But
    isn't there
anything else that follows this mother's wonder? Tell me.

ROSENCRANTZ

She would like to speak with you in her private room before
    you go to bed.

HAMLET

I shall obey even if she were my mother ten times over. Do you
    have anything
305   further to tell me?

ROSENCRANTZ

My lord, you were once very fond of me.

HAMLET

And I am still; I swear it by these thieving hands of mine.

ROSENCRANTZ

My good lord, why are you upset? You are certainly
denying yourself your own freedom if you conceal your sorrows
    from
310   your friend.

HAMLET

Sir, my ambitions are frustrated.

ROSENCRANTZ

How can that be, when the King himself
has declared that you're next in line for the throne of Denmark?
    Enter the Actors with recorders.

HAMLET

Yes sir, but "while the grass grows"—the old adage is a
315   bit stale. O the recorders, let me have one. (*To Rosencrantz and
    Guildenstern*) Let me speak privately to
you. Why are you trying to get down wind from me, as if you
wanted to drive me into a trap?

ROSENCRANTZ

O, my lord, if I offend you in doing my duty too well, it's because
    my friendship for you is too great to be confirmed by
    politeness.

HAMLET

I don't really know what you're talking about. Will you play
    this recorder?

---

314 *proverb*   "While the grass grows, the horse starves."

GUILDENSTERN

320   My lord, I cannot.

HAMLET

I pray you.

GUILDENSTERN

Believe me, I cannot.

HAMLET

I pray you.

GUILDENSTERN

Believe me, I cannot.

HAMLET

325   I do beseech you.

GUILDENSTERN

I know no touch of it, my lord.

HAMLET

It is as easy as lying. Govern these ventages with your fingers and thumb, give it breath with your mouth, and it will discourse most eloquent music. Look you, these are the stops.

GUILDENSTERN

330   But these cannot I command to any utt'rance of harmony; I have not the skill.

HAMLET

Why, look you now, how unworthy a thing you make of me! You would play upon me; you would seem to know my stops; you would pluck out the heart of my mystery; you would sound 335   me from my lowest note to the top of my compass; and there is much music, excellent voice, in this little organ, yet cannot you make it speak. 'Sblood, do you think I am easier to be played on than a pipe? Call me what instrument you will, though you can fret* me, you cannot play upon me.

Enter POLONIUS.

340   God bless you, sir!

POLONIUS

My lord, the Queen would speak with you, and presently.

---

339   *fret*   wordplay on "fret" meaning "annoy," and the "frets" or ridges that guide the fingers on stringed instruments.

GUILDENSTERN
320   My lord, I don't know how.
HAMLET
Please, play.
GUILDENSTERN
I swear to you, I don't know how.
HAMLET
Please, play.
GUILDENSTERN
I swear to you, I don't know how.
HAMLET
325   Please, I want you to play.
GUILDENSTERN
I have no skill to play it, my lord.
HAMLET
It is as easy as telling lies. Regulate these openings with your
    fingers
and thumb, blow through it with your mouth, and it will give out
very eloquent music. Look here, these are the openings. (*Holds
    up a recorder.*)
GUILDENSTERN
330   But I can't manage to play anything; I
don't know how.
HAMLET
Why, look then, what an inferior thing you think I am!
You want to play on me; you pretend to know the right openings.
You want to get to the bottom of my secret; you want to sound
    me out
335   from my lowest note to the highest one I can manage. And
    there is
a great deal of music and excellent tone in this little instrument
    (*holding up the recorder*), but you can't
play it. By God's blood, do you think I can be played on more
    easily
than a recorder? No matter what musical instrument you
    compare me to, you may
pluck at me, but you can't play me (i.e., you can't make me talk).
    Enter POLONIUS.
340   God bless you, sir!
POLONIUS
My lord, the Queen would like to speak with you, and right away.

HAMLET
Do you see yonder cloud that's almost in shape of a camel?

POLONIUS
By th' mass and 'tis, like a camel indeed.

HAMLET
Methinks it is like a weasel.

POLONIUS
345   It is backed like a weasel.

HAMLET
Or like a whale.

POLONIUS
Very like a whale.

HAMLET
Then I will come to my mother by and by.
[*Aside*] They fool me to the top of my bent.—I will come by
350   and by.

POLONIUS
I will say so.
        Exit.

HAMLET
"By and by" is easily said. Leave me, friends.
        [*Exeunt all but* HAMLET.]
'Tis now the very witching time of night,
When churchyards yawn, and hell itself breathes out
355   Contagion to this world. Now could I drink hot blood
And do such business as the bitter day
Would quake to look on. Soft, now to my mother.
O heart, lose not thy nature; let not ever
The soul of Nero* enter this firm bosom.
360   Let me be cruel, not unnatural;
I will speak daggers to her, but use none.
My tongue and soul in this be hypocrites:
How in my words somever she be shent,
To give them seals never, my soul, consent!
        Exit.

---

359 *Nero*   the Roman emperor, Nero (37-68 A.D.), accused his mother,
Agrippina, of poisoning her husband and had her executed.

HAMLET
Do you see that cloud up there that's almost
    shaped like a camel?

POLONIUS
By God, so it is, just like a camel.

HAMLET
I think it looks like a weasel.

POLONIUS
345 It has a back like a weasel's.

HAMLET
Or like a whale.

POLONIUS
Very much like a whale.

HAMLET
Then I will go to my mother's room very soon.
    (*To the audience*) They make me act as crazy as I possibly can.
      (*To Polonius*) I will come to my mother very
350 soon.

POLONIUS   .
I will tell her so.
    Exit POLONIUS.

HAMLET
"Very soon" is easily said. Leave me alone here, friends.
    Exit all except HAMLET.
Now is the time of night when the forces of evil are abroad,
    when graveyards open up, and hell itself spouts
355 disease to this world. Now I could drink hot blood
and do such terrible things that doomsday itself
would be afraid to look at them. Well, now to see my mother.
O my heart, don't forget yourself; never may
the soul of Nero possess my determined heart.
360 Let me be cruel, but not unnatural.
I will rip her up with words, not with knives.
My mouth and my soul shall be hypocrites in this:
no matter how much my words shall blame her,
may my soul never agree to confirm those words with deeds!
    Exit HAMLET.

[*Scene iii: The castle.*] *Enter* KING, ROSENCRANTZ, *and* GUILDEN-STERN.

KING
　　I like him not, nor stands it safe with us
　　To let his madness range. Therefore prepare you.
　　I your commission will forthwith dispatch,
　　And he to England shall along with you.
5　　The terms of our estate may not endure
　　Hazard so near's as doth hourly grow
　　Out of his brows.

GUILDENSTERN
　　We will ourselves provide.
　　Most holy and religious fear it is
　　To keep those many many bodies safe
10　　That live and feed upon your Majesty.

ROSENCRANTZ
　　The single and peculiar life is bound
　　With all the strength and armor of the mind
　　To keep itself from noyance, but much more
　　That spirit upon whose weal depends and rests
15　　The lives of many. The cess of majesty
　　Dies not alone, but like a gulf doth draw
　　What's near it with it; or it is a massy wheel
　　Fixed on the summit of the highest mount,
　　To whose huge spokes ten thousand lesser things
20　　Are mortised and adjoined, which when it falls,
　　Each small annexment, petty consequence,
　　Attends the boist'rous ruin. Never alone
　　Did the King sigh, but with a general groan.

KING
　　Arm you, I pray you, to this speedy voyage,
25　　For we will fetters put about this fear,
　　Which now goes too free-footed.

ROSENCRANTZ
　　　　　　　　　　　　　　　We will haste us.

　　　　Exeunt Gentlemen.
　　　　Enter POLONIUS.

Act III, Scene iii: The castle. Enter KING, ROSENCRANTZ, *and* GUILDENSTERN.

KING
    I don't trust Hamlet, nor is it safe for me
    to let him wander about freely in his madness. Therefore, get
        yourselves ready.
    I will draw up your orders without delay,
    and he'll go to England with you.
5   The conditions under which I hold my power cannot tolerate
    danger so close to me, danger such as every hour
    appears more plainly in his face.

GUILDENSTERN
    We'll get ready.
    It is a most solemn and religious duty to provide
    for the safety of those countless people
10   whose lives depend upon your Majesty.

ROSENCRANTZ
    The private individual is obliged
    to use all his mind's defensive strength and armor
    to protect himself from injury, but how much more of an
        obligation
    that person has upon whose well-being depends and rests
15   the lives of many others. The death of a king
    is not a solitary one, but like a whirlpool it sucks in
    those who are near. Or the king is like an enormous wheel
    planted on top of the highest mountain,
    to whose huge spokes are fixed and connected ten thousand
20   smaller beings, and when that wheel breaks loose,
    each small appendage, with its own minor effects,
    accompanies the wheel's noisy fall. Never by himself
    does the King sigh, but he groans for the entire commonwealth.

KING
    Prepare yourselves, please, for this hasty trip,
25   for I will put chains on this frightening person,
    who now runs around too freely.

ROSENCRANTZ
    We'll hurry.
        Exit ROSENCRANTZ *and* GUILDENSTERN.
        Enter POLONIUS.

POLONIUS
My lord, he's going to his mother's closet.
Behind the arras I'll convey myself
To hear the process. I'll warrant she'll tax him home,
30   And, as you said, and wisely was it said,
'Tis meet that some more audience than a mother,
Since nature makes them partial, should o'erhear
The speech of vantage. Fare you well, my liege.
I'll call upon you ere you go to bed
And tell you what I know.
KING
                                        Thanks, dear my lord.
35
Exit POLONIUS.
O, my offense is rank, it smells to heaven;
It hath the primal eldest curse upon't,
A brother's murder. Pray can I not,
Though inclination be as sharp as will.
40   My stronger guilt defeats my strong intent,
And like a man to double business bound
I stand in pause where I shall first begin,
And both neglect. What if this cursèd hand
Were thicker than itself with brother's blood,
45   Is there not rain enough in the sweet heavens
To wash it white as snow? Whereto serves mercy
But to confront the visage of offense?
And what's in prayer but this twofold force,
To be forestallèd ere we come to fall,
50   Or pardon being down? Then I'll look up.
My fault is past. But, O, what form of prayer
Can serve my turn? "Forgive me my foul murder"?
This cannot be, since I am still possessed
Of those effects for which I did the murder,
55   My crown, mine own ambition, and my queen.
May one be pardoned and retain th' offense?
In the corrupted currents of this world
Offense's gilded hand may shove by justice,
And oft 'tis seen the wicked prize itself
60   Buys out the law. But 'tis not so above.

POLONIUS

My lord, he's going to his mother's private room.
I'll place myself behind the wall-hanging
to overhear the proceedings. I guarantee she'll take him to task,
30   and as you said—so wisely—
it's fitting that someone else besides his mother,
since nature makes mothers biased, should overhear
the talk from an advantageous position. Goodbye, my lord.
I'll come to see you before you go to bed
and tell you what I have found out.

KING
35   Thanks, my dear lord.
                    Exit POLONIUS.
O, my sin is foul, it smells as high as heaven;
it has the curse of Cain on it,
the murder of a brother. I am unable to pray,
even though my desire to pray is as strong as my resolution to
        do it.
40   My feeling of guilt is stronger, and defeats my strong intention,
and like a man committed to two different tasks,
I wonder about where to begin
and neglect both. What if this cursed hand of mine
were caked thicker than itself with my brother's blood?
45   Isn't there enough rain in the sweet heavens
to wash it as white as snow? What purpose does mercy have
except to help the sinner face up to his sins?
And what is there in prayer except this double power:
to prevent us from sinning before we sin,
50   or to forgive us after we have sinned? Then I will look up.
My sin is over. But O what kind of prayer
can be suitable? "Forgive the foul murder I have committed"?
That cannot be right, since I still enjoy
those rewards for which I did the murder:
55   my crown, my ambition, and my queen.
May a man be forgiven and keep the results of his sin?
In this corrupt world of ours,
the sinner's wealthy hand can shove justice aside,
and it often happens that the ill-gotten gains of crime
are used to bribe the law. But it's not that way up above.

There is no shuffling; there the action lies
In his true nature, and we ourselves compelled,
Even to the teeth and forehead of our faults,
To give in evidence. What then? What rests?

65 Try what repentance can. What can it not?
Yet what can it when one cannot repent?
O wretched state! O bosom black as death!
O limèd* soul, that struggling to be free
Art more engaged! Help, angels! Make assay.

70 Bow, stubborn knees, and, heart with strings of steel,
Be soft as sinews of the newborn babe.
All may be well.
        [*He kneels.*]
        Enter HAMLET.

HAMLET
Now might I do it pat, now 'a is a-praying,
And now I'll do't. And so 'a goes to heaven,

75 And so am I revenged. That would be scanned.
A villain kills my father, and for that
I, his sole son, do this same villain send
To heaven.
Why, this is hire and salary, not revenge.

80 'A took my father grossly, full of bread,
With all his crimes broad blown, as flush as May;
And how his audit stands, who knows save heaven?
But in our circumstance and course of thought,
'Tis heavy with him; and am I then revenged,

85 To take him in the purging of his soul,
When he is fit and seasoned for his passage?
No.
Up, sword, and know thou a more horrid hent.
When he is drunk asleep, or in his rage,

90 Or in th' incestuous pleasure of his bed,
At game a-swearing, or about some act
That has no relish of salvation in't—

---

68 *limèd* caught, as in bird lime, a sticky substance used for trapping birds.

No deception is allowed in heaven; there the charge is considered
in its true nature, and we ourselves are forced,
even to the last detail, to describe the true features of our crimes,
and to testify against ourselves. What then? What remains that
    I can do?
65   Let me see what repentance can accomplish. What can't it?
Yet what good is it when one cannot repent?
O miserable condition! O heart as guilty as death!
O my soul is caught in birdlime, and the more it struggles to
    escape,
the more entangled it is! Help, angels! Let me give it a try.
70   Bend, you stubborn knees, and you my heart with your steel
    fibers,
may you become as soft as the tendons of a newborn baby.
Everything still may be well. (*He kneels.*)
    Enter HAMLET, *with his sword drawn.*
HAMLET (*to the audience*)
Now I could murder him easily, now that he's praying,
and now I'll do it. And so his soul goes to heaven,
75   and so I am revenged. That needs to be considered carefully.
A villain kills my father, and for that
I, his only son, send this same villain's soul
to heaven.
Why, this is like being a paid assassin and not a real revenger
    at all.
80   He killed my father when his soul was unprepared, full of earthly
    pleasures,
with all his sins in full bloom, as luxuriant as the month of May.
And who except heaven knows how his spiritual account stands?
But to the best of our knowledge and belief,
divine judgment has gone against him. And am I then revenged
85   to kill Claudius while he's cleansing his soul with prayer,
when he's ready and fully prepared for his journey to the other
    world?
No.
Into your scabbard, sword (*sheathing his sword*), and let me use
    you again on a more terrible occasion.
When the King is in a drunken sleep or raging about,
90   or in the incestuous pleasure of his bed,
or swearing while gambling, or doing something
that has no flavor of salvation in it—

Then trip him, that his heels may kick at heaven,
And that his soul may be as damned and black
95   As hell, whereto it goes. My mother stays.
This physic but prolongs thy sickly days.
            Exit.
KING [*rises*]
My words fly up, my thoughts remain below.
Words without thoughts never to heaven go.
            Exit.

[*Scene iv: The* QUEEN's *closet.*] *Enter* [QUEEN] GERTRUDE *and*
POLONIUS.

POLONIUS
'A will come straight. Look you lay home to him.
Tell him his pranks have been too broad to bear with,
And that your Grace hath screened and stood between
Much heat and him. I'll silence me even here.
5   Pray you be round with him.
HAMLET (*within*)
Mother, Mother, Mother!
QUEEN
I'll warrant you; fear me not. Withdraw; I hear him coming.
            [POLONIUS *hides behind the arras.*]
            Enter HAMLET.
HAMLET
Now, Mother, what's the matter?
QUEEN
Hamlet, thou hast thy father much offended.
HAMLET
10   Mother, you have my father much offended.
QUEEN
Come, come, you answer with an idle tongue.
HAMLET
Go, go, you question with a wicked tongue.
QUEEN
Why, how now, Hamlet?
HAMLET
                    What's the matter now?

then trip him up so that his heels will kick desperately toward
   heaven,
and so that his soul may be as damned and black
95   as the hell to which it's going. My mother is waiting for me.
This mercy that saves you only stretches out your sick existence.
   Exit HAMLET.
KING (*rising to his feet*)
   My words fly up to heaven, but my thoughts remain here on
      earth.
   Words without sincere thoughts can never reach heaven.
      Exit KING.

Act III, Scene iv: The QUEEN's *private room. Enter* QUEEN
and POLONIUS.

POLONIUS
   Hamlet will be here right away. Be sure to speak bluntly to him.
   Tell him that his tricks have been too wild to put up with,
   and that you have protected him and stood between
   him and the King's great anger. I'll hide quietly right in here.
5   Please, be direct with Hamlet.
HAMLET (*offstage*)
   Mother, mother, mother!
QUEEN
   Rest assured; don't worry about me. Hide yourself; I hear him
      coming.
      (*Polonius hides behind a wall-hanging*)
      Enter HAMLET.
HAMLET
   Well now, mother, what's wrong?
QUEEN
   Hamlet, you have greatly offended your father.
HAMLET
10   Mother, you have greatly offended *my* father.
QUEEN
   Come, come, you answer me with foolish words.
HAMLET
   Go on, go on, you ask your question with evil words.
QUEEN
   Why, what's wrong, Hamlet?
HAMLET
   What's the matter with you?

QUEEN
    Have you forgot me?

HAMLET
                    No, by the rood, not so!
15 You are the Queen, your husband's brother's wife,
    And, would it were not so, you are my mother.

QUEEN
    Nay, then I'll set those to you that can speak.

HAMLET
    Come, come, and sit you down. You shall not budge.
    You go not till I set you up a glass
20 Where you may see the inmost part of you!

QUEEN
    What wilt thou do? Thou wilt not murder me? Help, ho!

POLONIUS [*behind*]
    What, ho! Help!

HAMLET [*draws*]
    How now? A rat? Dead for a ducat, dead!
        [*Makes a pass through the arras and*] *kills* POLONIUS.

POLONIUS [*behind*]
    O, I am slain!

QUEEN
                O me, what hast thou done?

HAMLET
25 Nay, I know not. Is it the King?

QUEEN
    O, what a rash and bloody deed is this!

HAMLET
    A bloody deed—almost as bad, good Mother,
    As kill a king, and marry with his brother.

QUEEN
    As kill a king?

HAMLET
                Ay, lady, it was my word.
        [*Lifts up the arras and sees* POLONIUS.]
30 Thou wretched, rash, intruding fool, farewell!
    I took thee for thy better. Take thy fortune.
    Thou find'st to be too busy is some danger.—

QUEEN
Have you forgotten who I am?

HAMLET
No, by Christ's cross, I certainly haven't!
15   You are the Queen, your husband's brother's wife,
and—I wish it weren't so—you are my mother.

QUEEN
All right then, I'll have you questioned by people who can talk
to you better than I can.

HAMLET
Come on now, sit down. (*Taking her forcibly and making her
sit*) You shall not budge.
You won't go until I show you a mirror
20   in which you may see your innermost nature!

QUEEN
What will you do? You won't murder me? Help, oh!

POLONIUS (*behind the wall-hanging*)
What, oh! Help!

HAMLET (*draws his sword*)
What's this? A rat? I'll bet a dollar I kill it, kill it dead!
(*Runs his sword through the wall-hanging and kills Polonius.*)

POLONIUS (*behind the wall-hanging*)
O, I am killed!

QUEEN
O my God, what have you done?

HAMLET
25   Why, I don't know. Is it the King?

QUEEN
O, what a hasty and bloody deed this is!

HAMLET
Yes, a bloody deed—almost as bad, my good mother,
as killing a king and marrying his brother.

QUEEN
Killing a king?

HAMLET
Yes, lady, that is what I said. (*Lifts up wall-hanging and
sees the body of Polonius.*)
30   You poor, reckless, meddling fool, goodbye!
I thought you were the King. Take your fate as it comes.
You have discovered that to be too meddlesome is rather
dangerous.—

Leave wringing of your hands. Peace, sit you down
And let me wring your heart, for so I shall
35   If it be made of penetrable stuff,
If damnèd custom have not brazed it so
That it be proof and bulwark against sense.

QUEEN
What have I done that thou dar'st wag thy tongue
In noise so rude against me?

HAMLET
                                    Such an act
40   That blurs the grace and blush of modesty,
Calls virtue hypocrite, takes off the rose
From the fair forehead of an innocent love,
And sets a blister* there, makes marriage vows
As false as dicers' oaths. O, such a deed
45   As from the body of contraction plucks
The very soul, and sweet religion makes
A rhapsody of words! Heaven's face does glow,
Yea this solidity and compound mass
With heated visage, as against the doom
Is thoughtsick at the act.

QUEEN
50   Ay me, what act,
That roars so loud and thunders in the index?

HAMLET
Look here upon this picture, and on this,
The counterfeit presentment of two brothers.
See what a grace was seated on this brow:
55   Hyperion's curls, the front of Jove himself,
An eye like Mars, to threaten and command,
A station like the herald Mercury*
New lighted on a heaven-kissing hill—
A combination and a form indeed
60   Where every god did seem to set his seal
To give the world assurance of a man.
This was your husband. Look you now what follows.
Here is your husband, like a mildewed ear
Blasting his wholesome brother. Have you eyes?

---

43 *blister* the result of branding, such as prostitutes received on the
forehead as a punishment for sin.

(*To the Queen*) Stop wringing your hands. Be quiet, sit down
and let me wring your heart, for that's what I shall do
35   if it's made of sensitive stuff,
if evil habits haven't hardened it so much
that it has defensive armor against all feeling.

QUEEN
What have I done that you dare to shout
so violently at me?

HAMLET
An act so bad
40   that it dims the virtuous blushing of a modest woman,
declares that goodness is hypocritical, removes the rosy color
from the beautiful forehead of an innocent lover,
and puts a brand of shame there, makes marriage vows
as meaningless as the oaths of dice-players. O, an action that
45   snatches away the soul itself from the body of the marriage
        contract,
and turns the sacred marriage vows
into a jumble of words! The face of heaven glows,
yes, this solid and massive body
is hot with anger, as if it were Judgment Day,
and looks sick at heart over your act.

QUEEN
50   Oh my, what act is this
that has such a noisy and violent prologue?

HAMLET (*holding up a locket with miniature portraits*)
Look here at this picture, and at this one,
the painted likeness of two brothers.
Look at the attractive virtue that was expressed in his
        appearance:
55   Hyperion's curls, a forehead like Jove himself,
an eye like Mars, able to frighten and to command men;
he had a bearing like the herald Mercury,
just landed on a hill which touches the sky—
a combination of features and a shape on which
60   every god seemed to put his stamp of approval
to assure the world that this was a man.
This was your husband. Look at what follows.
Here is your new husband now, like a rotten ear of corn
destroying his healthy brother. Do you have eyes?

55-57 *Hyperion ... Mercury* Hyperion, the sun god and a model of
male beauty (see 1.2.140 and note); Jove, the chief of the gods; Mars, the
god of war; Mercury, the messenger of the gods.

65   Could you on this fair mountain leave to feed,
      And batten on this moor? Ha! Have you eyes?
      You cannot call it love, for at your age
      The heyday in the blood is tame, it's humble,
      And waits upon the judgment, and what judgment
70   Would step from this to this? Sense sure you have,
      Else could you not have motion, but sure that sense
      Is apoplexed, for madness would not err,
      Nor sense to ecstasy was ne'er so thralled
      But it reserved some quantity of choice
75   To serve in such a difference. What devil was't
      That thus hath cozened you at hoodman-blind?
      Eyes without feeling, feeling without sight,
      Ears without hands or eyes, smelling sans all,
      Or but a sickly part of one true sense
80   Could not so mope.
          O shame, where is thy blush? Rebellious hell,
      If thou canst mutine in a matron's bones,
      To flaming youth let virtue be as wax
      And melt in her own fire. Proclaim no shame
85   When the compulsive ardor gives the charge,
      Since frost itself as actively doth burn,
      And reason panders will.

QUEEN
                        O Hamlet, speak no more.
      Thou turn'st mine eyes into my very soul,
      And there I see such black and grainèd spots
      As will not leave their tinct.

HAMLET
90   Nay, but to live
      In the rank sweat of an enseamèd bed,
      Stewed in corruption, honeying and making love
      Over the nasty sty——

QUEEN
                        O, speak to me no more.
      These words like daggers enter in my ears.
      No more, sweet Hamlet.

65 How could you stop feeding on this beautiful mountain
 to gorge yourself on this swamp? Ha, tell me! Do you have eyes?
 You can't say it's love, for at your age
 the excitement of passion is tame, it's obedient,
 and it's subordinate to reason. And what kind of reason
70 would go from this to this? Surely your senses are still
  functioning,
 or else you wouldn't have any desires; but your feelings must
  certainly
 be paralyzed, for madness itself couldn't make such a mistake,
 nor did passion ever enslave the senses so
 that they didn't still have the power to choose
75 in such an obvious case. What devil was it
 who cheated you this way at blindman's buff?
 Eyes without any feeling, feeling without sight,
 ears without hands or eyes, the sense of smell without any other
  sense,
 or only a weakened part of one healthy sense
80 could not be so dull and imperceptive.
 O shame, where is your blush? O you rebellious evil impulses,
 if you can start a revolution in an older woman's body,
 then let virtue be like wax for passionate youth
 and melt away in the fire of their emotions. Let it not be called
  shameful
85 when compelling passion orders the attack,
 since coldness itself burns with passion just as readily,
 and reason pimps for desire.

QUEEN
 O Hamlet, don't say any more.
 You turn my eyes to look into my soul,
 and there I see spots so black and indelible
 that they can never be erased.

HAMLET
90 Well, but to live
 in the foul sweat of a greasy bed,
 soaked in corruption, embracing with honeyed sweetness
 in the nasty pig sty—

QUEEN
 O, don't tell me any more.
 These words pierce my ears like daggers.
 No more, dear Hamlet.

HAMLET

95   A murderer and a villain,
A slave that is not twentieth part the tithe
Of your precedent lord, a vice* of kings,
A cutpurse of the empire and the rule,
That from a shelf the precious diadem stole
And put it in his pocket——

QUEEN

100   No more.

      Enter GHOST.

HAMLET

A king of shreds and patches*——
Save me and hover o'er me with your wings,
You heavenly guards! What would your gracious figure?

QUEEN

Alas, he's mad.

HAMLET

105 Do you not come your tardy son to chide,
That, lapsed in time and passion, lets go by
Th' important acting of your dread command?
O, say!

GHOST

Do not forget. This visitation
110 Is but to whet thy almost blunted purpose.
But look, amazement on thy mother sits.
O, step between her and her fighting soul!
Conceit in weakest bodies strongest works.
Speak to her, Hamlet.

HAMLET

                    How is it with you, lady?

QUEEN

115 Alas, how is't with you,
That you do bend your eye on vacancy,
And with th' incorporal air do hold discourse?
Forth at your eyes your spirits wildly peep,
And as the sleeping soldiers in th' alarm
120 Your bedded hair like life in excrements
Start up and stand on end. O gentle son,

---

97 *vice* a character in the so-called "Morality" plays of the Middle Ages and the 16th century, who was a clown and a buffoon.

HAMLET

95   A murderer and a villain,
a slave who is not the twentieth part of a tenth
of your former husband, a fool of a king,
a pickpocket who stole the ruling power in Denmark,
who filched the precious crown from a shelf
and put it in his pocket—

QUEEN

100   No more.

> *Enter* GHOST.

HAMLET

A king dressed in a clown suit—
(*Seeing the Ghost*) Preserve my soul! and stay near me with
your wings,
you heavenly guardian angels! (*To the Ghost*) What do you
want, you royal personage?

QUEEN

Alas, he's insane.

HAMLET

105   Have you come to scold your lazy son,
who has allowed time to pass and emotion to subside, and who
delays
the urgent fulfillment of your fearful order?
O, speak!

GHOST

Do not forget. This visit
110   is only to sharpen your nearly blunted intention.
But look, your mother is utterly bewildered.
O preserve her from the ill effects of her anguished soul!
Imagination works most dangerously in the weakest bodies.
Speak to her, Hamlet.

HAMLET

How are you feeling, my lady?

QUEEN

115   Alas, how are you feeling,
since you stare at nothing
and talk to the bodiless air?
Your vital energies stare wildly out at your eyes,
and like sleeping soldiers when the call to arms is sounded,
120   your combed hair rises as if it were a living substance
and starts up and stands on end. O kind son,

---

101 *patches* Hamlet may refer to the "motley" costume worn by a
jester or a clown, or to the make-shift and patched-up kind of king he accuses Claudius of being.

Upon the heat and flame of thy distemper
Sprinkle cool patience. Whereon do you look?

HAMLET
On him, on him! Look you, how pale he glares!
125   His form and cause conjoined, preaching to stones,
Would make them capable. —Do not look upon me,
Lest with this piteous action you convert
My stern effects. Then what I have to do
Will want true color; tears perchance for blood.

QUEEN
To whom do you speak this?

HAMLET
130   Do you see nothing there?

QUEEN
Nothing at all; yet all that is I see.

HAMLET
Nor did you nothing hear?

QUEEN
                                  No, nothing but ourselves.

HAMLET
Why, look you there! Look how it steals away!
My father, in his habit as he lived!
135   Look where he goes even now out at the portal!
        Exit GHOST.

QUEEN
This is the very coinage of your brain.
This bodiless creation ecstasy
Is very cunning in.

HAMLET
                        Ecstasy?
My pulse as yours doth temperately keep time
140   And makes as healthful music. It is not madness
That I have uttered. Bring me to the test,
And I the matter will reword, which madness
Would gambol from. Mother, for love of grace,
Lay not that flattering unction to your soul,
145   That not your trespass but my madness speaks.

on the hot flames of your disordered mind
sprinkle cool self-control. What are you looking at?
HAMLET
At him, at him! Look, how pale his face is as he stares!
125   If his appearance and his message were joined, he could
        preach to stones,
and make them able to respond. (*To the Ghost*) Don't look at me.
You might with this pitying act transform
my fierce intentions. Then what I have to do
will look unconvincing; I will cry perhaps, instead of spilling
    blood.
QUEEN
To whom are you saying this?
HAMLET
130   Don't you see anything there?
QUEEN
I see nothing at all; yet I see everything that's there.
HAMLET
And didn't you hear anything?
QUEEN
No, nothing but you and I talking.
HAMLET
Why, look there! Look at how it slips away!
My father, dressed in the clothes he wore when he was alive!
135   Look, there he goes now right out the door!
        Exit GHOST.
QUEEN
This is only what your mind has invented.
Madness is very skillful
at imagining such disembodied things.
HAMLET
Madness?
My pulse is as normal as yours
140   and makes as healthy a beat as yours. It is not madness
that I have spoken. Put me to the test,
and I'll rephrase what I've said, an act that madness
would skip away from. Mother, for the love of God
don't deceive yourself by applying a soothing ointment to your
    guilty soul,
145   and tell yourself that it is not your guilt but my madness that
    disturbs you.

It will but skin and film the ulcerous place
Whiles rank corruption, mining all within,
Infects unseen. Confess yourself to heaven,
Repent what's past, avoid what is to come,
150   And do not spread the compost on the weeds
To make them ranker. Forgive me this my virtue.
For in the fatness of these pursy times
Virtue itself of vice must pardon beg,
Yea, curb and woo for leave to do him good.
QUEEN
155   O Hamlet, thou hast cleft my heart in twain.
HAMLET
O, throw away the worser part of it,
And live the purer with the other half.
Good night—but go not to my uncle's bed.
Assume a virtue, if you have it not.
160   That monster custom, who all sense doth eat,
Of habits devil, is angel yet in this,
That to the use of actions fair and good
He likewise gives a frock or livery*
That aptly is put on. Refrain tonight,
165   And that shall lend a kind of easiness
To the next abstinence; the next more easy;
For use almost can change the stamp of nature,
And either [master]* the devil, or throw him out
With wondrous potency. Once more, good night,
170   And when you are desirous to be blest,
I'll blessing beg of you.—For this same lord,
I do repent; but heaven hath pleased it so,
To punish me with this, and this with me,
That I must be their scourge and minister.
175   I will bestow him and will answer well
The death I gave him. So again, good night.
I must be cruel only to be kind.
Thus bad begins, and worse remains behind.
One word more, good lady.
QUEEN
                    What shall I do?

---

163   *livery*   wordplay on "habits" or customary acts/"habits" or customary clothing, a uniform.
168   *either* [*master*] a disputed phrase. As it stands here the phrase

That ointment will merely skin over the sore spot,
while foul guilt will undermine everything from inside
and infect you without being seen. Confess your sins to God,
repent what has passed, avoid the sin in the future,
150   and don't spread manure on the weeds of your guilt
to make them fouler. Forgive me for seeming self-righteous,
for in the grossness of these bloated and short-winded times,
virtue itself must ask forgiveness from vice,
indeed, bow low and ask permission to cure vice.

QUEEN
155   O Hamlet, you have cut my heart in two.

HAMLET
O, throw away the worse part of it,
and live more purely with the other half.
Good night—but don't go to my uncle's bed.
Pretend to be virtuous, even if you're not.
160   Custom is a monster which wears away all natural feeling;
and although it acts like a devil in establishing bad habits,
    custom is like an angel in this sense,
that when we acquire beautiful and good habits,
custom makes them like a garment or a uniform
that is easily put on. Don't go to his bed tonight,
165   and that shall give a sort of ease
to the next act of self-control, and make the next after that
    easier.
For habit can almost alter natural character,
and either master the devil or get rid of him
with miraculous power. Once again, good night,
170   and when you want to be repentant,
I'll ask you to forgive me. As for this lord (Polonius) here,
I'm sorry I killed him; but heaven has seen fit
to punish me with this task, and to punish others by me,
because I must be the instrument and agent of heaven's justice.
175   I will dispose of him and will think how to defend myself
for his murder. So again, good night.
I must be cruel to you only in order to be kind.
In this way bad things begin, and worse remain to come.
One word more for you, my good lady.

QUEEN
What shall I do?

---

represents a combination of words which appear in separate Elizabethan
editions of the play: "either" from the 1604 Quarto 2, and "master" from
the 1611 Quarto 3.

HAMLET

180   Not this, by no means, that I bid you do:
Let the bloat King tempt you again to bed,
Pinch wanton on your cheek, call you his mouse,
And let him, for a pair of reechy kisses,
Or paddling in your neck with his damned fingers,
185   Make you to ravel all this matter out,
That I essentially am not in madness,
But mad in craft. 'Twere good you let him know,
For who that's but a queen, fair, sober, wise,
Would from a paddock, from a bat, a gib,
190   Such dear concernings hide? Who would do so?
No, in despite of sense and secrecy,
Unpeg the basket on the house's top,
Let the birds fly, and like the famous ape,
To try conclusions, in the basket creep
195   And break your own neck down.*

QUEEN

Be thou assured, if words be made of breath,
And breath of life, I have no life to breathe
What thou hast said to me.

HAMLET

I must to England; you know that?

QUEEN

Alack,
200   I had forgot. 'Tis so concluded on.

HAMLET

There's letters sealed, and my two school-fellows,
Whom I will trust as I will adders fanged,
They bear the mandate; they must sweep my way
And marshal me to knavery. Let it work;
205   For 'tis the sport to have the enginer
Hoist with his own petar, and 't shall go hard
But I will delve one yard below their mines
And blow them at the moon. O, 'tis most sweet
When in one line two crafts directly meet.
210   This man shall set me packing:*
I'll lug the guts into the neighbor room.

191-95 *No, in despite ... neck down* Hamlet is referring to a story (now lost) in which an ape opens a bird cage and watches the birds fly away. The ape then tries to imitate the birds and falls to his death.

HAMLET

180   Whatever you do, by no means do what I just asked you to:
let the puffed-up King lure you again to bed,
pinch you lewdly on your cheek, call you his mouse.
Let him for a couple of filthy kisses,
or by caressing you fondly around your neck with his damned
     fingers,
185   cause you to disclose all of this:
that is, that I am not actually insane,
but only pretending cunningly to be so. (*Sarcastically*) That
     would be good if you told him,
for would anyone who was only a queen, beautiful, reasonable,
     and wise,
hide from a toad, a bat, a tomcat,
190   matters of such intense importance? Who would hide them?
No, despite common sense and a promise of secrecy,
anyone would open the door of the cage on the roof,
let the birds fly away, and like the famous ape,
crawl into the cage to experiment with flying
195   and break your own neck in falling down.

QUEEN

You can be confident that if words are made of breath,
and life is made of breath, I have no life to breathe
what you have told me.

HAMLET

I have to go to England. Do you know that?

QUEEN

I'm sorry,
200   I had forgotten. It is decided on.

HAMLET

A letter has been signed and sealed, and my two school-mates,
whom I will trust as much as poisonous snakes,
have their orders. They are directed to take me away
and lead me into a treacherous scheme. Let their plot proceed;
205   for it's amusing to see the plotter
blown up with his own bomb, and I will be in a tough spot
unless I dig a yard below their land mines
and blow them up to the moon. O, it's really marvelous
when two plots come together exactly at the same time.
210   (*Pointing to Polonius' body*) This man shall give me my send-off.
I'll lug his fat guts into the next room.

---

210 *packing* wordplay on contriving or plotting/leaving in a hurry,
"sent packing." It may also be a pun on packing in the sense of taking on a
load, since Hamlet has to pick up the body; and there is also the sense of
"packing the deck."

Mother, good night. Indeed, this counselor
Is now most still, most secret, and most grave,
Who was in life a foolish prating knave.
215   Come, sir, to draw toward an end with you.
Good night, Mother.
          [*Exit the* QUEEN. *Then*] *exit* HAMLET, *tugging in* POLONIUS.

[*Act IV, Scene i: The castle.*] *Enter* KING *and* QUEEN, *with* ROSEN-
CRANTZ *and* GUILDENSTERN.

KING
    There's matter in these sighs. These profound* heaves
    You must translate; 'tis fit we understand them.
    Where is your son?
QUEEN
    Bestow this place on us a little while.
          [*Exeunt* ROSENCRANTZ *and* GUILDENSTERN.]
5   Ah, mine own lord, what have I seen tonight!
KING
    What, Gertrude? How does Hamlet?
QUEEN
    Mad as the sea and wind when both contend
    Which is the mightier. In his lawless fit,
    Behind the arras hearing something stir,
10   Whips out his rapier, cries, "A rat, a rat!"
    And in this brainish apprehension kills
    The unseen good old man.
KING
                              O heavy deed!
    It had been so with us, had we been there.
    His liberty is full of threats to all,
15   To you yourself, to us, to every one.
    Alas, how shall this bloody deed be answered?
    It will be laid to us, whose providence
    Should have kept short, restrained, and out of haunt
    This mad young man. But so much was our love
20   We would not understand what was most fit,
    But, like the owner of a foul disease,

---

1 *profound* wordplay on deep in the literal sense / significant, full of
meaning.

Good night, mother. Oh yes, this counselor
is now very quiet, very discreet, and very serious,
who during his life was a silly, babbling rascal.
215   Come on, sir, let me finish my business with you.
Good night, mother.
> *Exit the* QUEEN. *Then* HAMLET *exits, dragging off*
> POLONIUS' *body.*

Act IV, Scene i: The castle. Enter KING *and* QUEEN, *with*
ROSENCRANTZ *and* GUILDENSTERN.

KING
There's some meaning in these sighs of yours. These deep sighs
have to be explained; it's right that I should know what they
   mean.
Where is your son?
QUEEN (*to Rosencrantz and Guildenstern*)
Leave us alone here for a little while.
> *Exit* ROSENCRANTZ *and* GUILDENSTERN.
5   Oh, my own dear lord, what I have seen tonight!
KING
What is it, Gertrude? How is Hamlet?
QUEEN
As insane as the sea and wind when they fight to see
which is stronger. During his uncontrolled fit,
hearing something moving behind the wall-hanging,
10   he whips out his sword, shouts, "A rat, a rat!"
and with this crazy notion kills
the good old man he didn't even see.
KING
O what a grievous act!
It would have happened to me if I had been there.
His freedom is full of danger for all of us,
15   for you yourself, for me, for everyone.
Alas, how shall I explain this bloody act to the people?
I will be blamed, because my foresight
should have told me to keep this crazy young man on a short
leash, controlled, and away from other people. But my affection
   for him was so great
20   that I refused to recognize what I should have done,
and like someone with a dreadful disease,

To keep it from divulging, let it feed
Even on the pith of life. Where is he gone?

QUEEN
    To draw apart the body he hath killed;
25 O'er whom his very madness, like some ore
    Among a mineral of metals base,
    Shows itself pure. 'A weeps for what is done.

KING
    O Gertrude, come away!
    The sun no sooner shall the mountains touch
30 But we will ship him hence, and this vile deed
    We must with all our majesty and skill
    Both countenance and excuse. Ho, Guildenstern!
        Enter ROSENCRANTZ *and* GUILDENSTERN.
    Friends both, go join you with some further aid:
    Hamlet in madness hath Polonius slain,
35 And from his mother's closet hath he dragged him.
    Go seek him out; speak fair, and bring the body
    Into the chapel. I pray you haste in this.
        [*Exeunt* ROSENCRANTZ *and* GUILDENSTERN.]
    Come, Gertrude, we'll call up our wisest friends
    And let them know both what we mean to do
40 And what's untimely done.* [So haply slander],
    Whose whisper o'er the world's diameter,
    As level as the canon to his blank
    Transports his poisoned shot, may miss our name
    And hit the woundless air. O, come away!
45 My soul is full of discord and dismay.
        Exeunt.

[*Scene ii: The castle.*] *Enter* HAMLET.

HAMLET
    Safely stowed.

GENTLEMEN
    (*Within*)
    Hamlet, Lord Hamlet!

---

40 *untimely done* . . .   something is missing here in the existing versions
of the play. In his 1734 edition of Shakespeare, Lewis Theobald inserted
"For, haply, Slander." In his 1768 edition of Shakespeare, Edward Capell

rather than reveal it, I let it eat away
the essential strength of life. Where has he gone?

QUEEN
  To hide the body he has killed;
25 over which body his insanity itself, like some vein of gold
  in a mine of ordinary metals,
  shows that it is pure. He weeps for what he has done.

KING
  O Gertrude, come away!
  As soon as the sun rises on the mountains,
30 I shall send him off, and this evil act
  I must use all my power and ability
  both to sanction and to explain. You there, Guildenstern!
     Enter ROSENCRANTZ *and* GUILDENSTERN.
  My two friends, get some others to help you.
  In his insanity, Hamlet has killed Polonius,
35 and dragged the body out of his mother's private room.
  Go find him; talk gently to him, and bring the body
  into the chapel. Please do this quickly.
     Exit ROSENCRANTZ *and* GUILDENSTERN.
  Let us go, Gertrude. I'll summon my wisest advisers
  and let them know both what I plan to do
40 and what has so inconveniently been done. Perhaps slander,
  whose gossip carries deadly bullets right through the world
  with an aim as good as a cannon at its target, may miss my
     reputation
  and hit the invulnerable air. O, come away!
45 My soul is full of conflict and sorrow.
     Exit KING *and* QUEEN.

Act IV, Scene ii: The castle. Enter HAMLET.

HAMLET
  It's safely hidden.

GENTLEMEN (*from offstage*)
  Hamlet! Lord Hamlet!

---

changed the "for" to "so," and that phrase is usually included in modern
editions to make sense of the line.

HAMLET
But soft, what noise? Who calls on Hamlet?
O, here they come.

Enter ROSENCRANTZ *and* GUILDENSTERN.

ROSENCRANTZ
5   What have you done, my lord, with the dead body?

HAMLET
Compounded it with dust, whereto 'tis kin.

ROSENCRANTZ
Tell us where 'tis, that we may take it thence
And bear it to the chapel.

HAMLET
Do not believe it.

ROSENCRANTZ
10   Believe what?

HAMLET
That I can keep your counsel and not mine own. Besides, to be
demanded of a sponge, what replication should be made by the
son of a king?

ROSENCRANTZ
Take you me for a sponge, my lord?

HAMLET
15   Ay, sir, that soaks up the King's countenance, his rewards, his
authorities. But such officers do the King best service in the end.
He keeps them, like an ape an apple, in the corner of his jaw,
first mouthed, to be last swallowed. When he needs what you
have gleaned, it is but squeezing you and, sponge, you shall be
20   dry again.

ROSENCRANTZ
I understand you not, my lord.

HAMLET
I am glad of it: a knavish speech sleeps in a foolish ear.

ROSENCRANTZ
My lord, you must tell us where the body is and go with us to
the King.

HAMLET
25   The body is with the King, but the King is not with the body.*
The King is a thing——

---

25 *body* Hamlet may merely be speaking nonsense; but like all of his
crazy speeches, these lines suggest various meanings: the King is only a

HAMLET
But what's that, what sound do I hear? Who is calling Hamlet?
O, here they come.
Enter ROSENCRANTZ *and* GUILDENSTERN.
ROSENCRANTZ
5   What have you done, my lord, with the dead body?
HAMLET
Mixed it with earth, to which it is related.
ROSENCRANTZ
Tell us where it is, so that we may take it from there
and carry it to the chapel.
HAMLET
Don't believe it.
ROSENCRANTZ
10   Believe what?
HAMLET
That I can keep your secret and not my own. Anyway, if I am
questioned by a sponge, what reply should I, the
son of a king, make?
ROSENCRANTZ
Do you think that I'm a sponge, my lord?
HAMLET
15   Yes, sir, one that soaks up the King's favor, his rewards, his
power of granting offices. But flunkies like you perform their
best service for the King in the end.
He keeps them the way an ape keeps an apple at the side of his
mouth,
the first to be eaten, the last to be swallowed. When he needs
the information you
have gathered for him, he has only to squeeze you and, like a
sponge, you shall be
20   dry again.
ROSENCRANTZ
I don't understand you, my lord.
HAMLET
I'm glad to hear it. A satirical speech is meaningless to a fool.
ROSENCRANTZ
My lord, you must tell us where the body is and go with us to see
the King.
HAMLET
25   The body is with the King, but the King is not with the body.
The King is a thing—

---

body, the mere external appearance of kingship; the real King is dead; or
the King is guilty of this death.

GUILDENSTERN
A thing, my lord?

HAMLET
Of nothing. Bring me to him. Hide fox, and all after.*
Exeunt.

[*Scene iii: The castle.*] *Enter* KING, *and two or three.*

KING
I have sent to seek him and to find the body:
How dangerous is it that this man goes loose!
Yet must not we put the strong law on him:
He's loved of the distracted multitude,
5   Who like not in their judgment, but their eyes,
And where 'tis so, th' offender's scourge is weighed,
But never the offense. To bear all smooth and even,
This sudden sending him away must seem
Deliberate pause. Diseases desperate grown
10   By desperate appliance are relieved,
Or not at all.
            Enter ROSENCRANTZ.
                How now? What hath befall'n?

ROSENCRANTZ
Where the dead body is bestowed, my lord,
We cannot get from him.

KING
                But where is he?

ROSENCRANTZ
Without, my lord; guarded, to know your pleasure.

KING
Bring him before us.

ROSENCRANTZ
15   Ho! Bring in the lord.
        They enter.

KING
Now, Hamlet, where's Polonius?

---

28 *Hide fox, and all after*   probably a cry from a game resembling
hide-and-seek.

GUILDENSTERN
What do you mean, a thing, my lord?

HAMLET
A thing made of nothing. Bring me to him. Catch me if you can.
Exit HAMLET *running.* ROSENCRANTZ *and* GUILDEN-
STERN *run after him.*

Act IV, Scene iii: The castle. Enter KING *with two or three
courtiers.*

KING
I have sent people to look for Hamlet and to find Polonius' body.
It's so dangerous that this man runs about free!
And yet I must not apply the harsh penalties against murder
    to him.
He's a favorite of the unstable common people,
5   who don't judge matters reasonably but only by appearances;
and where that's the case, the sinner's punishment is considered,
but never his sin. In order to make my attitude look quite calm
    and unruffled,
this sudden sending him away must appear to be a
maturely considered decision. When diseases turn desperate,
10   they're either cured by desperate remedies
or they're not cured at all (and we die).
Enter ROSENCRANTZ.
Well now, what's happened?

ROSENCRANTZ
We cannot make him tell us
where the dead body is hidden, my lord.

KING
But where is he?

ROSENCRANTZ
Outside, my lord, under guard until we know what you want
    to do with him.

KING
Bring him to me.

ROSENCRANTZ *(to the guards offstage)*
15   All right, bring in the lord.
Enter HAMLET, GUILDENSTERN, *and Attendants.*

KING
Now, Hamlet, where's Polonius?

HAMLET
At supper.

KING
At supper? Where?

HAMLET
20   Not where he eats, but where 'a is eaten. A certain convocation of politic worms are e'en at him. Your worm is your only emperor for diet. We fat all creatures else to fat us, and we fat ourselves for maggots. Your fat king and your lean beggar is but variable service—two dishes, but to one table. That's the end.*

KING
25   Alas, alas!

HAMLET
A man may fish with the worm that hath eat of a king, and eat of the fish that hath fed of that worm.

KING
What dost thou mean by this?

HAMLET
Nothing but to show you how a king may go a progress through
30   the guts of a beggar.

KING
Where is Polonius?

HAMLET
In heaven. Send thither to see. If your messenger find him not there, seek him i' th' other place yourself. But if indeed you find him not within this month, you shall nose him as you go up the
35   stairs into the lobby.

KING [*to Attendants*]
Go seek him there.

HAMLET
'A will stay till you come.
          [*Exeunt Attendants.*]

---

24   *end*   wordplay: the end of my story and the end of every man (i.e., death).

HAMLET
  At supper.

KING
  At supper? Where?

HAMLET
  Not where he's eating, but where he is eaten. A certain assembly
20   of crafty worms are just this minute getting to him. The worm
      is the
  emperor of us all, if you consider what it eats. We fatten every
      other creature to feed ourselves, and we fatten
  ourselves to feed maggots. The fat king and the thin beggar are
  just different courses of the same meal—two separate dishes, but
      meant for the same table. That's
  all there is to it.

KING (*to the others*)
25   Alas, alas!

HAMLET
  A man may go fishing with the worm that has dined on a king,
      and eat
  part of the fish that's fed on the worm.

KING
  What do you mean by this?

HAMLET
  Nothing except to show you how a king can take a royal journey
      of state through
30   a beggar's guts.

KING
  Where is Polonius?

HAMLET
  In heaven. Send someone there to look. If your messenger doesn't
      find him
  there, look for him in hell yourself. But if it happens that you
      really can't find
  him within a month, you'll smell him as you go up the
35   stairs into the lobby.

KING (*to Attendants*)
  Go look for him there.

HAMLET
  Don't hurry; he'll wait for you till you get there.
      Exit Attendants.

KING

Hamlet, this deed, for thine especial safety,
Which we do tender as we dearly grieve
40   For that which thou hast done, must send thee hence
With fiery quickness. Therefore prepare thyself.
The bark is ready and the wind at help,
Th' associates tend, and everything is bent
For England.

HAMLET
                    For England?

KING
                              Ay, Hamlet.

HAMLET
                                        Good.

KING
45   So is it, if thou knew'st our purposes.

HAMLET
I see a cherub that sees them. But come, for England! Farewell,
dear Mother.

KING
Thy loving father, Hamlet.

HAMLET
My mother—father and mother is man and wife, man and wife
50   is one flesh, and so, my mother.
Come, for England!
          Exit.

KING
Follow him at foot; tempt him with speed aboard.
Delay it not; I'll have him hence tonight.
Away! For everything is sealed and done
55   That else leans on th' affair. Pray you make haste.
          [*Exeunt all but the* KING.]
And, England, if my love thou hold'st at aught—
As my great power thereof may give thee sense,
Since yet thy cicatrice looks raw and red
After the Danish sword, and thy free awe
60   Pays homage to us—thou mayst not coldly set
Our sovereign process, which imports at full
By letters congruing to that effect

KING
>Hamlet, to preserve your special safety,
>which I hold as dear as I deeply regret

40
>what you have done—this act of yours makes it necessary to send
>   you away
>with fiery swiftness. Therefore, get yourself ready.
>The ship is ready and the wind is favorable,
>your companions are waiting, and everything is set
>for your trip to England.

HAMLET
>To England?

KING
>Yes, Hamlet.

HAMLET
>Good.

KING

45
>And it *is* good, as you would agree if you knew my motives.

HAMLET
>I see an angel that sees them. But let's go, to England! Goodbye,
>dear mother.

KING
>I am your loving father, Hamlet.

HAMLET
>You're my mother—father and mother are man and wife, man
>   and wife

50
>are united in one body, and so, you are my mother.
>Come on, to England!
>>   *Exit* HAMLET.

KING
>Follow him closely; persuade him to get on board quickly.
>Don't delay it; I want him to leave tonight.
>Get going! For everything else is signed and sealed

55
>that relates to this matter. Please hurry.
>>   *Exit everyone except the* KING.
>O England, if you at all value my friendship—
>since my great power may cause you to realize its value,
>and since your scar is still fresh and red
>from the Danish victory in battle and your fear

60
>makes you pay homage to us voluntarily—you cannot with
>   indifference set aside
>my royal command, the full meaning of which

The present death of Hamlet. Do it, England,
For like the hectic in my blood he rages,
65   And thou must cure me. Till I know 'tis done,
Howe'er my haps, my joys were ne'er begun.
             Exit.

[*Scene iv: A plain in Denmark.*] *Enter* FORTINBRAS *with his Army over the stage.*

FORTINBRAS
Go, Captain, from me greet the Danish king.
Tell him that by his license Fortinbras
Craves the conveyance of a promised march
Over his kingdom. You know the rendezvous.
5   If that his Majesty would aught with us,
We shall express our duty in his eye;
And let him know so.

CAPTAIN
                              I will do't, my lord.

FORTINBRAS
Go softly on.
             [*Exeunt all but the* CAPTAIN.]
             Enter HAMLET, ROSENCRANTZ, &c.

HAMLET
Good sir, whose powers are these?

CAPTAIN
10   They are of Norway, sir.

HAMLET
How purposed, sir, I pray you?

CAPTAIN
Against some part of Poland.

HAMLET
Who commands them, sir?

CAPTAIN
The nephew of old Norway, Fortinbras.

HAMLET
15   Goes it against the main of Poland, sir,
Or for some frontier?

is expressed in a letter which says
that Hamlet should be put to death instantly. Do it, O King of
    England,
for he burns in my blood like a fever,
65   and you must cure me of it. Until I know it's done,
whatever my fortune, I'll never be truly happy.
    Exit KING.

Act IV, Scene iv: A plain in Denmark. Enter FORTINBRAS,
marching with his army across the stage.

FORTINBRAS
Go, Captain, and take my greetings to the Danish king.
Tell him that Fortinbras, by our previous agreement,
requests an escort to accompany him and his army
through the kingdom of Denmark. You know the place where
    we'll meet.
5   If his Majesty wants to say anything to me,
I will pay my respects to him personally
and tell him what I wish to do.
CAPTAIN
I will do it, my lord.
FORTINBRAS (*to his troops*)
March on slowly.
    Exit all except the CAPTAIN.
    Enter HAMLET, ROSENCRANTZ, GUILDENSTERN,
    and Attendants.
HAMLET
Good sir, whose forces are these?
CAPTAIN
10   They belong to the King of Norway, sir.
HAMLET
What are they going to attack, sir, may I ask?
CAPTAIN
They march against a part of Poland.
HAMLET
Who commands them, sir?
CAPTAIN
The old king of Norway's nephew, Fortinbras.
HAMLET
15   Is the expedition against the main territory of Poland, sir,
or to fight for some frontier of the country?

CAPTAIN
  Truly to speak, and with no addition,
  We go to gain a little patch of ground
  That hath in it no profit but the name.
20 To pay five ducats, five, I would not farm it,
  Nor will it yield to Norway or the Pole
  A ranker rate, should it be sold in fee.

HAMLET
  Why, then the Polack never will defend it.

CAPTAIN
  Yes, it is already garrisoned.

HAMLET
25 Two thousand souls and twenty thousand ducats
  Will not debate the question of this straw.
  This is th' imposthume of much wealth and peace,
  That inward breaks, and shows no cause without
  Why the man dies. I humbly thank you, sir.

CAPTAIN
  God bye you, sir.
     Exit.

ROSENCRANTZ
30   Will't please you go, my lord?

HAMLET
  I'll be with you straight. Go a little before.
    [*Exeunt all but* HAMLET.]
  How all occasions do inform against me
  And spur my dull revenge! What is a man,
  If his chief good and market of his time
35 Be but to sleep and feed? A beast, no more.
  Sure he that made us with such large discourse,
  Looking before and after, gave us not
  That capability and godlike reason
  To fust in us unused. Now, whether it be
40 Bestial oblivion, or some craven scruple
  Of thinking too precisely on th' event—
  A thought which, quartered, hath but one part wisdom
  And ever three parts coward—I do not know
  Why yet I live to say, "This thing's to do,"

CAPTAIN

To tell you the truth, and to speak plainly,
we are going to fight for a little bit of ground
from which nothing is to be gained but its name.

20 For an annual rent of five dollars—not more than five—I would
not rent it,
nor will it supply either to the king of Norway or to the Polish
king
a higher profit, even if it were sold outright.

HAMLET

Why, then the Polish king will never defend it.

CAPTAIN

Yes, it is already prepared for an attack.

HAMLET

25 Two thousand lives and twenty thousand dollars
will scarcely be enough to settle this trivial question.
In a time of wealth and peace, this sort of thing is like a cancer;
it spreads inside the body and reveals no external cause
for the man's death. I thank you kindly, sir.

CAPTAIN

Goodbye to you, sir.
Exit the CAPTAIN.

ROSENCRANTZ

30 Would you like to go, my lord?

HAMLET

I'll be with you right away. Go on a little way before me.
Exit all except HAMLET.
How all events accuse me of inactivity
and remind me of my revenge! What is a man
if his main desire and the chief profit of his days
35 is merely to sleep and eat? An animal, nothing more.
Certainly God, who made us with such wide powers of reason
to consider the future and the past, did not give us
that power of godlike reasoning
to grow moldly in us with disuse. Now, whether it is
40 a matter of beast-like forgetfulness, or because of some cowardly
hesitation
from thinking too carefully about the outcome of action—
a thought which cut into quarters, is only one part wisdom
and always three parts cowardice—I don't know
why I am still alive to say, "This thing must be done,"

45   Sith I have cause, and will, and strength, and means
       To do't. Examples gross as earth exhort me.
       Witness this army of such mass and charge,
       Led by a delicate and tender prince,
       Whose spirit, with divine ambition puffed,
50   Makes mouths at the invisible event,
       Exposing what is mortal and unsure
       To all that fortune, death, and danger dare,
       Even for an eggshell. Rightly to be great
       Is not to stir without great argument,
55   But greatly to find quarrel in a straw
       When honor's at the stake. How stand I then,
       That have a father killed, a mother stained,
       Excitements of my reason and my blood,
       And let all sleep, while to my shame I see
60   The imminent death of twenty thousand men
       That for a fantasy and trick of fame
       Go to their graves like beds, fight for a plot
       Whereon the numbers cannot try the cause,
       Which is not tomb enough and continent
65   To hide the slain? O, from this time forth,
       My thoughts be bloody, or be nothing worth!
                 Exit.

[*Scene v: The castle.*] *Enter* HORATIO, [QUEEN] GERTRUDE, *and a
Gentleman.*

QUEEN
   I will not speak with her.

GENTLEMAN
   She is importunate, indeed distract.
   Her mood will needs be pitied.

QUEEN
                              What would she have?

GENTLEMAN
   She speaks much of her father, says she hears
5   There's tricks i' th' world, and hems, and beats her heart,

45   since I have reasons, and purpose, and strength, and the means
to do it. Examples as obvious as the earth urge me on.
Look at this huge and expensive army,
led by a slight and youthful prince,
whose spirit, blown up with ambition to be immortal,
50   treats the unforeseen outcome with scorn,
risking whatever is mortal and uncertain
in the face of all that circumstances, death, and danger
    challenge him with,
even for something as trivial as an eggshell. To be truly great
is not to require a powerful reason for fighting,
55   but to find (as a gentleman should) something to fight about in a
    trivial matter
when honor is involved. What is my situation, then,
whose father has been killed, whose mother has been corrupted—
emotional and rational spurs to revenge—
and yet I allow everything to lie still; while to my shame I see
60   twenty thousand men about to die,
who for a whim and a trifle of honor and reputation
go to their graves as calmly as if they were going to bed, who go
    to fight for a piece of ground
which isn't large enough for all of them to fight on, and
which cannot offer a large enough grave
65   in which to bury the dead? O, from this moment on,
let my thoughts be about revenge or else be worthless!
        Exit HAMLET.

Act IV, Scene v: The castle. Enter HORATIO, *the* QUEEN, *and
a Gentleman.*

QUEEN
    I won't speak to her.
GENTLEMAN
    She is insistent, indeed she's losing her mind.
    Her state must provoke pity.
QUEEN
    What does she want?
GENTLEMAN
    She talks a great deal about her father; she says she hears
5   that the world is deceitful, and she clears her throat and beats
    her breast,

Spurns enviously at straws, speaks things in doubt
That carry but half sense. Her speech is nothing,
Yet the unshapèd use of it doth move
The hearers to collection; they yawn at it,
10   And botch the words up fit to their own thoughts,
Which, as her winks and nods and gestures yield them,
Indeed would make one think there might be thought,
Though nothing sure, yet much unhappily.

HORATIO
'Twere good she were spoken with, for she may strew
15   Dangerous conjectures in ill-breeding minds.

QUEEN
Let her come in.
        [*Exit Gentleman.*]
[*Aside*] To my sick soul (as sin's true nature is)
Each toy seems prologue to some great amiss;
So full of artless jealousy is guilt
20   It spills itself in fearing to be spilt.
        Enter OPHELIA [*distracted.*]

OPHELIA
Where is the beauteous majesty of Denmark?

QUEEN
How now, Ophelia?

OPHELIA (*sings*)
        How should I your truelove know
            From another one?
25   By his cockle hat* and staff
            And his sandal shoon.

QUEEN
Alas, sweet lady, what imports this song?

OPHELIA
Say you? Nay, pray you mark.
        He is dead and gone, lady,   (*Song*)
30   He is dead and gone;
        At his head a grass-green turf,
            At his heels a stone.
        O, ho!

---

25 *cockle hat*   pilgrims returning from the famous shrine of St. James
of Compostela in Spain wore a cockle shell in their hat to mark their visit
there.

takes offense spitefully at trifles, says strange, disconnected
    things
that hardly make good sense. Her talk is nonsense,
yet its distracted manner leads
the hearers to guess at its meaning; they try to figure it out,
10   and patch the words together to suit their own thoughts.
Her winks and nods and gestures imply meanings,
indeed, make one think that there might be meaning in the
    words;
and although nothing in these words is certain, yet there is much
    that is jumbled together.

HORATIO
It would be good to talk to her, for she may throw
15   dangerous suspicions in minds apt to think the worst.

QUEEN
Let her come in.
    Exit Gentleman.
(*To the audience*) To my sick soul (for sin is truly a disease of
    the soul),
each trifling event looks like the introduction to some great
    calamity;
guilt is so full of clumsy suspicion
20   that it destroys itself in trying to ward off destruction.
    Enter OPHELIA, *speaking in a disconnected manner.*

OPHELIA
Where is the beautiful queen of Denmark?

QUEEN
What is it, Ophelia?

OPHELIA (*singing*)
How can I tell your true lover
from anyone else?
25   By his hat with a cockleshell in it, his walking stick
and his sandals.

QUEEN
Alas, dear lady, what do you mean by this song?

OPHELIA
What is that you say? But please listen.
(*Singing*) He is dead and gone, lady,
30   he is dead and gone;
at his head is green grass and earth,
at his heels a gravestone.
O, there!

QUEEN
Nay, but Ophelia——

OPHELIA
35   Pray you mark.
   [*Sings*] White his shroud as the mountain snow——
       Enter KING.

QUEEN
Alas, look here, my lord.

OPHELIA
       Larded all with sweet flowers   (*Song*)
       Which bewept to the grave did not go
40   With truelove showers.

KING
How do you, pretty lady?

OPHELIA
Well, God dild you! They say the owl was a baker's daughter.*
Lord, we know what we are, but know not what we may be. God
be at your table!

KING
45   Conceit upon her father.

OPHELIA
Pray let's have no words of this, but when they ask you what it
means, say you this:
       Tomorrow is Saint Valentine's day.*   (*Song*)
          All in the morning betime,
50   And I a maid at your window,
          To be your Valentine.

       Then up he rose and donned his clothes
          And dupped the chamber door,
       Let in the maid, that out a maid
55   Never departed more.

KING
Pretty Ophelia.

OPHELIA
Indeed, la, without an oath, I'll make an end on't:
[*Sings*] By Gis and by Saint Charity,
       Alack, and fie for shame!

---

42 *baker's daughter* refers to the legend of a baker's daughter whom
Jesus turned into an owl because she would not give him bread.

QUEEN
But wait, Ophelia—

OPHELIA
35   Please listen.
(*singing*) His grave clothing is as white as the mountain snow—
Enter KING.

QUEEN
Alas, look at this, my lord.

OPHELIA (*Singing*)
Adorned all over with pretty flowers
and with the tears of those who truly loved him,
40   he did not go to his grave.

KING
How are you, pretty lady?

OPHELIA
I'm well, God reward you! They say the owl was a baker's
daughter.
God, we know what we are but don't know what we may
become. May God
bless your meal!

KING
45   This is the result of brooding about her father.

OPHELIA
Please don't talk about this, but when they ask you what it
means, say this:
(*Singing*) Tomorrow is Saint Valentine's day.
Everyone will be up early in the morning,
50   and I was a virgin at your window,
in order to be your Valentine.

Then he got up and put on his clothes
and opened the door of his bedroom,
let in the virgin, who as a virgin
55   never left the room.

KING
Pretty Ophelia.

OPHELIA
Oh yes, look, without any swearing, I'll end my talking:
(*Singing*) By Jesus and by Saint Charity,
how sad, and oh what a shame!

---

48 *Saint Valentine's day*   the tradition was that a man would love the
first girl he saw on St. Valentine's day.

60   Young men will do't if they come to't,
　　　　　By Cock,* they are to blame.
　　　　Quoth she, "Before you tumbled me,
　　　　　You promised me to wed."
　　He answers:
65　　　　"So would I 'a' done, by yonder sun,
　　　　　An thou hadst not come to my bed."

KING
How long hath she been thus?

OPHELIA
I hope all will be well. We must be patient, but I cannot choose
but weep to think they would lay him i' th' cold ground. My
70   brother shall know of it; and so I thank you for your good counsel. Come, my coach! Good night, ladies, good night. Sweet
ladies, good night, good night.
　　　Exit.

KING
Follow her close; give her good watch, I pray you.
　　[*Exit* HORATIO.]
O, this is the poison of deep grief; it springs
75   All from her father's death—and now behold!
O Gertrude, Gertrude,
When sorrows come, they come not single spies,
But in battalions: first, her father slain;
Next, your son gone, and he most violent author
80   Of his own just remove; the people muddied,
Thick and unwholesome in their thoughts and whispers
For good Polonius' death, and we have done but greenly
In huggermugger to inter him; poor Ophelia
Divided from herself and her fair judgment,
85   Without the which we are pictures or mere beasts;
Last, and as much containing as all these,
Her brother is in secret come from France,
Feeds on his wonder, keeps himself in clouds,
And wants not buzzers to infect his ear
90   With pestilent speeches of his father's death,

---

61 *By Cock* a corruption of "by God," but also, in context, an obscene reference.

60   Young men will do it if they have the chance,
by God, they are to blame.
She said, "Before you bedded me,
you promised to marry me."
He answers:
65   And I would have, I swear by the sun up there,
if you had not come to my bed."

KING
How long has she been this way?

OPHELIA
I hope everything will turn out right. We must be patient, but I
   can only
cry to think that they would bury my father in the cold ground.
   My
70   brother will be told about it; and so I thank you for your good
   advice.
Come on, bring me my coach! Good night, ladies, good night.
   Sweet
ladies, good night, good night.
     Exit OPHELIA.

KING (*to Horatio*)
Follow her closely; guard her carefully, please.
     Exit HORATIO.
O, this is the poisonous result of deep sorrow; it is all the result
75   of her father's death—and now look!
O Gertrude, Gertrude,
when sorrows come, they don't come like single scouts (i.e.,
   ahead of the main force),
but in battalions. First, her father is killed;
next, your son leaves, and he himself the violent cause
80   of his own justly deserved exile; the people are confused,
suspicious, and unhealthy in their thoughts and gossip
about poor Polonius' death, and I have acted foolishly
in burying him secretly and hastily. Poor Ophelia
is beside herself and has lost her lovely powers of reason,
85   without which we are like pictures of ourselves or mere animals.
Last, and as important as all these other matters,
her brother has secretly returned from France,
lives on his suspicion, surrounds himself with cloudy guesses,
and doesn't lack gossipers to stir him up
90   with foul reports of his father's death.

Wherein necessity, of matter beggared,
Will nothing stick our person to arraign
In ear and ear. O my dear Gertrude, this,
Like to a murd'ring piece, in many places
Gives me superfluous death.
    A noise within.
    Enter a Messenger.

QUEEN
95   Alack, what noise is this?
KING
    Attend, where are my Switzers? Let them guard the door.
    What is the matter?
MESSENGER
                  Save yourself, my lord.
    The ocean, overpeering of his list,
    Eats not the flats with more impiteous haste
100   Than young Laertes, in a riotous head,
    O'erbears your officers. The rabble call him lord,
    And, as the world were now but to begin,
    Antiquity forgot, custom not known,
    The ratifiers and props of every word,
105   They cry, "Choose we! Laertes shall be king!"
    Caps, hands, and tongues applaud it to the clouds,
    "Laertes shall be king! Laertes king!"
        A noise within.
QUEEN
    How cheerfully on the false trail they cry!
    O, this is counter, you false Danish dogs!
        Enter LAERTES *with others.*
KING
110   The doors are broke.
LAERTES
    Where is this king?—Sirs, stand you all without.
ALL
    No, let's come in.
LAERTES
                I pray you give me leave.
ALL
    We will, we will.

And since the facts are not known, those reports
will naturally not hesitate to accuse me
to everybody who listens. O my dear Gertrude, these rumors,
like a cannon firing fragmentation shells,
wound me in more places than are necessary to kill me.
> *Noise and shouting offstage.*
> *Enter a Messenger.*

QUEEN

95   Oh my, what is the meaning of this noise?

KING

Wait, where are my Swiss guards? Let them defend the door.
(*To the Messenger*) What is wrong?

MESSENGER

Save yourself, my lord.
The ocean, in overflowing its shore,
does not flood the flatlands with more ruthless speed
100   than young Laertes, leading a rebellious force,
overwhelms your officers. The mob calls him lord;
and it is as if the world were just now beginning,
tradition forgotten, customs unknown
(those endorsers and supports of every kind of public order),
105   so that the mob shouts, "We shall choose! Laertes shall be king!'
Caps, hands, and tongues applaud this as high as the clouds,
"Laertes shall be king! Laertes king!"
> *Noise and shouting offstage.*

QUEEN

How cheerfully they shout, hunting a false trail!
O, that's the wrong scent, you unfaithful Danish dogs!
> *Enter* LAERTES *with his supporters, swords drawn.*

KING

110   They've broken open the doors.

LAERTES

Where is this king? (*To his men*) Gentlemen, all of you wait
outside.

ALL

No, let us come in.

LAERTES

Please, give me your permission to remain alone.

ALL

We will, we will.

LAERTES

    I thank you. Keep the door. [*Exeunt his Followers.*] O thou vile
       King,
    Give me my father.

QUEEN

115   Calmly, good Laertes.

LAERTES

    That drop of blood that's calm proclaims me bastard,
    Cries cuckold to my father, brands the harlot
    Even here between the chaste unsmirchèd brow
    Of my true mother.

KING

                  What is the cause, Laertes,

120   That thy rebellion looks so giantlike?
    Let him go, Gertrude. Do not fear our person.
    There's such divinity doth hedge a king
    That treason can but peep to what it would,
    Acts little of his will. Tell me, Laertes,

125   Why thou art thus incensed. Let him go, Gertrude.
    Speak, man.

LAERTES

    Where is my father?

KING

               Dead.

QUEEN

                  But not by him.

KING

    Let him demand his fill.

LAERTES

    How came he dead? I'll not be juggled with.

130   To hell allegiance, vows to the blackest devil,
    Conscience and grace to the profoundest pit!
    I dare damnation. To this point I stand,
    That both the worlds I give to negligence,
    Let come what comes, only I'll be revenged

135   Most throughly for my father.

KING

                  Who shall stay you?

LAERTES
I thank you. Stay by the door. (*Exit his followers.*) O you evil king,
hand over my father.

QUEEN
115   Be calm, good Laertes.

LAERTES
That drop of blood in me that's calm declares me a bastard,
shouts at my father that his wife was unfaithful to him, brands
   as a whore
right here (*touching his forehead*) between her chaste and pure
   brows
my faithful mother.

KING
Laertes, why does
120   your revolt take such an extravagant form?
(*The Queen holds Laertes to prevent him from attacking the
   King.*) Let him go, Gertrude. Don't be afraid for me.
There is such a divine aura around a king
that treason can only look from a distance and think about what
   it would like to do,
without accomplishing very much of its desire. Tell me, Laertes,
125   why you are so enraged? Let him go, Gertrude.
Speak up, man.

LAERTES
Where is my father?

KING
Dead.

QUEEN
But not killed by him.

KING
Let him ask whatever he wants.

LAERTES
How did he die? I won't be trifled with.
130   To hell with loyalty, my promises can go to the worst devil,
conscience and divine rewards to the lowest hole in hell!
I defy damnation. I take my stand on this resolution:
I don't care what the consequences are in this world or the next;
no matter what happens, I'll be completely revenged
135   for my father's death.

KING
Who shall prevent you?

LAERTES

   My will, not all the world's.

   And for my means, I'll husband them so well

   They shall go far with little.

KING

                            Good Laertes,

   If you desire to know the certainty

140   Of your dear father, is't writ in your revenge

   That swoopstake you will draw both friend and foe,

   Winner and loser?

LAERTES

   None but his enemies.

KING

                     Will you know them then?

LAERTES

   To his good friends thus wide I'll ope my arms

145   And like the kind life-rend'ring pelican*

   Repast them with my blood.

KING

                       Why, now you speak

   Like a good child and a true gentleman.

   That I am guiltless of your father's death,

   And am most sensibly in grief for it,

150   It shall as level to your judgment 'pear

   As day does to your eye.

           A noise within: "Let her come in."

LAERTES

   How now? What noise is that?

        Enter OPHELIA.

   O heat, dry up my brains; tears seven times salt

   Burn out the sense and virtue of mine eye!

155   By heaven, thy madness shall be paid with weight

   Till our scale turn the beam. O rose of May,

   Dear maid, kind sister, sweet Ophelia!

   O heavens, is't possible a young maid's wits

   Should be as mortal as an old man's life?

160   Nature is fine in love, and where 'tis fine,

   It sends some precious instance of itself

   After the thing it loves.

---

145 *pelican* the female pelican was thought to feed her young with her own blood.

LAERTES

Only my will, since not all the world's will could stop me.
And as for my methods of revenge, I'll use them so carefully
that a little shall go a long way.

KING

Good Laertes,
if you want to know the truth
140   about your dear father, does that mean that your revenge
will indiscriminately sweep up both friend and enemy,
winner and loser?

LAERTES

No one but my father's enemies.

KING

Do you, then, want to know who they are?

LAERTES

To his good friends I'll open wide my arms like this,
145   and like the kind pelican, which gives its life for its offspring,
feed them with my blood.

KING

Why, now you are speaking
like a good son and a true gentleman.
That I am not guilty of your father's death,
and that I am deeply grieving for it,
150   this shall appear as plain to your judgment
as the day does to your eyes.
      A noise offstage and someone shouts: "Let her come in."

LAERTES

What's this? What is that noise?
      *Enter the mad OPHELIA, dressed in a disheveled manner,
      carrying wild flowers.*
O heat of my passions, dry up my brains; let tears seven times
      more irritatingly salty than usual
burn out the feeling and visual power of my eyes!
155   By heaven, your insanity shall be paid for heavily
until the balance scale of justice is made even. O rose of May,
dear girl, kind sister, sweet Ophelia!
O heavens, is it possible that a young girl's mind
should be as mortal as an old man's life?
160   Human nature is purified by love, and where it is pure,
it sends some precious part of itself
after the person it loves.

OPHELIA

>They bore him barefaced on the bier   (*Song*)
>   Hey non nony, nony, hey nony
>And in his grave rained many a tear——
>Fare you well, my dove!

LAERTES

Hadst thou thy wits, and didst persuade revenge,
It could not move thus.

OPHELIA

You must sing "A-down a-down, and you call him a-down-a."
O, how the wheel becomes it! It is the false steward, that stole
his master's daughter.

LAERTES

This nothing's more than matter.

OPHELIA

There's rosemary, that's for remembrance. Pray you, love, remember. And there is pansies, that's for thoughts.

LAERTES

A document in madness, thoughts and remembrance fitted.

OPHELIA

There's fennel for you, and columbines. There's rue for you, and
here's some for me. We may call it herb of grace o' Sundays. O,
you must wear your rue with a difference. There's a daisy. I
would give you some violets,* but they withered all when my
father died. They say 'a made a good end.
[*Sings*]   For bonny sweet Robin is all my joy.

LAERTES

Thought and affliction, passion, hell itself,
She turns to favor and to prettiness.

OPHELIA

>And will 'a not come again?   (*Song*)
>And will 'a not come again?
>   No, no, he is dead,
>   Go to thy deathbed,
>He never will come again.

---

179 *violets* the flowers Ophelia mentions have symbolic meanings that
Shakespeare's audience would have been familiar with. These are the likely
meanings: fennel — flattery; columbine — cuckoldry, disloyalty, ingratitude;

Line numbers: 165, 170, 175, 180, 185

OPHELIA (*singing*)
They bore him barefaced in his coffin,
hey non nony, nony, hey nony,
165   and in his grave there fell many a tear—
goodbye my dove!

LAERTES
If you were still sane and argued logically for vengeance,
it couldn't persuade me like this sight.

OPHELIA
You must sing, "Down, down, and you call him down."
170   O, how well this refrain accompanies the song! It is about the
unfaithful steward, who stole
his master's daughter.

LAERTES
This meaningless nonsense is more moving than a recital of
her sorrows.

OPHELIA (*distributing her flowers*)
There's rosemary, that stands for a lover's remembrance.
Please, love,
remember me. And here are pansies, they stand for a lover's
troubled thoughts.

LAERTES
175   She is a lesson in the nature of insanity, driven to it by
thoughts and memory.

OPHELIA
There's fennel for you, and columbines. There's rue for you, and
here's some for me. We can call it a holy herb on Sundays. O,
you must now wear rue differently (i.e., in memory of my
father). There's a daisy. I
would give you some violets, but they all withered when my
180   father died. They say he died in a state of grace.
(*Singing*) For pretty dear Robin is all my joy.

LAERTES
She turns anxiety and trouble, grief, and hell itself,
into something charming and pretty.

OPHELIA (*singing*)
185   And won't he come again?
And won't he come again?
No, no, he is dead,
go to your deathbed.
He will never come again.

---

rue — sorrow and repentance; daisy — dissembling, infidelity; violets —
faithfulness.

His beard was as white as snow,
190 All flaxen was his poll.
   He is gone, he is gone,
   And we cast away moan.
  God 'a' mercy on his soul!

And of all Christian souls, I pray God. God bye you.
  Exit.
LAERTES
195 Do you see this, O God?
KING
 Laertes, I must commune with your grief,
 Or you deny me right. Go but apart,
 Make choice of whom your wisest friends you will,
 And they shall hear and judge 'twixt you and me.
200 If by direct or by collateral hand
 They find us touched, we will our kingdom give,
 Our crown, our life, and all that we call ours,
 To you in satisfaction; but if not,
 Be you content to lend your patience to us,
205 And we shall jointly labor with your soul
 To give it due content.
LAERTES
      Let this be so.
 His means of death, his obscure funeral—
 No trophy, sword, nor hatchment o'er his bones,
 No noble rite nor formal ostentation—
210 Cry to be heard, as 'twere from heaven to earth,
 That I must call't in question.
KING
       So you shall;
 And where th' offense is, let the great ax fall.
 I pray you go with me.
  Exeunt.

[*Scene vi: The castle.*] *Enter* HORATIO *and others.*

HORATIO
 What are they that would speak with me?

His beard was as white as snow,
190   his hair was as white as flax.
He is gone, he is gone,
and our moaning is in vain.
May God have mercy on his soul!

And on all Christian souls, I pray to God. Goodbye.
Exit OPHELIA.

LAERTES
195   O God, do you see this?

KING
Laertes, I must be allowed to talk to you about your grief,
or else you deny me my rights. Only, let's move away from the
    others,
while you choose a few of whatever wisest friends you like,
and they shall hear the case and judge between you and me.
200   If either directly or indirectly
they find me implicated, I will give you my kingdom,
my crown, my life, and everything that I call my own
to make up for it. But if they do not find me guilty,
you will be satisfied and patient with me,
205   and I will work with you
to give you what you want and deserve.

LAERTES
Let this take place.
How he died, his lowly and humble funeral—
no memorial, no ceremonial sword, nor coat of arms on his grave,
no noble ceremony, nor formal display—
210   these things cry out for an answer, as if from heaven to earth,
and so I must call them into question.

KING
So you shall;
and wherever the guilt is found, let the great ax fall.
Please come with me.
Exit KING, QUEEN, LAERTES, *Gentleman, and*
    Messenger.

Act IV, Scene vi: The castle. Enter HORATIO, *Gentleman, and*
Attendants.

HORATIO
Who are these people who wish to speak to me?

GENTLEMAN
Seafaring men, sir. They say they have letters for you.

HORATIO
Let them come in.
    [*Exit Attendant.*]
I do not know from what part of the world
I should be greeted, if not from Lord Hamlet.
    Enter Sailors.

SAILOR
God bless you, sir.

HORATIO
Let Him bless thee too.

SAILOR
'A shall, sir, an't please Him. There's a letter for you, sir—it
came from th' ambassador that was bound for England—if your
name be Horatio, as I am let to know it is.

HORATIO [*reads the letter*]
"Horatio, when thou shalt have overlooked this, give these fellows some means to the King. They have letters for him. Ere
we were two days old at sea, a pirate of very warlike appoint-
ment gave us chase. Finding ourselves too slow of sail, we put on
a compelled valor, and in the grapple I boarded them. On the
instant they got clear of our ship; so I alone became their
prisoner. They have dealt with me like thieves of mercy, but
they knew what they did: I am to do a good turn for them. Let
the King have the letters I have sent, and repair thou to me with
as much speed as thou wouldest fly death. I have words to speak
in thine ear will make thee dumb; yet are they much too light
for the bore of the matter. These good fellows will bring thee
where I am. Rosencrantz and Guildenstern hold their course for
England. Of them I have much to tell thee. Farewell.
                    He that thou knowest thine, HAMLET."
Come, I will give you way for these your letters,

GENTLEMAN
  Sailors, sir. They say they have a letter for you.

HORATIO
  Tell them to come in.
      Exit an Attendant.
  I don't know from what part of the world

5   I should receive a letter, except from Lord Hamlet.
      Enter Sailors.

SAILOR
  God bless you, sir.

HORATIO
  I hope he blesses you too.

SAILOR
  He shall, sir, if it pleases him. Here is a letter for you, sir—it
  came from the ambassador who was going to England—if your

10   name is Horatio, as I am told it is.

HORATIO (*reading the letter*)
  "Horatio, when you have read this, give these
  fellows some introduction to the King. They have a letter for
    him. Before
  we had been two days out at sea, a pirate ship fitted out in a very
    warlike way
  pursued us. Finding our ship too slow to escape, we were

15   forced to be brave and fight, and during the struggle I boarded
    their ship. At that
  moment, they pulled away from our ship; so I became their only
  prisoner. They have treated me like merciful thieves, but
  they knew what they were doing, since I will do a good turn for
    them. See that
  the King receives the letters I have sent, and come to where
    I am with

20   as much speed as you would run away from death. I have words
    to speak
  in your ear that will leave you speechless with amazement; and
    yet they are much too light
  for the importance of the matter. These good fellows will bring
    you
  to where I am. Rosencrantz and Guildenstern are on their way to
  England. I have much to tell you about them. Goodbye.

25   He who you know is your friend, HAMLET."
  Come, I will get you admitted to deliver this letter you carry,

And do't the speedier that you may direct me
To him from whom you brought them.
     Exeunt.

[*Scene vii: The castle.*] *Enter* KING *and* LAERTES.

KING
  Now must your conscience my acquittance seal,
  And you must put me in your heart for friend,
  Sith you have heard, and with a knowing ear,
  That he which hath your noble father slain
  Pursued my life.
LAERTES
5   It well appears. But tell me
  Why you proceeded not against these feats
  So criminal and so capital in nature,
  As by your safety, greatness, wisdom, all things else,
  You mainly were stirred up.
KING
                 O, for two special reasons,
10   Which may to you perhaps seem much unsinewed,
  But yet to me they're strong. The Queen his mother
  Lives almost by his looks, and for myself—
  My virtue or my plague, be it either which—
  She is so conjunctive to my life and soul,
15   That, as the star moves not but in his sphere,*
  I could not but by her. The other motive
  Why to a public count I might not go
  Is the great love the general gender bear him,
  Who, dipping all his faults in their affection,
20   Would, like the spring that turneth wood to stone,*
  Convert his gyves to graces; so that my arrows,
  Too slightly timbered for so loud a wind,
  Would have reverted to my bow again,
  And not where I had aimed them.
LAERTES
25   And so have I a noble father lost,
  A sister driven into desp'rate terms,

---

15 *sphere* according to the astronomy of the time, the planets were
thought to move within concentric, transparent, revolving globes which
contained them.

and I will do it quickly so that you can take me all the sooner
to him from whom you brought the letter.
  Exit HORATIO *and Sailors.*

Act IV, Scene vii: The castle. Enter KING *and* LAERTES.

KING
  Now your sound judgment must agree to my acquittal,
  and consider me your friend;
  since you have heard, and with a discriminating ear,
  that he who killed your noble father
  meant to kill me.

LAERTES
5 It clearly seems so. But tell me
  why you took no measures against these criminal acts,
  these deeds worthy of death;
  since consideration of your safety, your power and wisdom, and
      everything else,
  disturbed you so powerfully.

KING
  O, for two special reasons,
10 which may perhaps seem very feeble to you,
  but are strong to me. His mother the Queen
  is so fond of him that she almost lives on his looks, and as for
      myself—
  it's either my strength or my weakness—
  she is joined so closely to my life and soul
15 that, just as a star can only move in its sphere,
  I can only live by her influence. The other reason
  why I could not have a public reckoning with Hamlet
  is the great love the common people have for him.
  They dip all his faults in their affection,
20 and like the spring that turns wood to stone,
  they would, if he were in chains, transform his shackles into
      virtues and make a hero of him. So that my arrows,
  too light for so powerful a wind,
  would have been blown back to my bow again
  and not gone where I had aimed them.

LAERTES
25 And thus I have lost a noble father, and
  my sister has been driven into a desperate state of mind.

---

20 *wood to stone* there were several English springs whose waters were
so charged with lime that they would petrify wood placed in them.

Whose worth, if praises may go back again,
Stood challenger on mount of all the age
For her perfections. But my revenge will come.
KING
30   Break not your sleeps for that. You must not think
That we are made of stuff so flat and dull
That we can let our beard be shook with danger,
And think it pastime. You shortly shall hear more.
I loved your father, and we love ourself,
35   And that, I hope, will teach you to imagine——
        Enter a messenger with letters.
How now? What news?
MESSENGER
                    Letters, my lord, from Hamlet:
These to your Majesty; this to the Queen.
KING
From Hamlet? Who brought them?
MESSENGER
Sailors, my lord, they say; I saw them not.
40   They were given me by Claudio; he received them
Of him that brought them.
KING
                    Laertes, you shall hear them.——
Leave us.
        Exit messenger.
[*Reads*] "High and mighty, you shall know I am set naked on
your kingdom. Tomorrow shall I beg leave to see your kingly
45   eyes; when I shall (first asking your pardon thereunto) recount
the occasion of my sudden and more strange return.

                                HAMLET."
What should this mean? Are all the rest come back?
Or is it some abuse, and no such thing?
LAERTES
Know you the hand?
KING
50   'Tis Hamlet's character. "Naked"!
And in a postscript here, he says "alone."
Can you devise me?

Her worth, if I can praise her as she was before,
was such that it could stand up high and challenge the whole
   world
for its perfection. But my revenge will come.

KING

30   Don't lose sleep over that. You must not think
that I am made of such stupid and dull stuff
that I can let myself be dangerously defied
and think it a joke. You'll hear more of this soon.
I loved your father, and I love myself,

35   and I hope that will show you how to guess—
     Enter a Messenger carrying letters.
What's this? What is the news?

MESSENGER

Letters, my lord, from Hamlet.
This one for your Majesty; this one for the Queen.

KING

From Hamlet? Who brought them?

MESSENGER

Sailors, my lord, I am told; I did not see them.

40   The letters were given to me by Claudio; he received them
from the person who brought them.

KING

Laertes, you shall hear what's in this letter.—
(To the Messenger) Leave us.
    Exit Messenger.
(Reading the letter) "High and mighty King, this is to tell you
   that I have landed defenseless in
your kingdom. Tomorrow I shall ask permission to see you face
   to face,

45   when I shall (first begging your pardon to do it) describe
the reason for my very sudden and even stranger return.
                     HAMLET."
What can this mean? Have all the others come back?
Or is it some trick, and not what it appears to be?

LAERTES

Do you recognize the handwriting?

KING

50   It's Hamlet's handwriting. "Defenseless"!
And in a postscript here, he says "alone."
Can you explain it to me?

LAERTES

I am lost in it, my lord. But let him come.
It warms the very sickness in my heart
55   That I shall live and tell him to his teeth,
"Thus did'st thou."

KING

If it be so, Laertes
(As how should it be so? How otherwise?),
Will you be ruled by me?

LAERTES

Ay, my lord,
So you will not o'errule me to a peace.

KING

60   To thine own peace. If he be now returned,
As checking at his voyage, and that he means
No more to undertake it, I will work him
To an exploit now ripe in my device,
Under the which he shall not choose but fall;
65   And for his death no wind of blame shall breathe,
But even his mother shall uncharge the practice
And call it accident.

LAERTES

My lord, I will be ruled;
The rather if you could devise it so
That I might be the organ.

KING

It falls right.
70   You have been talked of since your travel much,
And that in Hamlet's hearing, for a quality
Wherein they say you shine. Your sum of parts
Did not together pluck such envy from him
As did that one, and that, in my regard,
Of the unworthiest siege.

LAERTES

75   What part is that, my lord?

KING

A very riband in the cap of youth,
Yet needful too, for youth no less becomes

LAERTES

I am confused by it, my lord. But let him come.
It cures the true sorrow in my heart
55 to know that I shall live and tell him face to face,
"This is what you have done."

KING

If it is true, Laertes
(and how can it be true that he's come back? How can it not
  be true?),
will you do what I say?

LAERTES

Yes, my lord,
as long as you don't force me to make my peace with Hamlet.

KING

60 Only your own peace. If he has now returned,
shying away from his voyage (i.e., like a falcon distracted from
  its proper prey), and if he intends
not to take the trip, I will manipulate him
into a scheme I have now worked out fully,
by which he must certainly be destroyed.
65 And no one will blame me in the least for his death,
but even his mother shall acquit me of treachery
and call it an accident.

LAERTES

My lord, I will do what you say;
and I will do it more readily if you can arrange it so
that I am the agent of his death.

KING

It's part of my plan.
70 You have been talked about a great deal since your travels,
and in Hamlet's presence, for an accomplishment
in which they say you shine. All your other accomplishments put
  together
did not make him so envious
as that one, which in my view
is of the lowest sort.

LAERTES

75 What accomplishment is that, my lord?

KING

A mere decoration in the cap of a young man,
yet a necessary one too, since a young man's

The light and careless livery that it wears
Than settled age his sables and his weeds,
80   Importing health and graveness. Two months since
Here was a gentleman of Normandy.
I have seen myself, and served against, the French,
And they can well on horseback, but this gallant
Had witchcraft in't. He grew unto his seat,
85   And to such wondrous doing brought his horse
As had he been incorpsed and deminatured
With the brave beast. So far he topped my thought
That I, in forgery of shapes and tricks,
Come short of what he did.

KING

LAERTES
                                        A Norman was't?

KING
90   A Norman.

LAERTES
Upon my life, Lamord.

KING
                                        The very same.

LAERTES
I know him well. He is the brooch indeed
And gem of all the nation.

KING
He made confession of you,
95   And gave you such a masterly report,
For art and exercise in your defense,
And for your rapier most especial,
That he cried out 'twould be a sight indeed
If one could match you. The scrimers of their nation
100   He swore had neither motion, guard, nor eye,
If you opposed them. Sir, this report of his
Did Hamlet so envenom with his envy
That he could nothing do but wish and beg
Your sudden coming o'er to play with you.
Now, out of this——

LAERTES
105   What out of this, my lord?

frivolous and careless dress is no less appropriate
than the sober and formal attire of an established older man,
80　　which signifies prosperity and dignity. Two months ago
a gentleman from Normandy was here.
I have seen them myself and fought against the French,
and they perform well on horseback; but this fine gentleman
rode as if by witchcraft. He seemed to be a part of the saddle,
85　　and made his horse do such marvellous things
that it seemed as if he himself were part
of the noble beast's body. He went so far beyond what I thought
　　could be done
that my imaginings of possible feats of horsemanship
fell short of his accomplishments.

LAERTES
Was he a Norman?

KING
90　　Yes, a Norman.

LAERTES
By my life, Lamord.

KING
That's the one.

LAERTES
I know him well. He is indeed the ornament
and jewel of all the French nation.

KING
He admitted that he knew your accomplishments,
95　　and described you as such a master
of the theory and practice of self-defense,
and especially in the use of your rapier,
that he cried out that it would be something indeed to see
if an equal match for you could be found. The fencers of his
　　country,
100　　he swore, had neither good movements, nor adequate defenses,
　　nor a sharp eye
when you fought with them. Sir, this report of his
poisoned Hamlet with such envy
that he could do nothing except wish and ask
for your quick return so that he could fence with you.
Now, from out of this—

LAERTES
105　　What can we do with this, my lord?

KING
Laertes, was your father dear to you?
Or are you like the painting of a sorrow,
A face without a heart?

LAERTES
                              Why ask you this?

KING
Not that I think you did not love your father,
110   But that I know love is begun by time,
And that I see, in passages of proof,
Time qualifies the spark and fire of it.
There lives within the very flame of love
A kind of wick or snuff that will abate it,
115   And nothing is at a like goodness still,
For goodness, growing to a plurisy,
Dies in his own too-much. That we would do
We should do when we would, for this "would" changes,
And hath abatements and delays as many
120   As there are tongues, are hands, are accidents,
And then this "should" is like a spendthrift sigh,*
That hurts by easing. But to the quick of th' ulcer—
Hamlet comes back; what would you undertake
To show yourself in deed your father's son
More than in words?

LAERTES
125   To cut his throat i' th' church!

KING
No place indeed should murder sanctuarize;
Revenge should have no bounds. But, good Laertes,
Will you do this? Keep close within your chamber.
Hamlet returned shall know you are come home.
130   We'll put on those shall praise your excellence
And set a double varnish on the fame
The Frenchman gave you, bring you in fine together
And wager on your heads. He, being remiss,
Most generous, and free from all contriving,
135   Will not peruse the foils, so that with ease,

---

121 *spendthrift sigh* sighs were thought to draw blood from the heart
and thereby to shorten life.

KING
> Laertes, did you really love your father?
> Or are you only like the picture of a grief-stricken person,
> a face without a heart?

LAERTES
> Why do you ask this?

KING
> Not because I think you did not love your father,
> 110 but because I know that love begins at a point in time,
> and because, as I have seen proved by examples,
> time modifies the intensity of its flames.
> There is right in the flame of love
> a sort of wick (or rather a bit of burnt wick) that will diminish
> the flame;
> 115 and there is nothing that remains always at the same point of
> perfection,
> for when perfection grows past its fullness,
> it dies of its own excess. When we want to do something,
> we ought to do it then, for this "want" changes,
> and has as many reductions and delays
> 120 as there are tongues, hands, and accidents to reduce and delay it.
> And then this "ought" is like a wasteful sigh,
> that injures us by giving us relief. But let's get to the core of
> this ulcer (i.e., the heart of the matter)—
> Hamlet is coming back; what are you willing to do
> to show yourself your father's son by your actions
> and not just by your words?

LAERTES
> 125 I'm ready to cut his throat in the church.

KING
> Right, no place should protect a murderer;
> revenge should have no limits. But, good Laertes,
> please do this for my sake: stay shut up in your room.
> When Hamlet returns, he'll find out you've come home.
> 130 I will have people praise your skill
> and even more brilliantly varnish the reputation
> Lamord gave you, and I will finally bring you together
> and bet on the match. Since he is careless,
> nobleminded, and innocent of all plotting,
> 135 he won't examine the swords, so that you may easily

Or with a little shuffling, you may choose
A sword unbated, and, in a pass of practice,
Requite him for your father.

LAERTES

I will do't,
And for that purpose I'll anoint my sword.
140   I bought an unction of a mountebank,
So mortal that, but dip a knife in it,
Where it draws blood, no cataplasm so rare,
Collected from all simples that have virtue
Under the moon, can save the thing from death
145   That is but scratched withal. I'll touch my point
With this contagion, that, if I gall him slightly,
It may be death.

KING

Let's further think of this,
Weigh what convenience both of time and means
May fit us to our shape. If this should fail,
150   And that our drift look through our bad performance,
'Twere better not assayed. Therefore this project
Should have a back or second, that might hold
If this did blast in proof. Soft, let me see.
We'll make a solemn wager on your cunnings—
155   I ha't!
When in your motion you are hot and dry—
As make your bouts more violent to that end—
And that he calls for drink, I'll have prepared him
A chalice for the nonce, whereon but sipping,
160   If he by chance escape your venomed stuck,
Our purpose may hold there.—But stay, what noise?
        Enter QUEEN.

QUEEN

One woe doth tread upon another's heel.
So fast they follow. Your sister's drowned, Laertes.

LAERTES

Drowned! O, where?

(or with a little clever switching), choose
an unblunted sword, and with a treacherous thrust
pay him back for your father's death.

LAERTES

I'll do it,
and for that purpose, I'll put something on my sword.

140 I bought an ointment from a seller of patent medicines
that is so deadly that if you just dip a knife in it,
when you draw blood there is no healing plaster, no matter how
    exceptional,
made up of all the medicinal herbs under the moon that have
    curative power,
that can save the thing from death

145 that is merely scratched with it. I'll taint my sword's point
with this disease, so that even if I graze him slightly,
it shall be his death.

KING

Let's think about this some more,
and consider the proper time and the means
which may best suit our purpose. If this should fail,

150 and our intention is evident from our poor execution,
it would better not be attempted at all. Therefore, this project
should have a back-up or second plot that might be put to work
if the first plan blows up in our hands. Wait, let's see.
I'll make a formal bet on your skill—

155 I have it!
When you become hot and thirsty from exerting yourselves—
and you should make your fencing more strenuous for that
    purpose—
and Hamlet asks for a drink, I'll have prepared for him
a special cup for the occasion, which if he only sips from—

160 should he by accident escape your poisoned thrust—
our purpose will be accomplished in that way. But wait, what is
    that noise? (*Cries from offstage.*)
     Enter QUEEN.

QUEEN

One sorrow walks on the heels of another—
they come so fast one after another. Your sister's drowned,
    Laertes.

LAERTES

Drowned! O, where?

QUEEN

165 There is a willow askant the brook,
That shows his hoar leaves in the glassy stream:
Therewith fantastic garlands did she make
Of crowflowers, nettles, daisies, and long purples,
That liberal shepherds give a grosser name,

170 But our cold maids do dead men's fingers call them.
There on the pendent boughs her crownet weeds
Clamb'ring to hang, an envious sliver broke,
When down her weedy trophies and herself
Fell in the weeping brook. Her clothes spread wide,

175 And mermaidlike awhile they bore her up,
Which time she chanted snatches of old lauds,
As one incapable of her own distress,
Or like a creature native and indued
Unto that element. But long it could not be

180 Till that her garments, heavy with their drink,
Pulled the poor wretch from her melodious lay
To muddy death.

LAERTES

Alas, then she is drowned?

QUEEN

Drowned, drowned.

LAERTES

Too much of water hast thou, poor Ophelia,

185 And therefore I forbid my tears; but yet
It is our trick; nature her custom holds,
Let shame say what it will: when these are gone,
The woman will be out. Adieu, my lord.
I have a speech o' fire, that fain would blaze,
But that this folly drowns it.

Exit.

KING

Let's follow, Gertrude.

190 How much I had to do to calm his rage!
Now fear I this will give it start again;
Therefore let's follow.

Exeunt.

QUEEN

165 There is a willow tree that grows slanting out over the brook,
and its gray-white leaves are reflected in the mirror-like stream.
With willow twigs, Ophelia made wild garlands
of cornflowers, nettles, daisies, and wild orchids,
which dirty-minded shepherds call by a filthier name,
170 but our chaste girls call them dead men's fingers.
When she climbed to hang her crown of wild flowers
on the overhanging limbs, a malicious branch broke,
and she and her garlands of wild flowers
fell into the tearful brook. Her clothes spread wide on the water,
175 and for a while they held her up like a mermaid,
during which time she sang snatches of old hymns,
like someone unable to understand her own danger,
or like a creature native to the water and adapted by nature
to that element. But that couldn't last for long,
180 and then her clothing, heavy from absorbing water,
dragged the unfortunate wretch from her melodious song
to muddy death.

LAERTES

Alas, then, is she drowned?

QUEEN

Drowned, drowned.

LAERTES

You have too much water already, poor Ophelia,
185 and therefore I will hold back my tears; but yet
weeping is a human weakness. Nature always works that way,
no matter how our embarrassment tries to hide it; when these
    tears are gone,
the womanly part of me will be gone for good. Goodbye, my lord.
I have a passionate speech that would like to blaze forth,
except that these foolish tears of mine drown it.
    Exit LAERTES.

KING

190 Let's go after him, Gertrude.
I had to work so hard to calm his rage!
Now I'm afraid that the death of Ophelia will inflame it again;
therefore, let's go after him.
    Exit KING *and* QUEEN.

[*Act V, Scene i: A churchyard.*] *Enter two* CLOWNS.

CLOWN

Is she to be buried in Christian burial* when she willfully seeks her own salvation?

OTHER

I tell thee she is. Therefore make her grave straight. The crowner hath sat on her, and finds it Christian burial.

CLOWN

5 How can that be, unless she drowned herself in her own defense?

OTHER

Why, 'tis found so.

CLOWN

It must be *se offendendo*;* it cannot be else. For here lies the point: if I drown myself wittingly, it argues an act, and an act
10 hath three branches—it is to act, to do, to perform. Argal,* she drowned herself wittingly.

OTHER

Nay, but hear you, Goodman Delver.

CLOWN

Give me leave. Here lies the water—good. Here stands the man—good. If the man go to this water and drown himself, it
15 is, will he nill he, he goes; mark you that. But if the water come to him and drown him, he drowns not himself. Argal, he that is not guilty of his own death, shortens not his own life.

OTHER

But is this law?

CLOWN

Ay marry, is't—crowner's quest law.

OTHER

20 Will you ha' the truth on't? If this had not been a gentlewoman, she should have been buried out o' Christian burial.

---

1 *Christian burial* church law denied Christian burial to suicides.
8 *se offendendo* the Gravedigger's blunder for *se defendendo*, "in self

Act V, Scene i: A graveyard. Enter two rustics, a Gravedigger and his young helper.

GRAVEDIGGER

Is she to be buried in consecrated ground with the proper ritual
  when she deliberately sought
her own salvation by killing herself?

HELPER

I tell you she is. Therefore dig her grave right away. The
  coroner
has ruled on her case, and he finds that she deserves Christian
  burial.

GRAVEDIGGER

5 How can that be, unless she drowned herself in self-defense?

HELPER

Why, that's the ruling.

GRAVEDIGGER

It must be a case of self-defense; it can't be otherwise. For here
  is the
crucial point: if I drown myself knowingly, that implies an
  action, and an action

10 has three parts—that is, to act, to do, to perform. Therefore, she
  drowned herself knowingly.

HELPER

Oh, listen to you, Mr. Digger.

GRAVEDIGGER

Let me go on. Here's the water—O.K. Here is the
man—O.K. If the man goes to this water and drowns himself,

15 whether he wants to drown or not, he has gone willfully.
  Remember that. But if the water comes
to him and drowns him, he does not drown himself. Therefore,
  he who
is not guilty of his own death does not shorten his own life.

HELPER

But is this the law?

GRAVEDIGGER

Yes, indeed it is—coroner's inquest law.

HELPER

20 Do you want to know the truth? If this had not been a
  gentlewoman,
she would have been buried without the rites of a Christian
  burial.

---

defense."
  10 *Argal* the Gravedigger's blunder for *ergo*, Latin for "therefore."

CLOWN
Why, there thou say'st. And the more pity that great folk should
have count'nance in this world to drown or hang themselves
more than their even-Christen. Come, my spade. There is no
25   ancient gentlemen but gard'ners, ditchers, and gravemakers. They
hold up Adam's profession.

OTHER
Was he a gentleman?

CLOWN
'A was the first that ever bore arms.

OTHER
Why, he had none.

CLOWN
30   What, art a heathen? How dost thou understand the Scripture?
The Scripture says Adam digged. Could he dig without arms?
I'll put another question to thee. If thou answerest me not to the
purpose, confess thyself——*

OTHER
Go to.

CLOWN
35   What is he that builds stronger than either the mason, the shipwright, or the carpenter?

OTHER
The gallowsmaker, for that frame outlives a thousand tenants.

CLOWN
I like thy wit well, in good faith. The gallows does well. But
how does it well? It does well to those that do ill. Now thou dost
40   ill to say the gallows is built stronger than the church. Argal,
the gallows may do well to thee. To't again, come.

OTHER
Who builds stronger than a mason, a shipwright, or a carpenter?

CLOWN
Ay, tell me that, and unyoke.

---

33 *confess thyself* "Confess thyself and be hanged," a common proverb,
is what the Clown would have said if he had not been interrupted.

GRAVEDIGGER

Why, there you say the truth indeed. And all the more pity it is that upper-class persons should

have more freedom in this world to drown or hang themselves than do their fellow Christians. Come on, give me my shovel. There are no

25   genuine gentlemen but gardeners, ditch-diggers, and grave-diggers. They

maintain Adam's profession.

HELPER

Was he a gentleman?

GRAVEDIGGER

He was the first who ever had a coat of arms.

HELPER

Why, he had none.

GRAVEDIGGER

30   What, are you a heathen? How do you understand the Bible? The Bible says that Adam dug. Could he dig without arms? I'll ask you another question. If you don't answer it correctly, confess yourself—

HELPER

Oh, come off it.

GRAVEDIGGER

35   Who builds more lastingly than either the mason, the shipbuilder, or the carpenter?

HELPER *(pauses, then with a triumphant tone)*

The gallows-maker, for that structure outlives a thousand tenants.

GRAVEDIGGER

I like your sense of humor, I really do. The gallows does well, that's a good answer. But

how does it do well? It does well to those who commit ill deeds. Now you do

40   ill to say that the gallows is built stronger than the church. Therefore,

the gallows may do well by you. Let's try it again, come on.

HELPER

Who builds more lastingly than a mason, a shipbuilder, or a carpenter?

GRAVEDIGGER

Yes, tell me that, and you can call it a day.

OTHER
Marry, now I can tell.

CLOWN
45   To't.

OTHER
Mass, I cannot tell.
    Enter HAMLET *and* HORATIO *afar off.*

CLOWN
Cudgel thy brains no more about it, for your dull ass will not
mend his pace with beating. And when you are asked this question next, say "a gravemaker." The houses he makes lasts till
50   doomsday. Go, get thee to Yaughan, and fetch me a stoup of
liquor.
    [*Exit other* CLOWN.]
    In youth when I did love, did love,   (*Song*)
        Methought it was very sweet
    To contract—O—the time for—a—my behove,
55   O, methought there—a—was nothing—a—meet.

HAMLET
Has this fellow no feeling of his business? 'A sings in grave-
making.

HORATIO
Custom hath made it in him a property of easiness.

HAMLET
'Tis e'en so. The hand of little employment hath the daintier
60   sense.

CLOWN
    But age with his stealing steps   (*Song*)
        Hath clawed me in his clutch,
    And hath shipped me into the land,
        As if I had never been such.
    [*Throws up a skull.*]

HAMLET
65   That skull had a tongue in it, and could sing once. How the
knave jowls it to the ground, as if 'twere Cain's jawbone, that
did the first murder!* This might be the pate of a politician,

---

67   *first murder*   see note for 1.2.105.

HELPER
Indeed, now I know.

GRAVEDIGGER
45 Go to it.

HELPER
Now that I come to think about it, I don't know.

Enter HAMLET *and* HORATIO, *at the rear of the stage.*

GRAVEDIGGER
Don't beat your brains any more about it, for your slow donkey won't

go any faster if it's beaten. And the next time you're asked this question,

say "a gravemaker." The houses he makes last till

50 doomsday. Go on now, go to Yaughan's (tavern) and get me a pitcher of

beer.

Exit HELPER.

(*Singing*) In youth when I was in love, in love,

I thought it was very sweet

to arrange—Oh—my time for—a—my benefit,

55 O, I thought there—a—was nothing—a—so fitting.

HAMLET
Doesn't this fellow have any feelings about his work. He sings while gravedigging.

HORATIO
Habit has made it something that he can do with complete ease of mind.

HAMLET
That's just the way it is. The hand that doesn't work at something has more delicate and sensitive

60 feeling.

GRAVEDIGGER (*singing*)
But old age, stealing up on me,

has grabbed me in his clutches,

and has sent me into the ground,

as if I had never been in love. (*Throws up a skull.*)

HAMLET
65 Once, that skull had a tongue in it and could sing. How this

clod throws it to the ground, as if it were Cain's jawbone, with which

he did the first murder! This might be the skull of a politician which this ass now o'erreaches, one that would circumvent God, might it not?

HORATIO
70   It might, my lord.

HAMLET
Or of a courtier, which could say "Good morrow, sweet lord! How dost thou, sweet lord?" This might be my Lord Such-a-one, that praised my Lord Such-a-one's horse when 'a meant to beg it, might it not?

HORATIO
75   Ay, my lord.

HAMLET
Why, e'en so, and now my Lady Worm's, chapless, and knocked about the mazzard with a sexton's spade. Here's fine revolution, an we had the trick to see't. Did these bones cost no more the breeding but to play at loggets* with them? Mine ache to think
80   on't.

CLOWN
A pickax and a spade, a spade,   (*Song*)
  For and a shrouding sheet;
O, a pit of clay for to be made
  For such a guest is meet.
          [*Throws up another skull.*]

HAMLET
85   There's another. Why may not that be the skull of a lawyer? Where be his quiddities now, his quillities, his cases, his tenures, and his tricks? Why does he suffer this mad knave now to knock him about the sconce with a dirty shovel, and will not tell him of his action of battery? Hum! This fellow might be in's time a
90   great buyer of land, with his statutes, his recognizances, his fines, his double vouchers, his recoveries.* Is this the fine of his fines,

79 *loggets*   a game, something like quoits, in which blocks of wood were thrown at a stake.
90-91 *statutes . . . recoveries*   these are technical legal terms of the time: *statutes* — bonds by which a creditor collects from a debtor by attaching his land and goods; *recognizances* — bonds by which a debtor acknowledges

which this fool now triumphs over—a politician who wanted to
   bypass God's laws,
might it not?

HORATIO

70   It might, my lord.

HAMLET

Or it might be the skull of a courtier, who could say "Good
   morning, dear lord!
How are you, dear lord?" This might be my Lord what's his
   name,
the one who praised my Lord what's his name's horse when he
   really meant to ask him for it,
might it not?

HORATIO

75   Yes, my lord.

HAMLET

Why, that's it, and now he belongs to my Lady Worm, lacks his
   lower jaw, and is knocked
on the noodle with a sexton's shovel. Here is a subtle change,
if only we had the knack to see it. Were these bones worth
bringing up just to play loggets with? My own bones ache to
   think
80   about it.

GRAVEDIGGER (*singing*)

A pickax and a shovel, a shovel,
and a shrouding sheet to wrap the body in;
O, to make a pit in the dirt
is fitting for such a guest. (*Throws up another skull.*)

HAMLET

85   There's another. Why couldn't that be the skull of a lawyer?
Where are his subtleties now, his fine distinctions, his cases,
   his real estate deeds,
and his tricks? Why does he let this crazy fellow knock
him now on the skull with a dirty shovel without suing
him for assault and battery? Hah! This fellow might have been
   during his life a
90   great buyer of land, with his statutes, his recognizances, his
   fines,
his double vouchers, his recoveries. Is this the fine end of his
   fines,

---

his indebtedness to a creditor; *fines, recoveries* — procedures for converting
an entailed estate (one limited in its transmission to a certain succession of
heirs) to fee simple or unrestricted ownership; *double vouchers* — documents signed by two persons testifying to the ownership of land.

and the recovery of his recoveries, to have his fine pate full of fine dirt? Will his vouchers vouch him no more of his purchases, and double ones too, than the length and breadth of a pair of indentures? The very conveyances of his lands will scarcely lie in this box, and must th' inheritor himself have no more, ha?

HORATIO
Not a jot more, my lord.

HAMLET
Is not parchment made of sheepskins?

HORATIO
Ay, my lord, and of calveskins too.

HAMLET
They are sheep and calves which seek out assurance in that. I will speak to this fellow. Whose grave's this, sirrah?

CLOWN
Mine, sir.
        [*Sings*]   O, a pit of clay for to be made
                        For such a guest is meet.

HAMLET
I think it be thine indeed, for thou liest* in't.

CLOWN
You lie out on't, sir, and therefore 'tis not yours. For my part, I do not lie in't, yet it is mine.

HAMLET
Thou dost lie in't, to be in't and say it is thine. 'Tis for the dead, not for the quick; therefore thou liest.

CLOWN
'Tis a quick lie, sir; 'twill away again from me to you.

HAMLET
What man dost thou dig it for?

CLOWN
For no man, sir.

HAMLET
What woman then?

CLOWN
For none neither.

---

105 *liest*   wordplay on lie (be situated) / lie (tell an untruth).

and what he recovers from his recoveries—to have his subtle head full of

fine dirt? Will his vouchers get him no more of his holdings —and double vouchers too—than the length and breath of a pair of

95   contracts? The deeds themselves of his lands will hardly fit in this coffin, and must the owner himself have no more room, eh?

HORATIO
Not a bit more, my lord.

HAMLET
Isn't parchment made from sheepskins?

HORATIO
Yes, my lord, and from calveskins too.

HAMLET

100   They are sheep and calves themselves who look for security in parchment. I

will speak to this fellow. (*To the Gravedigger*) Whose grave is this, my good fellow?

GRAVEDIGGER
Mine, sir.
(*Singing*) O to make a pit in the dirt
is fitting for such a guest.

HAMLET

105   I think it is indeed yours, for you are lying in it.

GRAVEDIGGER
You are lying outside of it, sir, and therefore it isn't yours. As for me,
I do not lie in it, and yet it is mine.

HAMLET
You tell lies in it, to stand in it and say that it is yours. It's for the dead,
not for the living; therefore you're lying.

GRAVEDIGGER

110   It's a lively lie, sir; it will fly away again from me to you.

HAMLET
What man do you dig it for?

GRAVEDIGGER
For no man, sir.

HAMLET
What woman then?

GRAVEDIGGER
For no woman either.

HAMLET

115   Who is to be buried in't?

CLOWN

One that was a woman, sir; but, rest her soul, she's dead.

HAMLET

How absolute the knave is! We must speak by the card,* or equivocation will undo us. By the Lord, Horatio, this three years I have took note of it, the age is grown so picked that the

120   toe of the peasant comes so near the heel of the courtier he galls his kibe. How long hast thou been a gravemaker?

CLOWN

Of all the days i' th' year, I came to't that day that our last king Hamlet overcame Fortinbras.

HAMLET

How long is that since?

CLOWN

125   Cannot you tell that? Every fool can tell that. It was that very day that young Hamlet was born—he that is mad, and sent into England.

HAMLET

Ay, marry, why was he sent into England?

CLOWN

Why, because 'a was mad. 'A shall recover his wits there; or, if

130   'a do not, 'tis no great matter there.

HAMLET

Why?

CLOWN

'Twill not be seen in him there. There the men are as mad as he.

HAMLET

How came he mad?

CLOWN

Very strangely, they say.

HAMLET

135   How strangely?

---

117 *by the card* by the points of the compass, marked exactly on a navigator's card.

HAMLET

115 Who is to be buried in it?

GRAVEDIGGER

Someone who was a woman, sir; but, God rest her soul, she's
dead.

HAMLET

How exact the fellow is! We must speak very precisely, or
double meanings will ruin us. By the Lord, Horatio, these
last three
years I have noticed that the times have become so refined
that the

120 common man's toe comes close enough to the courtier's heel
to make
the back of his heel sore. (*To the Gravedigger*) How long have
you been a gravedigger?

GRAVEDIGGER

Of all the days in the year, I began on that day that our last king
Hamlet defeated Fortinbras.

HAMLET

How long ago was that?

GRAVEDIGGER

125 Don't you know that? Every fool knows that. It was the same
day that young Hamlet was born—he who is crazy and sent to
England.

HAMLET

Yes, to be sure. Why was he sent to England?

GRAVEDIGGER

Why, because he was crazy. He shall get back his sanity there;
or, if

130 he doesn't, it doesn't much matter there.

HAMLET

Why?

GRAVEDIGGER

It won't be noticed in him there. There the people are as crazy
as he is.

HAMLET

How did he go crazy?

GRAVEDIGGER

Very strangely, they say.

HAMLET

135 What do you mean, strangely?

CLOWN
Faith, e'en with losing his wits.

HAMLET
Upon what ground?

CLOWN
Why, here in Denmark. I have been sexton here, man and boy, thirty years.

HAMLET

140   How long will a man lie i' th' earth ere he rot?

CLOWN
Faith, if 'a be not rotten before 'a die (as we have many pocky corses nowadays that will scarce hold the laying in), 'a will last you some eight year or nine year. A tanner will last you nine year.

HAMLET

145   Why he, more than another?

CLOWN
Why, sir, his hide is so tanned with his trade that 'a will keep out water a great while, and your water is a sore decayer of your whoreson dead body. Here's a skull now hath lien you i' th' earth three and twenty years.

HAMLET

150   Whose was it?

CLOWN
A whoreson mad fellow's it was. Whose do you think it was?

HAMLET
Nay, I know not.

CLOWN
A pestilence on him for a mad rogue! 'A poured a flagon of Rhenish on my head once. This same skull, sir, was, sir, Yorick's

155   skull, the King's jester.

HAMLET
This?

CLOWN
E'en that.

GRAVEDIGGER

By my faith, exactly by losing his wits.

HAMLET

What was the cause, the grounds?

GRAVEDIGGER

Why, right here in Denmark. I have been sexton here, as a man and a boy,

for thirty years.

HAMLET

140   How long can a man's body lie in the earth before it rots?

GRAVEDIGGER

By my faith, if he's not rotten before he dies (as we have many corpses

nowadays, rotten with venereal disease, that will scarcely stay together for the burial), he will

last for about eight years or nine. A tanner will last

for nine years.

HAMLET

145   Why he more than another person?

GRAVEDIGGER

Why, sir, his skin is so cured from plying his trade that it will keep

out water for a long time, and water is a great decayer of your goddam dead body. Here's a skull now that has been in the ground

for twenty-three years.

HAMLET

150   Whose was it?

GRAVEDIGGER

It was a damned crazy fellow's. Whose do you think it was?

HAMLET

No, I don't know.

GRAVEDIGGER

A plague on him for being such a crazy rascal! He poured a jug of Rhine wine on my head once. This same skull, sir, was, sir, Yorick's

155   skull, the King's jester.

HAMLET

This?

GRAVEDIGGER

The very same.

HAMLET
> Let me see. [*Takes the skull.*] Alas, poor Yorick! I knew him,
> Horatio, a fellow of infinite jest, of most excellent fancy. He
160 hath borne me on his back a thousand times. And now how
> abhorred in my imagination it is! My gorge rises at it. Here
> hung those lips that I have kissed I know not how oft. Where be
> your gibes now? Your gambols, your songs, your flashes of
> merriment that were wont to set the table on a roar? Not one
165 now to mock your own grinning? Quite chapfall'n*? Now get
> you to my lady's chamber, and tell her, let her paint an inch
> thick, to this favor she must come. Make her laugh at that.
> Prithee, Horatio, tell me one thing.

HORATIO
> What's that, my lord?

HAMLET
170 Dost thou think Alexander looked o' this fashion i' th' earth?

HORATIO
> E'en so.

HAMLET
> And smelt so? Pah!
> [*Puts down the skull.*]

HORATIO
> E'en so, my lord.

HAMLET
> To what base uses we may return, Horatio! Why may not im-
175 agination trace the noble dust of Alexander till 'a find it stopping
> a bunghole?

HORATIO
> 'Twere to consider too curiously, to consider so.

HAMLET
> No, faith, not a jot, but to follow him thither with modesty

---

165 *chapfall'n* wordplay: lacking the lower jaw or chap / downcast,
glum.

HAMLET

Let me see it (*taking the skull*). Alas, poor Yorick! I knew him,
Horatio. He was a fellow who knew endless jokes, and had a
wonderful sense of humor. He

160 carried me on his back a thousand times. And now how
disgusting his skull is to my imagination! I could vomit at the
thought. (*Holding up the skull*) Here
hung those lips that I have kissed I don't know how often.
Where are
your jokes now? Your playful remarks, your songs, your quick,
witty replies that always used to make the dinner guests at the
table roar with laughter? Not even one jest left

165 now to make fun of your own grin? Do you lack your lower jaw?
Now run
to my lady's bedroom and tell her this: even if she paints herself
with an inch
thick of cosmetics, she will come to look like you. Make her laugh
at that.
Listen, Horatio, tell me one thing.

HORATIO

What's that, my lord?

HAMLET

170 Do you think Alexander the Great looked like this when he was
dead and buried?

HORATIO

Just like that.

HAMLET

And smelled this way? Pah! (*Throws down the skull in disgust.*)

HORATIO

Just like that, my lord.

HAMLET

What degrading uses we may be put to after we're dead,
Horatio! Why can't our

175 imagination trace the noble dust of Alexander the Great's body
until we find it corking
a beer barrel?

HORATIO

It would be too minute an investigation to think that way.

HAMLET

No, by my faith, not in the least, not if we followed him there
with sufficient moderation

enough, and likelihood to lead it; as thus: Alexander died,
180   Alexander was buried, Alexander returneth to dust; the dust is
earth; of earth we make loam; and why of that loam whereto
he was converted might they not stop a beer barrel?
Imperious Caesar, dead and turned to clay,
Might stop a hole to keep the wind away.
185   O, that that earth which kept the world in awe
Should patch a wall t' expel the winter's flaw!
But soft, but soft awhile! Here comes the King.

> *Enter* KING, QUEEN, LAERTES, *and a coffin, with Lords*
> *attendant and a Priest.*

The Queen, the courtiers. Who is this they follow?
And with such maimèd rites? This doth betoken
190   The corse they follow did with desp'rate hand
Fordo its own life. 'Twas of some estate.
Couch we awhile, and mark.

> *[Retires with Horatio.]*

LAERTES
What ceremony else?

HAMLET
That is Laertes,
A very noble youth. Mark.

LAERTES
195   What ceremony else?

PRIEST
Her obsequies have been as far enlarged
As we have warranty. Her death was doubtful,
And, but that great command o'ersways the order,
She should in ground unsanctified been lodged
200   Till the last trumpet. For charitable prayers,
Shards, flints, and pebbles should be thrown on her.
Yet here she is allowed her virgin crants,
Her maiden strewments, and the bringing home
Of bell and burial.

and with plausibility leading the way. For example: Alexander
died,
180   Alexander was buried, Alexander returns to dust; the dust is
earth; of earth we make clay. And why from that clay into which
he was converted shouldn't someone plug up a beer barrel?
(*Singing*) Imperial Caesar, dead and turned to clay,
might plug up a hole to keep the wind out.
185   O, that that piece of earth which kept the world in awe
should patch a wall to keep out the winter wind.
But wait a minute, just a minute! Here comes the King.
  Enter KING, QUEEN, LAERTES, *and a coffin carried by*
  pall-bearers, with Lords attending, and a Priest.
And the Queen and the courtiers. Who is in that coffin they
follow?
And with such curtailed burial rites? This is a sign that
190   the corpse they follow desperately
destroyed its own life. It must be a person of high rank.
Let's conceal ourselves for a while and watch.
  (*Stands to one side of the stage with Horatio.*)

LAERTES
Are there to be no other ceremonies?

HAMLET (*to Horatio*)
That is Laertes,
a very noble youth. Observe.

LAERTES
195   Are there to be no other ceremonies?

PRIEST
Her funeral rites have been extended as far
as we have permission. Her death was suspicious,
and were it not that a powerful command prevails over
customary procedure,
she would certainly have been buried in unsanctified ground
200   until the last trumpet on Judgment Day. Instead of prayers
for her salvation,
broken bits of pottery, stones, and pebbles would have been
thrown on her coffin.
Yet here she is allowed to have the garlands proper to a
virgin and
flowers scattered on her grave, and she is laid to rest
with the bell tolling.

LAERTES
Must there no more be done?
PRIEST

205   No more be done.
We should profane the service of the dead
To sing a requiem and such rest to her
As to peace-parted souls.
LAERTES
                              Lay her i' th' earth,
And from her fair and unpolluted flesh
210   May violets spring! I tell thee, churlish priest,
A minist'ring angel shall my sister be
When thou liest howling!
HAMLET
                                    What, the fair Ophelia?
QUEEN
Sweets to the sweet! Farewell.
          [*Scatters flowers.*]
I hoped thou shouldst have been my Hamlet's wife.
215   I thought thy bride bed to have decked, sweet maid,
And not have strewed thy grave.
LAERTES
                                        O, treble woe
Fall ten times treble on that cursèd head
Whose wicked deed thy most ingenious sense
Deprived thee of! Hold off the earth awhile,
220   Till I have caught her once more in mine arms.
          Leaps in the grave.
Now pile your dust upon the quick and dead
Till of this flat a mountain you have made
T'o'ertop old Pelion or the skyish head
Of blue Olympus.*
HAMLET [*coming forward*]
                                    What is he whose grief
225   Bears such an emphasis, whose phrase of sorrow
Conjures the wand'ring stars, and makes them stand
Like wonder-wounded hearers? This is I,
Hamlet the Dane.

223-24 *Pelion ... Olympus*   mountains in Greece. Laertes alludes to the
legend of the Titans, giants in classical mythology, who tried to reach

LAERTES

Can't any more be done?

PRIEST

205   No more can be done.

We would profane the burial service

if we sang a requiem and wished such rest for her

as we do for souls who have made their peace with God.

LAERTES

Lay her in the earth,

and from her beautiful and undefiled body

210   may violets grow! I tell you, snarling priest,

my sister shall be an angel of mercy

when you are howling in hell!   ·

HAMLET *(to Horatio)*

What, is this the beautiful Ophelia?

QUEEN

Sweet flowers for the sweet! Farewell.

     (Scatters flowers on the coffin.)

I hoped that you would have been my Hamlet's wife.

215   I thought I would have adorned your bridal bed with flowers,

     sweet girl,

not scattered them on your grave.

LAERTES

O, may triple misfortune

fall ten times triple on that accursed head

whose evil deed deprived you of your most delicate spirit!

Don't cover her with earth yet,

220   until I have held her once more in my arms.

     (Leaps into the grave.)

Now pile the earth on the living and the dead

until you've made a mountain of this flat ground

rising higher than Mount Pelion or than that mountain with its

     head in the skies,

blue Mount Olympus.

HAMLET *(coming forward)*

Who is he whose grief

225   has such an exaggerated emphasis, whose sorrowful words

call upon the planets as they move and order them to stand

like listeners struck with wonder? This is I,

Hamlet the Dane.

     (Leaps in the grave with Laertes.)

---

heaven (the top of Mt. Olympus) by piling Mt. Ossa on Mt. Pelion (compare Hamlet's allusion in 5.2.253).

LAERTES

             The devil take thy soul!

    [*Grapples with him.*]

HAMLET

    Thou pray'st not well.

230   I prithee take thy fingers from my throat,

    For, though I am not splenitive and rash,

    Yet have I in me something dangerous,

    Which let thy wisdom fear. Hold off thy hand.

KING

    Pluck them asunder.

QUEEN

              Hamlet, Hamlet!

ALL

    Gentlemen!

HORATIO

235   Good my lord, be quiet.

    [*Attendants part them.*]

HAMLET

    Why, I will fight with him upon this theme

    Until my eyelids will no longer wag.

QUEEN

    O my son, what theme?

HAMLET

    I loved Ophelia. Forty thousand brothers

240   Could not with all their quantity of love

    Make up my sum. What wilt thou do for her?

KING

    O, he is mad, Laertes.

QUEEN

    For love of God forbear him.

HAMLET

    'Swounds, show me what thou't do.

245   Woo't weep? Woo't fight? Woo't fast? Woo't tear thyself?

    Woo't drink up eisel? Eat a crocodile?

    I'll do't. Dost thou come here to whine?

    To outface me with leaping in her grave?

    Be buried quick with her, and so will I.

250   And if thou prate of mountains, let them throw

LAERTES
>The devil take your soul!
>>(*They grapple with one another in Ophelia's grave.*)

HAMLET
>You don't pray very well.
>Please take your fingers off my throat;
>for although I am not hot-tempered and rash,
>I do have something dangerous in me
>which you would be wise to fear. Take your hands off.

KING
>Pull them apart.

QUEEN
>Hamlet, Hamlet!

ALL
>Gentlemen!

HORATIO
>My good lord, calm yourself.
>>(*Attendants separate them, and they come out of the grave.*)

HAMLET
>Why, I will fight with him on this matter
>until my eyelids no longer close.

QUEEN
>O, my son, what matter?

HAMLET
>I loved Ophelia. Forty thousand brothers
>could not with all their quantity of love
>add up to my total. What will you do for her?

KING
>O, he is insane, Laertes.

QUEEN
>For the love of God, don't provoke him.

HAMLET
>By God's wounds, show me what you would do.
>Would you shed tears? Would you fight? Would you fast? Would
>>you tear your hair?
>Would you drink vinegar? Eat a crocodile?
>I'll do it. Do you come here to whine?
>To humiliate me by leaping in her grave?
>Be buried alive with her, and so will I.
>And if you chatter about mountains, let them throw

230

235

240

245

250

> Millions of acres on us, till our ground,
> Singeing his pate against the burning zone,
> Make Ossa like a wart! Nay, an thou'lt mouth,
> I'll rant as well as thou.

QUEEN

>   This is mere madness;
255   And thus a while the fit will work on him.
> Anon, as patient as the female dove
> When that her golden couplets are disclosed,
> His silence will sit drooping.

HAMLET

>   Hear you, sir.
> What is the reason that you use me thus?
260   I loved you ever. But it is no matter.
> Let Hercules* himself do what he may,
> The cat will mew, and dog will have his day.

KING

> I pray thee, good Horatio, wait upon him.
>   *Exit* HAMLET *and* HORATIO.
> [*To Laertes*] Strengthen your patience in our last night's speech.
265   We'll put the matter to the present push.
> Good Gertrude, set some watch over your son.
> This grave shall have a living monument.
> An hour of quiet shortly shall we see;
> Till then in patience our proceeding be.
>   *Exeunt.*

[*Scene ii: The castle.*] *Enter* HAMLET *and* HORATIO.

HAMLET

> So much for this, sir; now shall you see the other.
> You do remember all the circumstance?

HORATIO

> Remember it, my lord!

---

261 *Hercules* Hamlet may be comparing Laertes' exaggerated behavior and language to that of Hercules, who was sometimes depicted on stage as a boasting and ranting tyrant.

millions of acres on us, till our mound of earth
singes its head against the sun's orbit
and makes Mount Ossa look like a wart! No, if you want to
  talk big,
I can rant as well as you can.

QUEEN
  This is pure insanity;
255 and the fit affects him this way for a little while.
  Soon, as patient as the female dove
  when she hatches her two downy golden chicks,
  his silence will make him sit quietly.

HAMLET (*to Laertes*)
  Listen to me, sir.
  Why do you treat me this way?
260 I always thought well of you. But it's not important.
  Let Hercules brag and shout all he can,
  the cat will mew, and the dog will have his day.

KING
  Please, good Horatio, look after him.
      Exit HAMLET *and* HORATIO.
  (*To Laertes*) Let your patience be strengthened by remembering
    our talk last night.
265 We'll put our plot to an immediate test.
  (*To the Queen*) Good Gertrude, have someone keep an eye on
    your son.
  Ophelia's grave shall have a lasting monument to mark it.
  Soon we shall have quiet times;
  until then let's go on patiently.
      Exit KING, QUEEN, LAERTES, *and the others.*

Act V, Scene ii: Inside the castle. Enter HAMLET *and* HORATIO.

HAMLET
  So much for this part of my story, sir; now you shall hear
    the other.
  Do you remember all the details?

HORATIO
  Of course I remember them, my lord!

HAMLET
Sir, in my heart there was a kind of fighting
That would not let me sleep. Methought I lay
Worse than the mutines in the bilboes. Rashly—
And praised be rashness for it—let us know,
Our indiscretion sometime serves us well
When our deep plots do pall, and that should learn us
There's a divinity that shapes our ends,
Rough-hew them how we will.

HORATIO
                                        That is most certain.

HAMLET
Up from my cabin,
My sea gown scarfed about me, in the dark
Groped I to find out them, had my desire,
Fingered their packet, and in fine withdrew
To mine own room again, making so bold,
My fears forgetting manners, to unseal
Their grand commission; where I found, Horatio—
Ah, royal knavery!—an exact command,
Larded with many several sorts of reasons,
Importing Denmark's health, and England's too,
With, ho, such bugs and goblins in my life,
That on the supervise, no leisure bated,
No, not to stay the grinding of the ax,
My head should be struck off.

HORATIO
                                        Is't possible?

HAMLET
Here's the commission; read it at more leisure.
But wilt thou hear now how I did proceed?

HORATIO
I beseech you.

HAMLET
Being thus benetted round with villains,
Or I could make a prologue to my brains,
They had begun the play. I sat me down,

5

10

15

20

25

30

HAMLET
Sir, in my heart there was a kind of uneasiness
that wouldn't let me sleep. I felt
worse than mutineers in chains. On impulse—
and thank goodness impulses work that way—let's acknowledge
that our imprudence sometimes assists us quite well
when our secret plots fail. And that should teach us
that there's a divine force that gives final shape to our designs,
no matter how we rough them out beforehand.

HORATIO
That is certainly true.

HAMLET
On an impulse, then, I left my cabin,
my sailor's cloak around my shoulders, and in the dark,
I groped around to find Rosencrantz and Guildenstern, got
what I wanted,
stole their papers, and finally returned
to my own room again. Then I was bold enough,
since my fear made me forget about good manners, to break the
seal
of their grand commission. There I found, Horatio—
ah, royal trickery!—a precise order,
embellished with many different kinds of reasons
concerning the King of Denmark's welfare and the King of
England's too,
with, oh, such warnings of dire consequences—goblins and
bugaboos—if I were allowed to live.
So that when the letter was read, without any delay,
no, not even to wait for the sharpening of the ax,
my head should be cut off.

HORATIO
Is it possible?

HAMLET
Here's the order; read it when you have more time.
But do you want to hear now what I did?

HORATIO
Please go on.

HAMLET
Since I was thus surrounded by villains;
before I could even write a prologue for myself,
they had begun the play. I sat myself down,

5

10

15

20

25

30

Devised a new commission, wrote it fair.
I once did hold it, as our statists do,
A baseness to write fair, and labored much
35   How to forget that learning, but, sir, now
It did me yeoman's service. Wilt thou know
Th' effect of what I wrote?

HORATIO

Ay, good my lord.

HAMLET

An earnest conjuration from the King,
As England was his faithful tributary,
40   As love between them like the palm might flourish,
As peace should still her wheaten garland wear
And stand a comma 'tween their amities,
And many suchlike as's* of great charge,
That on the view and knowing of these contents,
45   Without debatement further, more or less,
He should those bearers put to sudden death,
Not shriving time allowed.

HORATIO

How was this sealed?

HAMLET

Why, even in that was heaven ordinant.
I had my father's signet in my purse,
50   Which was the model of that Danish seal,
Folded the writ up in the form of th' other,
Subscribed it, gave't th' impression, placed it safely,
The changeling never known. Now, the next day
Was our sea fight, and what to this was sequent
55   Thou knowest already.

HORATIO

So Guildenstern and Rosencrantz go to't.

HAMLET

Why, man, they did make love to this employment.
They are not near my conscience; their defeat
Does by their own insinuation grow.
60   'Tis dangerous when the baser nature comes
Between the pass and fell incensèd points
Of mighty opposites.

---

43   *as's*   wordplay on the plural of "as" and "asses."

invented a new set of orders, and wrote them out like a
    professional scribe.
I once thought, as our politicians do,
that it was demeaning to have a good handwriting and worked
    hard
35   to forget penmanship. But, sir, now
it did me a good turn. Do you want to know
the gist of what I wrote?

HORATIO
Yes, my good lord.

HAMLET
A solemn appeal from the King,
that whereas England was his faithful ally,
40   whereas love between them might thrive like a palm tree,
whereas peace should continue to be adorned like the goddess of
    agriculture
and remain a link between their friendships,
and many similar "as's" carrying great loads,
that upon reading and understanding the contents of this letter,
45   without any further consideration, more or less,
he should put those who brought it to immediate death,
allowing them no time for confession.

HORATIO
How did you make this official?

HAMLET
Why, even in that heaven showed its interest in my success.
I had my father's signet ring in my wallet,
50   a small copy of the official Danish seal.
I folded up the document in the same way the other one was,
signed it, sealed it with the signet, and replaced it safely,
without the switch being noticed. Now, the next day
our sea fight took place, and what happened after this
55   you already know about.

HORATIO
So Guildenstern and Rosencrantz go to their death.

HAMLET
Why, man, they were overjoyed to be sent on this mission.
They're not on my conscience; their defeat
grows out of their own meddling.
60   It's dangerous when inferior people come
between the thrusts of the fiercely angry swords
of powerful opponents.

HORATIO

Why, what a king is this!

HAMLET

Does it not, think thee, stand me now upon—

He that hath killed my king, and whored my mother,

65   Popped in between th' election and my hopes,

Thrown out his angle for my proper life,

And with such coz'nage—is't not perfect conscience

To quit him with this arm? And is't not to be damned

To let this canker of our nature come

70   In further evil?

HORATIO

It must be shortly known to him from England

What is the issue of the business there.

HAMLET

It will be short; the interim's mine,

And a man's life's no more than to say "one."*

75   But I am very sorry, good Horatio,

That to Laertes I forgot myself,

For by the image of my cause I see

The portraiture of his. I'll court his favors.

But sure the bravery of his grief did put me

Into a tow'ring passion.

HORATIO

80   Peace, who comes here?

Enter young OSRIC, *a courtier.*

OSRIC

Your lordship is right welcome back to Denmark.

HAMLET

I humbly thank you, sir. [*Aside to Horatio*] Dost know this waterfly?

HORATIO [*Aside to Hamlet*]

No, my good lord.

HAMLET [*Aside to Horatio*]

85   Thy state is the more gracious, for 'tis a vice to know him. He hath much land, and fertile. Let a beast be lord of beasts, and his crib shall stand at the king's mess. 'Tis a chough, but, as I say, spacious in the possession of dirt.

---

74   *"one"*   Hamlet may mean that a man can be killed in no more time than it takes to deliver one sword thrust. See 5.2.253.

HORATIO
Why, what kind of king is this Claudius!

HAMLET
Don't you think that it is now my duty—
he who has killed my king and seduced my mother,
65   squeezed his way into election as king and thereby frustrated
              my hopes,
thrown out his hook for my own life,
and with such trickery—isn't it absolutely right
that I pay him back with this arm of mine? And isn't it sinful
to allow this cancerous sore on human nature
70   to do more evil?

HORATIO
He will soon hear from England
what the result is of the business there.

HAMLET
It will be soon, but the intervening time is mine,
and a man can be killed in no more time than it takes to
              say "one."
75   But I am very sorry, my dear Horatio,
that I forgot myself with Laertes;
for in picturing my cause for revenge I understand
what his looks like. I'll try to win his friendship.
But it was clearly the exaggeration of his grief that made me
uncontrollably angry.

HORATIO
80   Wait a minute, who's coming here?
                  Enter young OSRIC, *a fantastically dressed courtier.*

OSRIC (*with an elaborate bow and flourish*)
Your lordship is truly welcome back to Denmark.

HAMLET
I humbly thank you, sir. (*To Horatio*) Do you know this
vain insect?

HORATIO (*to Hamlet*)
No, my good lord.

HAMLET (*to Horatio*)
85   You're very lucky, because it's a vice to know him. He
owns a lot of fertile land. If an animal should own a lot of
              animals,
his trough shall be at the king's table. He's a chattering
              jackdaw; but, as I
say, richly possessed of dirt, of land.

OSRIC

90   Sweet lord, if your lordship were at leisure, I should impart a thing to you from his Majesty.

HAMLET

I will receive it, sir, with all diligence of spirit. Put your bonnet to his right use. 'Tis for the head.

OSRIC

I thank your lordship, it is very hot.

HAMLET

No, believe me, 'tis very cold; the wind is northerly.

OSRIC

95   It is indifferent cold, my lord, indeed.

HAMLET

But yet methinks it is very sultry and hot for my complexion.

OSRIC

Exceedingly, my lord; it is very sultry, as 'twere—I cannot tell how. But, my lord, his Majesty bade me signify to you that 'a has laid a great wager on your head. Sir, this is the matter—

HAMLET

100   I beseech you remember.

[HAMLET *moves him to put on his hat.*]

OSRIC

Nay, good my lord; for my ease, in good faith. Sir, here is newly come to court Laertes—believe me, an absolute gentleman, full of most excellent differences, of very soft society and great showing. Indeed, to speak feelingly of him, he is the card or
105   calendar of gentry; for you shall find in him the continent of what part a gentleman would see.

HAMLET

Sir, his definement* suffers no perdition in you, though, I know, to divide him inventorially would dozy th' arithmetic of memory, and yet but yaw neither in respect of his quick sail. But, in the
110   verity of extolment, I take him to be a soul of great article, and

---

107 ff.   *definement* . . .   by imitating it, Hamlet is making fun of Osric's extravagant and affected way of talking.

OSRIC (*taking off his hat out of respect for Hamlet*)
Sweet lord, if your lordship had the time, I would like to give
90   you a message from his Majesty.
HAMLET
I will receive it, sir, with a spirit ready and eager to serve.
Put your hat
to its right use. It's for the head.
OSRIC
I thank your lordship; it is very hot.
HAMLET
No, believe me, it's very cold. The wind is from the north.
OSRIC
95   It is rather cold, my lord, yes indeed.
HAMLET
But yet I think it is very sultry and hot for someone of my
temperament.
OSRIC
Very much so, my lord, it is very sultry, as it were—I cannot say
why or how. But, my lord, his Majesty asked me to inform you
that he
has bet a large sum on you. Sir, here's what it concerns—
HAMLET
100   I ask you, please, remember your hat.
(*Hamlet motions for him to put on his hat.*)
OSRIC
No, my good lord; I'm all right this way, by my good faith. Sir,
Laertes has just arrived at the court—believe me, he is a
complete gentleman, full
of most excellent personal qualities, with very agreeable
manners and a splendid
appearance. Indeed, to speak justly of him, he is the map or
105   guide to what a gentleman should be. You shall find him to be
the sum total of
every quality a gentleman should have.
HAMLET
Sir, his definition undergoes no loss by your description of him,
although I know
that to analyze him in detail would make the mathematical
powers of the mind dizzy.
And yet the mind would stagger and fall for all that because of
the rapid increase of his achievements. But to
110   praise him truly, I consider him to be a soul of great scope.

his infusion of such dearth and rareness as, to make true diction
of him, his semblable is his mirror, and who else would trace
him, his umbrage, nothing more.

OSRIC
Your lordship speaks most infallibly of him.

HAMLET
115   The concernancy, sir? Why do we wrap the gentleman in our
more rawer breath?

OSRIC
Sir?

HORATIO
Is't not possible to understand in another tongue? You will to't,
sir, really.

HAMLET
120   What imports the nomination of this gentleman?

OSRIC
Of Laertes?

HORATIO [*Aside to Hamlet*]
His purse is empty already. All's golden words are spent.

HAMLET
Of him, sir.

OSRIC
I know you are not ignorant——

HAMLET
125   I would you did, sir; yet, in faith, if you did, it would not much
approve me. Well, sir?

OSRIC
You are not ignorant of what excellence Laertes is——

HAMLET
I dare not confess that, lest I should compare with him in excellence; but to know a man well were to know himself.

OSRIC
130   I mean, sir, for his weapon; but in the imputation laid on him
by them, in his meed he's unfellowed.

His essence is so scarce and rare that, to speak of him truly,
no one is like him but his reflection in his mirror. And if anyone
tries to follow or imitate
him, they are merely a shadow of him, nothing more.

OSRIC
Your lordship speaks very confidently about him.

HAMLET
115   What is the relevance of this, sir? Why do we wrap the
gentleman in our
words, which are too crude to do him justice?

OSRIC
What do you mean, sir?

HORATIO
Can't you understand your own way of speaking when someone
else uses it? You can do it if you try,
sir, really.

HAMLET
120   What does your naming of this gentleman signify?

OSRIC
My naming of Laertes?

HORATIO *(to Hamlet)*
His purse is empty already. All his golden words are spent.

HAMLET
Yes, of him, sir.

OSRIC
I know that you are not unaware—

HAMLET
125   I wish you did know that, sir; yet, by my faith, if you did
know, it would not be very much
to my credit. Well, what is it, sir?

OSRIC
You are not unaware of how excellent Laertes is—

HAMLET
I dare not admit that, for fear that I should seem to claim
the same
excellence for myself; for to know a man well means to know him
just as thoroughly (as yourself).

OSRIC
130   I mean, sir, to speak of his skill with his weapon; that in the
reputation given him
by others, in his worth he is without equal.

HAMLET
What's his weapon?

OSRIC
Rapier and dagger.

HAMLET
That's two of his weapons—but well.

OSRIC
135   The King, sir, hath wagered with him six Barbary horses, against
the which he has impawned, as I take it, six French rapiers and
poniards, with their assigns, as girdle, hangers, and so. Three of
the carriages,* in faith, are very dear to fancy, very responsive
to the hilts, most delicate carriages, and of very liberal conceit.

HAMLET
140   What call you the carriages?

HORATIO [*Aside to Hamlet*]
I knew you must be edified by the margent ere you had done.

OSRIC
The carriages, sir, are the hangers.

HAMLET
The phrase would be more germane to the matter if we could
carry a cannon by our sides. I would it might be hangers till then.
145   But on! Six Barbary horses against six French swords, their
assigns, and three liberal-conceited carriages—that's the French
bet against the Danish. Why is this all impawned, as you call it?

OSRIC
The King, sir, hath laid, sir, that in a dozen passes between yourself and him he shall not exceed you three hits; he hath laid on
150   twelve for nine, and it would come to immediate trial if your
lordship would vouchsafe the answer.

HAMLET
How if I answer no?

OSRIC
I mean, my lord, the opposition of your person in trial.

---

138 *carriages* an affected synonym for "hangers." "Carriages" usually
refer to guns or cannons.

HAMLET
What's his weapon?
OSRIC
Sword and dagger.
HAMLET
That's two of his weapons—but go on.
OSRIC
135   The King, sir, has bet him six Barbary horses, against
which Laertes has pawned, as I hear, six French swords and
daggers, with their accessories, such as belts, straps, and so on. Three of
the carriages, by my faith, are in very exquisite taste, matched well
to the sword hilts, very finely made carriages, and elegantly
designed.
HAMLET
140   What are these things you call "carriages"?
HORATIO (*to Hamlet*)
I knew you would need notes in the margin to explain the
original before you were through.
OSRIC
The carriages, sir, are the straps that hold the sword.
HAMLET
The expression would be more appropriate to the matter if we could
carry a cannon by our sides. I hope we can call them sword straps
until then.
145   But go on! Six Barbary horses against six French swords, their
accessories, and three elegantly designed carriages—that's the French bet
against the Danish one. Why is all this "pawned," as you call it?
OSRIC
The King, sir, has bet, sir, that in a dozen rounds between
yourself and Laertes, he shall not outscore you by more than
three hits. Laertes has bet that
150   out of twelve exchanges he will win at least nine, and this bet
could be played out immediately if your
lordship would bestow the answer.
HAMLET
Suppose I answer no?
OSRIC
I mean, my lord, once you agree to fight.

HAMLET

155 Sir, I will walk here in the hall. If it please his Majesty, it is the breathing time of day with me. Let the foils be brought, the gentleman willing, and the King hold his purpose, I will win for him an I can; if not, I will gain nothing but my shame and the odd hits.

OSRIC

Shall I deliver you e'en so?

HAMLET

160 To this effect, sir, after what flourish your nature will.

OSRIC

I commend my duty to your lordship.

HAMLET

Yours, yours. [*Exit* OSRIC.] He does well to commend it himself; there are no tongues else for's turn.

HORATIO

This lapwing* runs away with the shell on his head.

HAMLET

165 'A did comply, sir, with his dug before 'a sucked it. Thus has he, and many more of the same breed that I know the drossy age dotes on, only got the tune of the time and, out of an habit of encounter, a kind of yeasty collection, which carries them through and through the most fanned and winnowed opinions; and do

170 but blow them to their trial, the bubbles are out.
        Enter a Lord.

LORD

My lord, his Majesty commended him to you by young Osric, who brings back to him that you attend him in the hall. He sends to know if your pleasure hold to play with Laertes, or that you will take longer time.

---

164 *lapwing* the newly hatched lapwing was thought to run from the nest with part of the eggshell still over its head. Osric has apparently put on his hat at last.

HAMLET

    Sir, I am going to walk here in the hall of the castle. If his
        Majesty will excuse me, it is

155   my usual time for exercise. Let the fencing foils be brought, and
        if the

    gentleman is still willing and the King is still ready to bet, I will
        win for

    him if I can. If not, I will gain nothing but my own
        embarrassment and a

    couple of hits.

OSRIC

    Shall I report this as your answer?

HAMLET

160   To this effect, sir, using whatever rhetorical embellishments your
        temperament delights in.

OSRIC

    I offer your lordship my dutiful respects.

HAMLET

    I remain yours, yours. (*Exit* OSRIC.) He has to praise his own
        dutiful respects;

    there's no one else who will.

HORATIO

    This foolish bird runs away with the shell still on its head.

HAMLET

165   He bowed ceremoniously to his mother's breast before he sucked
        it. Thus he,

    and many others of the same sort that I know who are made
        much of in these worthless days,

    only mimic the fashionable talk of the times. And out of these
        superficial

    contacts, they accumulate a sort of frothy collection of fine
        phrases, by which they manage to fool

    the most judicious and refined judgments. But if you

170   just blow on these phrases to test them, the bubbles all pop.

        Enter a Lord.

LORD

    My lord, his Majesty sent you his respects by young Osric,
    who tells him that you are waiting for him in the main hall.
        He sends me

    to ask if you are still ready to fence with Laertes, or whether you
    would like more time.

HAMLET

175   I am constant to my purposes; they follow the King's pleasure. If his fitness speaks, mine is ready; now or whensoever, provided I be so able as now.

LORD

The King and Queen and all are coming down.

HAMLET

In happy time.

LORD

180   The Queen desires you to use some gentle entertainment to Laertes before you fall to play.

HAMLET

She well instructs me.
      [*Exit Lord.*]

HORATIO

You will lose this wager, my lord.

HAMLET

185   I do not think so. Since he went into France I have been in continual practice. I shall win at the odds. But thou wouldst not think how ill all's here about my heart. But it is no matter.

HORATIO

Nay, good my lord——

HAMLET

It is but foolery, but it is such a kind of gain-giving as would
190   perhaps trouble a woman.

HORATIO

If your mind dislike anything, obey it. I will forestall their repair hither and say you are not fit.

HAMLET

Not a whit, we defy augury. There is special providence in the fall of a sparrow.* If it be now, 'tis not to come; if it be not to
195   come, it will be now; if it be not now, yet it will come. The readiness is all. Since no man of aught he leaves knows, what is't to leave betimes? Let be.

---

194 *sparrow* an allusion to the well known passage: "Are not two sparrows sold for a farthing? and one of them shall not fall on the ground without your Father" (Matthew 10:29).

HAMLET

175 I am still ready to do what I promised; my intentions follow
the King's wishes.

If Laertes is ready, so am I; now or whenever, provided that
I am as strong as I am now.

LORD

The King and Queen and all the court are coming down.

HAMLET

I'm glad.

LORD

180 The Queen would like you to greet Laertes courteously
before you begin to fence.

HAMLET

She advises me well.

Exit Lord.

HORATIO

You will lose this bet, my lord.

HAMLET

185 I don't think so. Since Laertes went to France, I have been in
continual practice. I shall win with the handicap I have. But
you can't

imagine how apprehensive I feel here in my heart. But it doesn't
matter.

HORATIO

But wait, my good lord—

HAMLET

It's just an absurdity, but it's the sort of misgiving that would
190 perhaps trouble a woman.

HORATIO

If your instinct tells you something is wrong with this fencing
match, obey it. I will prevent their coming

here and say that you aren't able to fight.

HAMLET

Not at all, I despise a superstitious belief in premonitions. There
is a special divine plan at work even in the

fall of a sparrow. If my death is to be now, it won't occur in
the future; if it won't occur

195 in the future, it will happen now; if it doesn't happen now, yet
it will come. Being

ready is all that matters. Since no man knows anything of what
will happen after his death, what difference does it make
to die early? Let it be.

A table prepared. [Enter] Trumpets, Drums, and Officers with cushions; KING, QUEEN, [OSRIC,] *and all the State, [with] foils, daggers, [and stoups of wine borne in]; and* LAERTES.

KING
Come, Hamlet, come, and take this hand from me.
[*The King puts Laertes' hand into Hamlet's.*]

HAMLET
Give me your pardon, sir. I have done you wrong,
200   But pardon't, as you are a gentleman.
This presence knows, and you must needs have heard,
How I am punished with a sore distraction.
What I have done
That might your nature, honor, and exception
205   Roughly awake, I here proclaim was madness.
Was't Hamlet wronged Laertes? Never Hamlet.
If Hamlet from himself be ta'en away,
And when he's not himself does wrong Laertes,
Then Hamlet does it not, Hamlet denies it.
210   Who does it then? His madness. If't be so,
Hamlet is of the faction that is wronged;
His madness is poor Hamlet's enemy.
Sir, in this audience,
Let my disclaiming from a purposed evil
215   Free me so far in your most generous thoughts
That I have shot my arrow o'er the house
And hurt my brother.

LAERTES
                    I am satisfied in nature,
Whose motive in this case should stir me most
To my revenge. But in my terms of honor
220   I stand aloof, and will no reconcilement
Till by some elder masters of known honor
I have a voice and precedent of peace
To keep my name ungored. But till that time
I do receive your offered love like love,
And will not wrong it.

A table is brought in, with mugs of wine on it. Enter Musicians playing trumpets and drums, and Servants with cushions, swords, and daggers; then enter KING, QUEEN, LAERTES, OSRIC, *and all the court.*

KING
Come, Hamlet, come and take this hand from me.
The King puts Laertes' hand into Hamlet's.

HAMLET
Grant me your pardon, sir. I have done you wrong,
200   but pardon me, as you are a gentleman.
This assembled court knows, and you must have heard,
how I am punished with great mental distress.
Whatever I have done
that might have thoughtlessly offended your feelings and your
     honor, and provoked your disapproval,
205   I here declare was because of my madness.
Was it Hamlet who wronged Laertes? It was never Hamlet.
If Hamlet is taken away from his true self,
and when he's not himself wrongs Laertes,
then Hamlet does not do it, Hamlet denies doing it.
210   Who does it then? His madness. If this is true,
Hamlet is on the side that is wronged;
his own madness is poor Hamlet's enemy.
Sir, in this royal presence,
let my declaration that I meant no deliberate evil
215   free me of guilt in your very generous feelings.
Let it be as if I had shot an arrow over the house
and accidentally hurt my brother.

LAERTES
My feelings are satisfied,
whose promptings in this case should move me very powerfully
to my revenge. But so far as my honor is concerned,
220   I stand aloof, and I will agree to no reconciliation
until some older experts in the rules of honor
give me an authoritative opinion with precedents for making
     peace,
so that I can keep my good name uninjured. But until that time
I accept your offered friendship as friendship,
and will not reject it.

HAMLET

225   I embrace it freely,
And will this brother's wager frankly play.
Give us the foils. Come on.

LAERTES

                                Come, one for me.

HAMLET

I'll be your foil,* Laertes. In mine ignorance
Your skill shall, like a star i' th' darkest night,
Stick fiery off indeed.

LAERTES

230   You mock me, sir.

HAMLET

No, by this hand.

KING

Give them the foils, young Osric. Cousin Hamlet,
You know the wager?

HAMLET

                          Very well, my lord.
Your grace has laid the odds o' th' weaker side.

KING

235   I do not fear it, I have seen you both;
But since he is bettered, we have therefore odds.

LAERTES

This is too heavy; let me see another.

HAMLET

This likes me well. These foils have all a length?
               Prepare to play.

OSRIC

Ay, my good lord.

KING

240   Set me the stoups of wine upon that table.
If Hamlet give the first or second hit,
Or quit in answer of the third exchange,
Let all the battlements their ordnance fire.
The King shall drink to Hamlet's better breath,

245   And in the cup an union* shall he throw
Richer than that which four successive kings
In Denmark's crown have worn. Give me the cups,

---

228 *foil* wordplay: a fencing foil/a background, like dark velvet, which shows a jewel to advantage.

HAMLET

225 I welcome it without reservation,
and will play freely for this friendly bet.
Give us the fencing foils. Come on.

LAERTES

Come, give me one.

HAMLET

I'll serve as a foil for you, Laertes. My clumsiness
shall make your skill, like a star in the darkest night,
really blaze out brilliantly.

LAERTES

230 You're making fun of me, sir.

HAMLET

No, I swear by this hand of mine.

KING

Give them the fencing foils, young Osric. My dear kinsman
Hamlet,
you know the terms of the bet?

HAMLET

Very well, my lord.
Your grace has given odds to the weaker side.

KING

235 I don't think so. I have seen you both fight,
but since he has improved himself so much, I therefore have
placed the odds on Laertes' side.

LAERTES

This foil is too heavy; let me see another.

HAMLET

This one pleases me. Are these foils all the same length?
They prepare to fence.

OSRIC

Yes, my good lord.

KING

240 Put the cups of wine on that table.
If Hamlet wins the first or second bout,
or repays Laertes' previous wins in the third bout,
let all the battlements fire their cannons.
The King shall drink to Hamlet's staying power,
245 and he shall throw a pearl in the cup
more valuable than the one which four successive kings
have worn in Denmark's crown. Give me the cups,

---

245 *union* presumably, a trick pearl, which has poison concealed in it.

And let the kettle to the trumpet speak,
The trumpet to the cannoneer without,
250   The cannons to the heavens, the heaven to earth,
"Now the King drinks to Hamlet." Come, begin.
        Trumpets the while.
And you, the judges, bear a wary eye.
HAMLET
    Come on, sir.
LAERTES
                Come, my lord.
        They play.
HAMLET
                                One.
LAERTES
                                    No.
HAMLET
                                        Judgment?
OSRIC
    A hit, a very palpable hit.
        Drum, trumpets, and shot. Flourish; a piece goes off.
LAERTES
                        Well, again.
KING
255   Stay, give me drink. Hamlet, this pearl is thine.
Here's to thy health. Give him the cup.
HAMLET
    I'll play this bout first; set it by awhile.
    Come. [*They play.*] Another hit. What say you?
LAERTES
    A touch, a touch; I do confess't.
KING
    Our son shall win.
QUEEN
260   He's fat, and scant of breath.
Here, Hamlet, take my napkin, rub thy brows.
The Queen carouses to thy fortune, Hamlet.
HAMLET
    Good madam!
KING
            Gertrude, do not drink.

and let the kettledrum say to the trumpet,
the trumpet to the cannoneer outside,
250 the cannons to the sky, the sky echoing the sound to the earth,
"Now the King drinks to Hamlet." Come, begin.
> *Trumpets in the background as the King speaks.*

And you judges, keep close watch.

HAMLET
Come on, sir.

LAERTES
Come, my lord.
> *They fence.*

HAMLET
That's one hit.

LAERTES
No.

HAMLET
Can we have a decision?

OSRIC
A hit, a very clear hit.
> *Drums, trumpets, and ceremonial shooting are heard. A flourish of trumpets; a cannon goes off.*

LAERTES
All right, let's fence again.

KING
255 Wait, give me a cupful of wine. Hamlet, this pearl is yours.
Here's to your health. (*To Attendants*) Give him the cup.

HAMLET
I'll play this round first; put it aside for a while.
Come on. (*They fence.*) Another hit. What do you say?

LAERTES
A touch, a touch; I admit it.

KING
Our son will surely win.

QUEEN
260 He's out of condition and will soon be out of breath.
Here, Hamlet, take my handkerchief, wipe your brow.
The Queen drinks a toast to your good luck, Hamlet.

HAMLET
Thank you, good madam!

KING
Gertrude, do not drink!

QUEEN

I will, my lord; I pray you pardon me.

[*Drinks.*]

KING [*aside*]

265   It is the poisoned cup; it is too late.

HAMLET

I dare not drink yet, madam—by and by.

QUEEN

Come, let me wipe thy face.

LAERTES

My lord, I'll hit him now.

KING

I do not think't.

LAERTES [*aside*]

And yet it is almost against my conscience.

HAMLET

270   Come for the third, Laertes. You do but dally.

I pray you pass with your best violence;

I am sure you make a wanton of me.

LAERTES

Say you so? Come on.

[*They play.*]

OSRIC

Nothing neither way.

LAERTES

Have at you now!

In scuffling they change rapiers, [and both are wounded.]

KING

275   Part them. They are incensed.

HAMLET

Nay, come—again!

[*The Queen falls.*]

OSRIC

Look to the Queen there, ho!

HORATIO

They bleed on both sides. How is it, my lord?

OSRIC

How is't, Laertes?

LAERTES

Why, as a woodcock* to mine own springe, Osric.

280   I am justly killed with mine own treachery.

---

279   *woodcock*   proverbially stupid bird. See 1.3.115.

QUEEN
I will, my lord; please, with your permission. (*Drinks.*)

KING (*to the audience*)
265   It is the poisoned cup; it is too late.

HAMLET
I mustn't drink yet, madam—a little later.

QUEEN
Come, let me wipe your face.

LAERTES (*to the King*)
My lord, I'll hit him now.

KING
I don't think so.

LAERTES (*to the audience*)
And yet it is almost against my conscience.

HAMLET
370   Come on, let's have the third bout, Laertes. You're just fooling
around with me.

Come on, please show me your best moves;
I am sure you're treating me like a spoiled child (i.e., holding
back to let me win).

LAERTES
Do you think so? Come on.
They fence.

OSRIC
Nothing either way.

LAERTES
I'll get you now!
In the struggle they exchange swords, and both are wounded.

KING
275   Separate them. They are angry.

HAMLET
No, come on—again.
The Queen falls.

OSRIC
Take care of the Queen over there!

HORATIO
They're both bleeding. How are you, my lord?

OSRIC
How are you, Laertes?

LAERTES
Why, I am like a foolish woodcock caught in my own trap, Osric.
280   I am justly killed by my own treachery.

HAMLET
How does the Queen?

KING
　　　　　　　　　　She sounds to see them bleed.

QUEEN
No, no, the drink, the drink! O my dear Hamlet!
The drink, the drink! I am poisoned.
　　　[Dies.]

HAMLET
O villainy! Ho! Let the door be locked.
285 Treachery! Seek it out.
　　　[Laertes falls.]

LAERTES
It is here, Hamlet. Hamlet, thou art slain;
No med'cine in the world can do thee good.
In thee there is not half an hour's life.
The treacherous instrument is in thy hand,
290 Unbated and envenomed. The foul practice
Hath turned itself on me. Lo, here I lie,
Never to rise again. Thy mother's poisoned.
I can no more. The King, the King's to blame.

HAMLET
The point envenomed too?
295 Then, venom, to thy work.
　　　Hurts the King.

ALL
Treason! Treason!

KING
O, yet defend me, friends. I am but hurt.

HAMLET
Here, thou incestuous, murd'rous, damnèd Dane,
Drink off this potion. Is thy union here?
Follow my mother.
　　　King dies.

LAERTES
　　　　　　　　　　He is justly served.
300 It is a poison tempered by himself.
Exchange forgiveness with me, noble Hamlet.

HAMLET
How is the Queen?

KING
She faints to see them bleed.

QUEEN
No, no, the drink, the drink! O my dear Hamlet!
The drink, the drink! I am poisoned.
> *Queen dies.*

HAMLET
O villainy! Look out! Lock the door.
285   Treachery! Let's find it.
> *Laertes falls.*

LAERTES
It is here, Hamlet. Hamlet, you've been killed;
no antidote in the world can save you.
You don't have half an hour's life left.
The treacherous instrument of your death is in your hand,
290   unblunted and poisoned. The vicious plot
has turned itself on me. Look, here I lie,
never to rise again. Your mother is poisoned.
I can't talk any more. The King, the King's to blame.

HAMLET
Was the point poisoned too?
295   Then, poison, get to work.
> *Stabs the King.*

ALL
Treason! Treason!

KING
O, you can still defend me, friends. I am only wounded.

HAMLET
Here, you incestuous, murderous, damned Dane,
finish drinking this poisoned cup. Is your pearl in here?
Follow my mother.
> *Forces the King to drink, and King dies.*

LAERTES
300   He has gotten what he deserves.
It is a poison he mixed himself.
Let us forgive each other, noble Hamlet.

> Mine and my father's death come not upon thee,
> Nor thine on me!
>> *Dies.*

HAMLET

305   Heaven make thee free of it! I follow thee.
    I am dead, Horatio. Wretched Queen, adieu!
    You that look pale and tremble at this chance,
    That are but mutes or audience to this act,
    Had I but time (as this fell sergeant, Death,
310   Is strict in his arrest) O, I could tell you—
    But let it be. Horatio, I am dead;
    Thou livest; report me and my cause aright
    To the unsatisfied.

HORATIO
                   Never believe it.
    I am more an antique Roman* than a Dane.
    Here's yet some liquor left.

HAMLET

315   As th' art a man,
    Give me the cup. Let go. By heaven, I'll ha't!
    O God, Horatio, what a wounded name,
    Things standing thus unknown, shall live behind me!
    If thou didst ever hold me in thy heart,
320   Absent thee from felicity awhile,
    And in this harsh world draw thy breath in pain,
    To tell my story.
        A march afar off.
               What warlike noise is this?

OSRIC
    Young Fortinbras, with conquest come from Poland,
    To th' ambassadors of England gives
    This warlike volley.

HAMLET

325   O, I die, Horatio!
    The potent poison quite o'ercrows my spirit.
    I cannot live to hear the news from England,
    But I do prophesy th' election lights
    On Fortinbras. He has my dying voice.

---

314 *antique Roman* Horatio alludes to the Roman tradition, which considered suicide an honorable death in preference to a dishonorable existence.

May you be free of guilt for my death and that of my father,
and may I be guiltless for yours!
> *Laertes dies.*

HAMLET

305   May heaven absolve you from it. I follow you.
I am dying, Horatio. Unhappy Queen, goodbye.
(*To the courtiers*) You who look pale and tremble at this event,
you who are only silent actors or spectators of this action,
if I had more time(since this cruel police sergeant, Death,
310   is strict when he arrests you), O, I could tell you—
but let it be. Horatio, I am dying;
you're alive. Give a true account of me and my cause
to the uninformed.

HORATIO

Never believe that I will live to do it.
I am more like an ancient Roman than a Dane.
There is still some poisoned liquor left in the cup.

HAMLET

315   If you are a man,
give me the cup. Let go of it. By heaven, I'll have it!
> (*Seizes the cup from Horatio.*)

O God, Horatio, what a disgraced name,
with things remaining unknown this way, shall live behind me
    when I'm gone!
If you ever cared for me deeply,
320   keep yourself a while from the happiness of death,
and breathe painfully in this harsh world
to tell my story.
> *A march and a volley of shooting are heard from offstage.*

What warlike sound is this?

OSRIC

Young Fortinbras, arriving from his conquest in Poland,
gives the English ambassadors
this military salute.

HAMLET

325   O, I am dying Horatio!
The powerful poison triumphs over my spirit.
I cannot live to hear the news from England,
but I predict that Fortinbras will be elected the new king of
    Denmark.
He has my dying vote.

330   So tell him, with th' occurrents, more and less,
Which have solicited—the rest is silence.
            Dies.

HORATIO
Now cracks a noble heart. Good night, sweet Prince,
And flights of angels sing thee to thy rest.
            [*March within.*]
Why does the drum come hither?
            Enter FORTINBRAS, *with the Ambassadors, with Drum,*
            Colors, and Attendants.

FORTINBRAS
Where is this sight?

HORATIO
335   What is it you would see?
If aught of woe or wonder, cease your search.

FORTINBRAS
This quarry cries on havoc. O proud Death,
What feast is toward in thine eternal cell
That thou so many princes at a shot
So bloodily hast struck?

AMBASSADOR
340   The sight is dismal;
And our affairs from England come too late.
The ears are senseless that should give us hearing
To tell him his commandment is fulfilled,
That Rosencrantz and Guildenstern are dead.
Where should we have our thanks?

HORATIO
345   Not from his mouth,
Had it th' ability of life to thank you.
He never gave commandment for their death.
But since, so jump upon this bloody question,
You from the Polack wars, and you from England,
350   Are here arrived, give order that these bodies
High on a stage be placèd to the view,
And let me speak to th' yet unknowing world
How these things came about. So shall you hear
Of carnal, bloody, and unnatural acts,

So tell him that, along with the events, great and small,
which have caused—the rest is silence.
> *Hamlet dies.*

HORATIO
Now crack the strings of Hamlet's noble heart. Good night,
    sweet Prince,
may flights of angels sing you to your eternal rest.
> *Sound of marching music comes nearer.*

Why do the drummers come this way?
> *Enter* FORTINBRAS, *with the English Ambassadors,*
> *Attendants, and Soldiers carrying drums and flags.*

FORTINBRAS
Where is this sight?

HORATIO
What do you want to see?
If anything tragic or incredible, stop your search.

FORTINBRAS
This pile of bodies proclaims that a massacre has taken place.
    O proud Death,
what feast is being prepared in your eternal dwelling place
that you have, like a hunter at a single blow, killed so many
    princes
and so bloodily?

AMBASSADOR
The sight is woeful,
and our report of success in England comes too late.
The ears cannot hear that should listen to us
tell him that his orders are carried out,
that Rosencrantz and Guildenstern are dead.
From whom shall we receive our thanks?

HORATIO
Not from the King's mouth,
even if it had the power of life to thank you.
He never ordered their death.
But since you have arrived so soon after this bloody quarrel,
you from war with Poland, and you from England,
give orders that these bodies
be placed in view high on a platform;
and let me tell the still uninformed world
how these things came about. That way you shall hear
of sensual, bloody, and unnatural acts,

355   Of accidental judgments, casual slaughters,
      Of deaths put on by cunning and forced cause,
      And, in this upshot, purposes mistook
      Fall'n on th' inventors' heads. All this can I
      Truly deliver.
FORTINBRAS
                    Let us haste to hear it,
360   And call the noblest to the audience.
      For me, with sorrow I embrace my fortune.
      I have some rights of memory in this kingdom,
      Which now to claim my vantage doth invite me.
HORATIO
      Of that I shall have also cause to speak,
365   And from his mouth whose voice will draw on more.
      But let this same be presently performed,
      Even while men's minds are wild, lest more mischance
      On plots and errors happen.
FORTINBRAS
                    Let four captains
      Bear Hamlet like a soldier to the stage,
370   For he was likely, had he been put on,
      To have proved most royal; and for his passage
      The soldiers' music and the rite of war
      Speak loudly for him.
      Take up the bodies. Such a sight as this
375   Becomes the field, but here shows much amiss.
      Go, bid the soldiers shoot.

         Exeunt marching; after the which a peal of ordnance are
           shot off.

                    FINIS

355 of accidental retributions, murders which happened by chance,
of deaths brought about by plots and by contrivance;
and, in this concluding episode, intentions gone wrong,
destroying the devisers. All of this I can
report accurately.

FORTINBRAS
Tell us quickly,
360 and call the most important nobles to listen as well.
As for me, with sorrow I accept my good fortune.
I have some traditional rights to this kingdom,
which my opportunity now invites me to claim.

HORATIO
About that I shall also have reason to speak,
365 and about what I heard from Hamlet's mouth, whose choice for
king will set an example for others.
But let these (arrangements for revealing the truth) be made
at once,
right now while men's minds are confused, to prevent more
unfortunate accidents
from happening because of new plots and mistakes.

FORTINBRAS
Let four captains
carry Hamlet like a soldier to the platform;
370 for had he been put to the test as king, he would
have behaved royally. And to mark his death,
the soldiers' music and the ceremonies of war
shall speak loudly for him.
Lift up the bodies. A sight like this
375 is fitting for the battlefield, but is all wrong in a kingly court.
(*To a soldier*) Go, tell the soldiers to shoot the cannons.
Exit all, FORTINBRAS *and the soldiers marching. Then
cannons are heard firing from offstage.*

THE PLAY IN REVIEW:
A Teacher and Student Supplement

Between Acts: Study Questions

Act I

1. **What mood is stressed at the outset of the play?**

   With the sentries on guard, the drama creates an effect of vigilance against evil; the exact nature of that evil is unspecified. In spite of the explanation that the guards are protecting the castle from outside invasion, it is apparent that some inner evil also plagues the court. Hamlet is all too aware of this. Francisco speaks the key words during the first few minutes of the drama: "'Tis bitter cold and I am sick at heart," reflecting the play's overriding imagery of sickness and corruption. The exchange between the men on guard stresses the tension that began even before the opening curtain, and the description of "this thing" leaves a note of mystery that is to plague Hamlet. He must decide for himself exactly what manner of "thing" the ghost really is.

2. **Why does Marcellus tell Horatio to speak to the ghost?**

   The Elizabethans believed that ghosts must be addressed in Latin, so Marcellus turned the responsibility over to Horatio, a scholar. Shakespeare's audience would have accepted the ghostly apparition with some credulity, dependent upon their religious beliefs. Protestants did not believe in Purgatory and would have dismissed this part of the ghost's story; Roman Catholics might have found it more acceptable. Skepticism existed, though, as evidenced by Hamlet's later doubt as to whether or not to trust the ghost. The Elizabethan audience, however, would not have dismissed the ghost as unimportant.

3. **What current events are discussed as the men await the ghost?**

King Hamlet, whose ghost they await, had slain King Fortinbras of Norway in battle and laid claim to his lands. Fortinbras' son has been leading a guerilla movement to hold the lands and, at present, all Denmark is preparing for war. This conversation introduces Fortinbras, later to claim the Danish throne, and shows a son avenging his father, a role Hamlet is to emulate.

4. **What possible reasons for the ghost's appearance are discussed?**

In the sixteenth century, there were four reasons for a ghost's walking: to tell of hidden treasure, to gain revenge, to warn loved ones, or to offer aid when the state was in danger. With Denmark on the brink of war, the last reason seemed a viable one to Horatio and the sentries. At any rate, they mention that the ghost comes armed; the equipage identifies the ghost as the late king because of his distinctive armor and shows that his spirit is not at rest.

5. **What unnatural happenings does Horatio equate with the ghost's appearance?**

Eclipses, meteors, and walking dead were signs of discord. For the Elizabethans, nature and man were linked as part of the "great chain of being." All entities — human, animal, and mineral — were joined, and each had to function properly in its own sphere to insure universal harmony. If something fundamentally evil took place within the world of man, if the chain were disrupted, all nature would be affected and would show signs of protest.

6. **What is the atmosphere of the court routine that begins Scene 2?**

In his speech, Claudius provides exposition, revealing that as brother to the late king, he has wed his brother's widow and assumed the throne. His complacency covers up a shocking circumstance in its day — "Our sometime sister, now our queen" — but shows that Claudius is firmly in control. He then explains the war with Fortinbras to a court he knows he can count on for support. His conversation with Laertes shows his complete assumption of power.

Each of these subjects foreshadows events to come: the reference to Fortinbras sets up the youth's later claim to the Danish throne, while his chat with Laertes and Polonius introduces the family which figures so largely in the drama. But most of all, the whole court scene is invested with pomp, courtesy, and normality, so that Hamlet's bleak and bitter alienation is in graphic contrast.

✓ 7. **What attitude dominates Hamlet's personality in Scene 2?**

He is alone and apart from the others, dressed in the "nighted color." He alone is still in mourning, so that his black clothing separates him from the rest of the court. He alienates himself totally, refusing to join in the good humor so much in evidence between King, Queen, and courtiers.

His bitter sarcasm with his stepfather, close to insolence, is weighted by unhappiness and a sense of injustice, as is his rebuff to his mother. "Seems? I know not seems," he says, refusing to hide behind the cloak of subterfuge and intrigue assumed by the rest of the court. He is so bitterly unhappy and out of place at court that Claudius' smooth reference to Gertrude's remarriage echoes now with new impact. Hamlet is bereft, stunned by grief for a loved father and cut off from the comfort of his mother, the person whose love should most sustain him now. He is cut off, in fact, by her own betraying act. That he has also been deprived of his lawful birthright, the throne of Denmark, seems almost superfluous.

8. **How does Hamlet's soliloquy betray his melancholy?**

In a soliloquy, one bares one's inmost thoughts. Though Hamlet has managed to keep his replies to the King and Queen within the bounds of common civility, he releases the full measure of his agony as soon as he is left alone. He has completely lost faith in human nature; his mother's action has destroyed any fragment of belief in fidelity. In this first soliloquy he describes the evil in which his world is enmeshed, "an unweeded garden," a disgusting place, rife with corruption. He is helpless against the actions which have taken place; his father's death is an accomplished fact, as is his mother's remarriage. All he can do is curse the world that permitted such vile happenings.

9. **What historical event might Shakespeare be using as reference?**

This play was written during the reign of Elizabeth I. Her father, Henry VIII, had been able to marry her mother only by divorcing his first wife, on the grounds that she had previously been married to his brother. At the time, this was against custom and against canon law. Thus Hamlet's remarks about the Queen's "incestuous" union and its repugnant nature would have met with general understanding and royal approval.

10. **What is Hamlet's personality when he is with Horatio?**

Here is a glimpse of what Hamlet might really be. He uses no mask with Horatio, nor does he protect himself with darts of sarcasm or seek to wound in retaliation. He is open, friendly, interested; Horatio is a man he both loves and trusts.

Horatio's virtue and good will are unquestioned, and his function throughout the play is that of disinterested bystander. He takes no real part in the action, but serves as a sounding board for Hamlet's thoughts. By the end of the play he is the only major character left alive, still an impartial observer and commentator.

11. **What is the effect of Horatio's news of the ghost?**

Hamlet seems to awaken as if from a sleep. Here is something to which he can respond with verve and movement. His exchange with the two guards comes in brief questions and answers, a staccato effect heightening the tension as his excitement grows. His determined avowal to face the ghost includes the ominous line "Foul deeds will rise," although at this point he has no idea how foul the deeds will be.

12. **What is the effect of Laertes' talk with Ophelia in Scene 3?**

The scene shows Ophelia in her role as puppet, moving on the whim of others, and his words are ominous, for Laertes believes that her relationship with Hamlet bodes evil. In the main thought, the dialogue between brother and sister is rather charming and creates sympathy for both. Laertes' argument is not offensive; he sincerely feels that class differences doom Ophelia's future with Hamlet, and that she can only endanger her virtue by responding to his interest. She has spirit enough to answer him in kind, with pointed reference to his own dalliances, and the fondness between them is apparent. Laertes' extreme grief at Ophelia's death is more real because of the loving concern displayed in this scene.

13. **What is the significance of Polonius' advice to Laertes?**

The words themselves, superficially eloquent and thoughtful, are in contradictory context, revealing Polonius' hypocrisy and stressing the distinction between appearance and reality. Beginning with the admonition that Laertes should fly off to his ship, but stay till the father has spoken, the speech continues in double-talk.

The words form a self-serving guide to living: Laertes should construct an outer shell to win others to him, ignoring his true character. This is obviously the code by which Polonius lives, false to every man, concerned only about his own advancement. This code brings success in the corrupt world Hamlet despises.

His words to Ophelia are similarly cynical: he is interested only in practical results, not human feelings. Her response, "I do not know, my lord, what I should think," characterizes her aptly and totally.

14. **In Scene 4, what facts emerge from Hamlet's conversation with Horatio?**

Again, Hamlet is free to drop the watchful guile he assumes with others for self-protection. He can relax in detached, philosophical analysis of the local customs. He disdains the drinking bout taking place within the castle; it offends his sensibilities, though it does not produce the sharp outrage evoked by more personal events. He assesses the virtues of the nation, but feels such customs as the drinking are detrimental to Denmark's public image. He compares this to the reputation of a single individual, whose many good points may be blasted by a single fault.

15. **How does Hamlet approach the ghost?**

He begins with a demi-religious, demi-superstitious incantation against evil; this foreshadows his lingering uncertainty about acting on the ghost's testimony. How can he be sure the ghost is sincere? What if it serves the devil? When he follows the apparition, the others protest. Their disquieting assertion that "something is rotten in the state of Denmark" acknowledges that beneath the glittering surface of Claudius' court lies rank corruption. A glorious appearance conceals an appalling reality.

16. **In Scene 5, why is the ghost's reminder about his descent to Hell significant?**

According to the ghost's report of the murder, Claudius killed him with no chance for the last rites; so his death brought the curse of eternal damnation. This foreshadows Hamlet's reluctance to kill Claudius at prayer. Hamlet feels strongly — though mistakenly — that it will not be vengeance to take Claudius' life when his soul is prepared for Heaven.

17. **What is the unknowing irony in Hamlet's reply to the ghost?**

Hamlet makes a dramatic declaration that he "with wings as swift As meditation or the thoughts of love, May sweep to [his] revenge." The irony lies in the length of time that passes before he accomplishes that revenge. Procrastination slows his "sweep" to vengeance.

18. **Hamlet seems genuinely horrified at the ghost's revelation. Has he had no hint of evil?**

During the ghost's shocking account, he says, "O my prophetic soul!" implying that he had guessed the truth. However, there is no previous textual reference to an accusation of murder against his uncle; perhaps his inability to accept his father's death and mother's remarriage, his general foreboding and misery, have made him receptive to the idea that something is wrong.

19. **What does Hamlet realize after talking with the ghost?**

"That one may smile, and smile, and be a villain!" The shocking gulf between appearance and reality is grimly obvious to him, as is the fact that one dare not trust appearances. He seems to be walking through a mine field, fully aware of the perilous unreliability of the world around him. He realizes that time is "out of joint" and that it is his task to act in this milieu and change it for the better.

Act II

20. What change of mood occurs with Scene 1?

From the dark tension of the previous scene, with its unbelievable treachery that seems to color the whole world black, the mood shifts. It focuses on the pettiness of a sly old man, Polonius, preparing with painstaking calculation to spy on his own son. This microcosmic example justifies Hamlet's cynical vision of the world, a corrupt, vicious place where a father might use devious means against his own child.

21. What news does Ophelia bring Polonius?

Hamlet has told Horatio that he may put on an "antic disposition," counterfeit madness to cloak his real intention. This attitude reported by Ophelia might seem an actualization of Hamlet's scheme. However, in light of Hamlet's later grief at her death, it may be a sincere reflection of his real mood. Perhaps he went with a heart full of agony to the woman he loved, hoping that he could trust her. His fear of the world in which she is enmeshed prevented this trust and he departed in misery.

This scene, though reported secondhand, is the forerunner of the image Hamlet cunningly constructs for himself, a Hamlet no one understands. Polonius, as usual, interprets it to his own advantage, and decides that he can use Ophelia as bait. Innocent as she may be, her deployment by Polonius and the king seems to justify Hamlet's cynicism in the later "nunnery" scene.

22. What is the significance of the meeting between the royal couple and Rosencrantz and Guildenstern?

Their meeting parallels the scene in which Polonius spies on his son. Although Gertrude may be acting from the best of motives, spying on Hamlet seems an unworthy act. This attempt is more sinister than Polonius' since Hamlet is not Claudius' son. Different motives are in operation; Claudius has more power and perhaps a guilty secret to protect. The scene reveals that Hamlet has made good his proposal facade of madness, while their manipulation of his affection for friends reinforces Hamlet's view of an untrustworthy world.

23. Why is Fortinbras mentioned again?

Although he takes no part in the action of the drama — Denmark's royal house destroys itself from within — Fortinbras will be the ultimate ruler of the state. It will fall to him to restore stability, so the audience must be reminded of his power.

24. What is Hamlet's reception of Rosencrantz and Guildenstern?

Hamlet greets them warmly, alluding to his present condition and hinting that his madness does not blunt his awareness. Beginning to mistrust their motives because of their meeting with the King and Queen, he entreats them to be truthful. Hamlet longs to be able to trust somebody; he might have faith in Ophelia, were it not for her family associations, and he does trust Horatio. But Rosencrantz and Guildenstern fail him; they change the subject and distract him with news of the players' arrival.

25. Why is Hamlet excited about the players?

It is a touch of the world outside his "prison," Denmark, and again a glimpse of the relaxed Hamlet is revealed — gay, vibrantly alive, and awake to new stimuli. However, he does not completely forget his present dilemma. His final words to Rosencrantz and Guildenstern before joining the players tell the pair, or warn them, that his madness has an underlying purpose.

26. **What is the importance of the reference to Jephthah?**

Polonius, like Jephthah in the Bible, is willing to sacrifice his daughter for worldly gain. Polonius misses the analogy, however, seeing only that Hamlet's comment can be put to his own use.

27. **What is the import of Hamlet's speech to the players?**

The speech sharpens audience interest in the play, since at this point the relevance of the performance is not known. The passage also reveals Shakespeare, as playwright and actor, sharing an enthusiasm for his craft and enumerating his standards for the drama.

28. **What emotion dominates the soliloquy that follows when Hamlet is alone?**

While the first soliloquy dealt with the evil surrounding him, the second major soliloquy concerns the flaws Hamlet recognizes within himself. He is now consumed by guilt at his failure to obey the ghost's dictates. He contrasts the emotions of the actor, motivated by a fictional stimulus, with his own lack of action though he is driven by a real and pressing agony.

He finishes the soliloquy by revealing his plan for the performance. The plan extenuates his apparent procrastination: the ambiguity of the ghost must be resolved before Hamlet can take action. The spirit might have been sent by the devil to tempt him, so he will have the players enact a scene very much like his uncle's alleged crime. If Claudius responds with recognition, Hamlet may then assume him guilty and feel justified in taking revenge.

Act III

29. **What feeling permeates the first part of Scene 1?**

   The atmosphere that Hamlet fears and distrusts is all too apparent here. The King, Queen, Ophelia, and Polonius prepare to use Hamlet's affection for Ophelia against him, to broach his defenses and learn his motives. Though Gertrude is acting with good intent — with love and worry and the hope of cure — and Ophelia is manipulated by her father, their action is a repugnant one.

30. **What meaning is given to Claudius' aside as they plan Ophelia's actions?**

   This comment is important, if ambiguous. Claudius concurs with Polonius' comment about the ease of hiding an evil reality with a virtuous appearance, realizing that his own actions prove the statement. However, though he clearly reveals his guilt, the confession is fragmented. Does he admit to murder, or to marrying his brother's widow, an act then considered incestuous?

31. **What major philosophical points dominate Hamlet's soliloquy in Scene 1?**

   In this most famous of all Shakespearean speeches, Hamlet departs completely from thoughts of the revenge he has promised the ghost. His preoccupation here is with suicide. Only ecclesiastical law and the fear of Hell prevent him from taking his own life, and in view of this philosophy, Hamlet's conscience becomes a new and paramount consideration. Perhaps it is something more than the establishment of Claudius' guilt that has prevented him from taking precipitate action: must he not also deal with his own conscience? In opposing evil, must he himself become part of that evil? While the speech itself is a forthright exploration of suicide, the question of conscience must be examined. Otherwise, the soliloquy becomes merely a detour. Hamlet is clearly reluctant to "take arms against a sea of troubles," for by doing so he must participate in the evildoing he condemns in others.

32. Why is Hamlet so brutal to Ophelia?

There is some possibility that Hamlet overheard the plan of Claudius and Polonius to use Ophelia and has decided to turn the plot to his own advantage. The only textual reference supporting this explanation is that Hamlet asks her "Where's your father?" When she answers with a lie, his treatment of her becomes increasingly rough.

His tirade against Ophelia may also be spurred by his general disgust with the world and with women in particular. In many ways his horror at his mother's behavior is reflected in his attitude toward Ophelia. Whatever his feelings toward her as an individual, she remains Polonius' daughter and a member of Gertrude's treacherous sex.

It is also likely that he wants to sever the links between the girl and the contaminating world she inhabits. By putting her firmly out of his own cursed life, he may somehow protect her; if brutal treatment is required, he will be cruel now in order to be kind in the end.

33. Is Ophelia, as far as the text reveals, guilty of any of the "womanly" sins of which Hamlet accuses her?

For the most part she is innocent. She is not wanton, her chastity is unquestioned, her beauty is not put to any conniving use — except in obedience to her father. Her pathetic statement that Hamlet made her believe in his love is a poignant revelation of the pain his denunciation must cause.

34. What is the purpose of Ophelia's remembrance of the former Hamlet?

Her reflection provides another viewpoint of the nobility that once was Hamlet. It stresses the fact that his present state is indeed a grievous change. And this picture of Hamlet, painted in Ophelia's words, is ample justification for the love she feels; when he spurns her and later kills her father, her lapse into madness seems logical and credible.

35. How do Claudius and Polonius view the meeting?

Polonius seems reluctant to admit that Ophelia was not the cause of Hamlet's moodiness; he at least has no guilty secret to consider. For Claudius, however, certain things are becoming clearer, and his suspicion is growing. If Hamlet's problem does not stem from thwarted love, perhaps it has a more sinister source. The King means to protect himself with quick action.

36. What incidents occur in the scene with the players?

Hamlet's instructions to the actors seem unnecessary as far as action is concerned. The scene, in part, reflects Shakespeare's preoccupation with the thespian art; but its main thrust is to focus attention and suspense upon the play-within-a-play to come. Hamlet's shrewd instructions to the players reveal that he is becoming more adept at transforming reality into appearance. He himself has been acting a part ever since his conference with the ghost.

37. How does Hamlet behave before the play begins?

He ridicules Polonius mercilessly and engages in bawdy repartee with Ophelia. Here, his "madness" is less a subterfuge than an excuse for disregarding the conventions of respect and obedience. A direct insult to Polonius, an important courtier, is disregarded because the old man thinks the prince is "not himself." Such behavior does not further Hamlet's plan of vengeance. He is in a mood of nervous playfulness, an almost hysterical anticipation, though his antics seem merely a continuation of previous aberrations.

38. **What is the purpose of the scene with Horatio?**

This scene explains the importance of the play that is to follow, as Hamlet spells out for Horatio exactly what he wants to learn from the maneuver. The contrast between his attitude toward Horatio and his feelings about Rosencrantz and Guildenstern is significant. He knows he can trust Horatio, but not the other two. His reasoning here reveals much about his personality. It is not only that Rosencrantz and Guildenstern serve the King, while Horatio is faithful to the prince. Hamlet's reasons for valuing Horatio reflect his inner turmoil. Horatio is a calm person, a man of equanimity who is not slave to whims and passions as Hamlet feels himself to be. The qualities Hamlet admires in his friend reveal his priorities.

39. **What is Hamlet hoping to accomplish in the speech of the Player Queen to the Player King?**

He wants Gertrude to acknowledge her disloyalty to her first husband. Although he told Horatio that he planned the play to establish evidence against Claudius, the play he selected has a double thrust. The protestations of undying love the Player Queen makes to her husband are intended to wound Gertrude, to remind her of her vows to her first husband, and to impress upon her the disloyalty of her remarriage. The Elizabethans' religious and political backgrounds let them affirm the evil of such remarriage far more readily than a modern audience would.

40. **How does the performance temporarily shift circumstances?**

The scene which began with Claudius' smug "How fares our cousin Hamlet?" has changed radically.

Claudius was secure in his royal estate, master of all before him. Now he flees in panic from what must seem a public rehearsal of his crime. The balance of power has changed so that the Queen, noting his distress, must cry "How fares my lord?" For the moment, at least, Hamlet is in control. His jubilance shows his awareness of this fact.

41. **What stress is laid on Hamlet's confrontation with Gertrude?**

Claudius and Polonius have plotted it before the play. When Gertrude sends Rosencrantz and Guildenstern to summon Hamlet, she reveals the intrigue which surrounds their meeting, although she herself is not knowingly part of the plot. Claudius intends the meeting as Hamlet's last chance, and though Hamlet is unaware of this, it is his big chance. He knows with certainty, at last, that the king is guilty.

42. **What extended simile does Hamlet employ with Rosencrantz and Guildenstern?**

He tells them that they must not try to "play him like a pipe." He is warning them that he is aware of their treacherous intent, but, at the same time, he is imploring them to be the loyal friends he once thought them. They feign ignorance of the intrigue and continue to use his previous affection as a basis for spying.

43. **What is the irony of Hamlet's concluding remarks in Scene 2?**

He makes a ferocious declaration of his intentions toward Claudius, using words captains employ to spur their men on before battle. Yet when Hamlet soon has the opportunity to "drink hot blood," he fails to do so. Each time he can directly oppose evil, he shrinks from the necessity of committing an evil act himself.

44. What action does Claudius take against Hamlet after the play?

Hamlet is jubilant about "exposing" the king in the mouse-trap scene, but he is actually no closer to avenging his father than he was before. In high spirits, he does not see that he has accomplished nothing except putting Claudius on his guard. Though Hamlet concludes the preceding scene with fine words, it is Claudius who takes immediate action with another plot against the prince. Hamlet's madness has turned public opinion against him, boomeranged; now Claudius' decision to banish Hamlet from court seems understandable and justified. Rosencrantz and Guildenstern, the king's tools, might be expected to support the king because of patriotism and political necessity; but almost any citizen of Denmark would have encouraged their support. Hamlet has alienated those around him and caused serious doubts about his sanity.

45. What is the effect of Claudius' soliloquy?

It is the first clear proof that the ghost was speaking truth. Claudius' previous fears and the prince's odd behavior, and the King's acknowledged guilt might have stemmed from his "incestuous union" with Gertrude. Now, however, Claudius admits the murder of his brother. Note the manner in which Shakespeare shapes this confession: Claudius emerges a fully developed character with passions and drives, understandable motives, justifiable griefs. He is not a one-dimensional villain but a complete character who evokes a certain sympathy. He regrets his crime but cannot bring himself to relinquish the rewards of evil and so cannot achieve true repentance.

46. What is the irony of Hamlet's decision while Claudius is at prayer?

Seeing Claudius at prayer, as he thinks, he cannot bring himself to kill the King. His father was murdered without absolution and his spirit must now descend to Hell; Hamlet seeks a similar fate for Claudius. It seems too generous to kill the King when his soul is cleansed by prayer. The irony, of course, is that Claudius, aware of his guilt and unwilling to expiate his crime, has been unable to pray. He is far from the state of grace Hamlet imagines.

Critics have speculated, however, that Hamlet's reasoning at this point is too pat and easy. His is an ethical philosophy of life; is not cold-blooded murder repugnant, so that he will grasp at any straw that affords him an excuse? Whatever his motives, this is the turning point of the play. Hamlet fails to kill the King when he might; Claudius is now aware of the danger Hamlet represents and will take action against him.

47. What fact emerges from Hamlet's talk with his mother in Scene 4?

Did Gertrude know of Claudius' crime? The question is open to interpretation. At any rate, Hamlet soon drops that speculation and harangues Gertrude with what he considers her real crime: marrying Claudius. He puts aside the question of incest and concentrates on the disparity between the two husbands. He describes the superiority of King Hamlet and tries to persuade her to end her relationship with Claudius. When Gertrude recoils, frightened and grieved by his accusations, the ghost appears to protect her and again warn Hamlet not to distress her. This is part of Hamlet's philosophical dilemma: the ghost wants Hamlet to leave the Queen's punishment to heaven. Yet how is he to expose Claudius' crime or end the incestuous marriage without implicating his mother? Again Hamlet's problem is how to combat crime without taking up the weapons of evil himself.

48. What is the importance of Polonius' death?

Hamlet is unwittingly drawn into the morass of evildoing. Perhaps Polonius causes his own death by playing with intrigue, but Hamlet is still the agent of murder. In killing Polonius, he incurs the disapproval of the public and gives Claudius the upper hand. For the King now has an unimpeachable reason to expel the prince from court, hiding his true motives behind a desire to "protect" Hamlet.

Act IV

49. **What explanation does Gertrude offer for Polonius' murder?**

She tells Claudius that Hamlet is mad, ignoring completely the accusations against herself and Claudius. Her explanation allows two interpretations. Either she believes her son truly insane, or she simply cannot face the brutal facts behind his painful accusations. Whatever her beliefs, she chooses to say only that Hamlet, in a fit of madness, has taken Polonius' life.

50. **In what mood does Hamlet speak with Rosencrantz and Guildenstern?**

He is again hiding behind his facade of madness. There is an almost surrealistic humor in his banter about Polonius being "at supper." There is little strategic benefit to be gained from the mask of madness at this point, since he must know that he can no longer deceive Claudius about his motives. Considering Rosencrantz and Guildenstern mere empty shells entirely under the King's command, perhaps he considers discussion with them unworthy of his time.

51. **What is Claudius' attitude in Scene 3?**

He acts as a practical man, seeking a pragmatic solution to his problems. Hamlet realizes that he is not dealing with Rosencrantz and Guildenstern, meaningless nonentities, but with a powerful king. After a preliminary attempt to maintain the counterfeit madness and conceal Polonius' body, apparently for no purpose, he reveals the body's hiding place and is sent from court. Then Claudius, alone, discloses his true pragmatic solution: once abroad, Hamlet will be killed by the English, tributaries to Denmark. So will Claudius rid himself of an ever-growing danger and retain control of his kingdom.

52.   How does Fortinbras compare with Hamlet?

Fortinbras is a man of action, and Hamlet acknowledges the other's superiority. Hamlet berates himself for his own failure to take action; Claudius still lives, holds power, and claims Gertrude for his wife. Fortinbras has seized control of events and guided them to his own ends, while Hamlet is swept one way or another by accidents of fortune and the will of others. In this soliloquy Hamlet is ashamed to see Fortinbras head an army in a cause not really worthy, while, he, prince of Denmark, has taken inadequate action against a greater wrong. Again — once again — he vows to achieve the revenge which has long motivated him.

53.   What new insight does Ophelia's grief evoke?

Polonius had been portrayed as a hypocrite, a panderer, a man who would spy on his son and use his daughter in court intrigue. His death had been a meaningless accident and had brought grim humor from Hamlet. Now a more complete picture is drawn; with all his faults, Polonius was evidently a warm human being, loved by both daughter and son. Polonius was not merely the King's prop, a dupe used to manipulate the prince; he was a man whose death deeply grieves those who love him.

54.   How is Ophelia's madness portrayed?

Hamlet's "antic disposition" had been a thing of foolishness, an excuse for taking liberties at the expense of others. Now Shakespeare shows true madness, the tragedy of a broken mind. There is nothing silly or laugh-provoking here; Ophelia elicits concern and pity. Hers is authentic aberration and touches the emotions to the quick. Her father's death, with her beloved Hamlet its cause, has destroyed her control. Her bawdy songs hint that perhaps her feelings for Hamlet were as carnal as Laertes and Polonius feared.

55. What does Laertes' anger show?

Like Fortinbras, he acts as foil to Hamlet. He is a man of action and would "sweep to his revenge" as Hamlet has sworn to do. He returns posthaste after learning of his father's death and bursts upon the court, demanding reasons for his father's secret burial. His behavior may be rash, but it is understandable and direct. Claudius immediately assumes control, manipulating Laertes' pain at Ophelia's madness, boding ill for Hamlet.

56. What is the function of Scene 6 with Horatio?

This is an interim scene, in which the promise of action is all. Hamlet's letter predicts strange news and serves to whet the interest without revealing any news. Hamlet's imminent return, with Laertes and Claudius united against him, presages a dramatic and dangerous conclusion.

57. What final plans are arranged in Scene 7?

The duel which is to silence Hamlet forever is set in motion here. The arrangement makes Hamlet's death inevitable; they will leave no escape from the treachery of poisoned weapons. Claudius, who truly loves Gertrude, must camouflage her son's murder. But murder it remains. Laertes, who joins Claudius in this plot, is not lost in villainy. His real and affecting grief at Ophelia's death redeems him. Claudius may be driven by self-interest, but Laertes' motives have a certain understandable purity to them.

Act V

58. What is the effect of the "clowns' " conversation?

First, the gravediggers function as a sort of comic relief after the tension of Ophelia's breakdown and the high-pitched intrigue of the plot. Some pause is necessary before the ascent to the highest peak, the dueling scene. Previously, Polonius and — to a lesser degree — Rosencrantz and Guildenstern have provided humor of sorts, but they are now dead. The carefree banter of the gravediggers provides a relaxation of atmosphere.

Second, the juxtaposition of clowns and graveyard is startling, though no more so than the following conversation. The gravediggers chatter about their work, and what they say is revealing. Their discussion of Ophelia's burial as a suicide is important but less so than their rambling about death. Their casual acceptance of death and its leveling power presages Hamlet's calm new attitude and leads toward the drama's conclusion.

59. How is Hamlet changed?

Hamlet is no longer obsessed and weighed down by the paradox of good and evil, nor does his attitude toward death show his previous turbulence. He muses about the skull of his old acquaintance Yorick and notes the equality of all men in death, an end which awaits everyone. Ophelia's death is a blow to him and produces a moment of true aberration as he grapples with Laertes in the grave. Then he composes himself, apologizes, and suggests that life must run its course.

Claudius parts the two and it is his ominous speech to Laertes which ends the scene.

60. What new philosophy motivates Hamlet?

During his absence Hamlet has taken on a new attitude toward life. He left Denmark marked for death but, by the sheerest accident of fate, has avoided death on the high seas and execution in England as well. Perhaps these brushes with mortality have claimed him or given him a new perspective of the questions which had so haunted him. Forgotten now are his former obsessions with mortality and the hereafter. He now believes in some "divinity that shapes our end," is willing to accept his fate; no longer does he rant against injustices of life. He prepares instead to endure whatever may happen, for "the readiness is all." He makes no specific reference to the vengeance that motivated him for so long, but when forced to a confrontation, he acts.

61. How is a final solution achieved?

Although the final scene is one of carnage, every major character except Horatio dead, some semblance of normality has been restored. The evil which permeated Denmark has been exorcised. With the advent of Fortinbras a virtuous, reasonable government may be established. Horatio, a bystander but a man of integrity and judgment, makes the final evaluation of Hamlet — a "noble heart." Thrown into a world consumed by evil for which he is not responsible, Hamlet has at least made protest and fought for redemption. If he was not successful in restoring virtue and order to his world, perhaps he accomplished all that can be expected of any human. He took arms against the evil which encompassed him. He rose to the struggle.

315

The Play's the Thing: Discussion Questions

Motivation:

1. **What is Hamlet's original opinion of Gertrude?**

   At the beginning of the play Hamlet is aghast at his mother's marriage to Claudius. That she betrayed him by marrying the man who usurped Hamlet's right to the throne is never a major issue. He first criticizes her action in terms of its hastiness; he believes she has shown disloyalty to her first husband by remarrying so quickly. However, his subsequent behavior shows that her disrespectful haste is not at the heart of his disgust.

   He then claims that the union between Gertrude and Claudius is an incestuous one, abhorrent in the sight of God and man. This too is a rational explanation, but perhaps it also serves to cloak the primary reason for his disgust.

   In his climactic interview with Gertrude, he concentrates on the disparity between her first husband and her second, on Claudius' apparent inferiority. This gulf prompts Hamlet's inability to accept his mother's remarriage; but it is also possible that any man would have seemed unfit to assume his father's role as husband to Gertrude.

2. **How does Hamlet's attitude toward Gertrude change?**

   From the beginning, the ghost has cautioned Hamlet not to accuse Gertrude; apart from his sardonic remarks and general coldness, he has done so. However, flushed with the triumph of the "mousetrap" and his new assurance of Claudius' guilt, he loses self-control and berates his mother mercilessly. At this point the ghost intervenes to protect her. Still, Hamlet's attitude toward her does not change until after he returns from the pirate ship and his brush with death. Then, in keeping his new philosophy, he is able to mute his anger and recall some of the love they shared.

3. **What is the conflict in Hamlet's feelings for Ophelia?**

Since the drama begins *"in media res,"* the audience can only deduce their previous relationship. Several comments make it clear that Hamlet had been involved in a romance with Ophelia: first, her father and brother note the fact and warn her against it; she reminds Hamlet poignantly that he had made declarations of love in the past; and finally, his first action after encountering the ghost is to seek out Ophelia. Stricken by the knowledge of the evil surrounding him, he searches out the woman he loves; according to her description, he stares at her as if he would plumb her soul. This action reflects the two facets of Hamlet's feelings toward Ophelia: he loves her and wishes to trust her, but — female and child of Polonius — she seems a danger to him. Feeling she is part of the intrigue and subterfuge of the court, he turns viciously on her and orders her out of his life.

4. **How do Hamlet's feelings toward Ophelia change?**

When he learns of Ophelia's death, he is stricken both by grief and by conscience. He finally admits his love for her when he leaps into her grave, challenging Laertes with the cry that his love was much greater than any brother's could be. For Ophelia has proved her love for the prince; her emotions have been sincere and so profound that they have led to her death.

5. **Describe Hamlet's personality during the first four acts.**

He grows increasingly bitter and distraught. The agony of his father's death and mother's marriage have flung him into an abyss of bleak despair. Then

317

comes the shock of the ghost's dire accusations. Hamlet is pledged to action but unsure of what to do. He seems wildly agitated and engages in much futile activity — striking out brutally at Ophelia, indulging in malicious gibes at Polonius. But he accomplishes very little of consequence.

In taking on the responsibility of righting all the wrongs of the world, he is engaging in a kind of egocentricity. The universe seems to him totally wicked, and he has assumed the duty of abolishing that wickedness; he will instruct his mother in her wrongdoing, cast off his sweetheart for unproved guilt, and not only condemn Claudius to death but to eternal damnation. Hamlet's task is clearly beyond any human's power, and it is this frustration which absorbs him and defeats his efforts.

6. **In retrospect, what had Hamlet been like before his father's death?**

Hamlet's previous personality shows in his friendship with Horatio, his conversation with the players, and Ophelia's memories of his former behavior. With Horatio he is hearty, affectionate, and completely at ease. He is capable of calm observations on important national issues, showing intelligence and perceptivity. His conversation with the players reveals him as a sophisticated man of the world, interested in the arts and culture, with a shrewd grasp of public affairs. Ophelia, fearing him mad, mourns the loss of what he once was: "The expectancy and rose of the fair state, The glass of fashion and the mould of form, The observed of all observers — quite, quite down!" He had been in short the complete Renaissance hero: interested in a variety of subjects, eager to do his best, regarding the world as a treasure house of enjoyment and enlightenment. He had, however, lacked the maturity and experience to cope with the worst that life has to offer; he even failed to realize that this underside existed. His confrontation with evil outlines his growth from smooth sophistication to perceptive maturity.

7. **What is Hamlet's final attitude toward good and evil?**

He learns to accept that he is bound, as are all men, by the human condition. When he returns from the sea voyage, impressed by the closeness of death and the intervention of fate, he has become a gentler, more understanding person. He has become reconciled with his mother, although she has not corrected the behavior for which he once denounced her; and he is capable of asking Laertes' pardon where he once would not. He still recognizes the existence of evil but now is capable of action against it. He verbally deflates the self-important, posturing Osric, and strikes out finally at Claudius, taking vengeance for his mother's death and, at last, for his father's. Hamlet has learned that man must do his utmost to seek good within his limited sphere, rather than despair at a totality of evil against which he is powerless. Horatio recommends for him "soldier's rites," for he has been a participant in the battle against evil. A futile battle, perhaps, but one from which no contestant retires without honor.

Appearance and Reality:

1. **What is Hamlet's fundamental problem with appearance and reality?**

His mother's remarriage shows Hamlet that she is not the person he thought her, and, with the ghost's shocking revelations, Hamlet faces new gulfs between appearance and reality. In the past he had always accepted appearance as inseparable from reality. Now he is forced to a new maturity with the recognition that surface is not always substance. In an extremely brief time, he is confronted with a number of enigmatic surfaces which he must decipher before the plotters kill him. This is his first experience with evil, a traumatic maelstrom, and he must cultivate new senses to discern hidden truths.

2. **In what ways does Claudius illustrate the basic disparity between appearance and reality?**

The first court scene exemplifies Shakespeare's thematic statement about the difference between appearance and reality. The court is calm, good-humored, with an outward appearance of splendid stability. Yet all this is superficial. Claudius urges Hamlet to accept nature — his father's death — when he himself has committed an unnatural murder. The danger to Denmark merely appears to be approaching from outside; actually the kingdom is rotting from within, contaminated by its unlawful ruler, Claudius. Hamlet, learning of Claudius' crime and recalling the man's affability mourns "That one may smile, and smile, and be a villain."

3. **How is the appearance-reality theme expressed by the ghost?**

The appearance-reality question is at the heart of Hamlet's dilemma about the ghost. If the ghost is his father's spirit, Hamlet must take action. But is the ghost really what it seems? After all, as Hamlet muses, "The devil hath power to assume a pleasing shape." The prince must evaluate the ghost's words with the new awareness that outward surfaces do not always match inward realities.

4. **What is the importance of the players?**

The players are clearly a high point for the thespian Shakespeare, whose life was centered around the theater. More important, they provide an intriguing comment on the appearance-reality theme. In Hamlet's second soliloquy ("Oh what a rogue and peasant slave am I"), he berates himself for his lack of action. The visiting player shows a simulated grief more convincing than the real grief evinced by Hamlet. "What's he to Hecuba or Hecuba to him," the prince wonders, in awe at the agony the player rouses over an impersonal tragedy. For the players hold the "mirror up to nature"; they thus emphasize the difficulty which is confounding Hamlet, that of separating appearance from reality. The mouse trap, the "play-within-a-play," is a climactic scene, while Hamlet's failure to kill the king afterwards because he seems to be at prayer is the turning point. Appearance has, again, distorted Hamlet's perception of reality.

5. **Are Hamlet's friends what they seem to be?**

Hamlet displays trust only in one friend, Horatio, who is exactly what he seems. Ophelia raises strong misgivings. Is she the innocent girl he has loved, or is she a scheming decoy? In Act II, Scene 1, she says he stares at her as if he would "read" her face and judge the substance it hides. Later, in a frenzy, he scathingly tells her that "God has given you one face and you make yourself another," fearing that she too has hidden her real self behind a sham he cannot trust. Rosencrantz and Guildenstern he dismisses almost immediately; they are far from being what they seem.

6. **How does Polonius reinforce the appearance-reality theme?**

He epitomizes the successful man of affairs whose code is one of hypocrisy. He speaks to Laertes specifically of hiding the inner self behind a virtuous exterior to win favor and promotion. Then he sends Reynaldo to spy upon Laertes, explaining that he must "by indirection find direction out," use insincerity to ascertain truth. This is the sort of two-faced intrigue which Hamlet sees strangling human civilization. He will have none of it.

7. **Is Hamlet really mad, or does he merely pretend to be insane?**

    He speaks of "putting on" an antic disposition, and he makes Horatio and the sentries swear not to reveal by their appearance what the reality is. In Act V, however, he tells Laertes that when he hurt Ophelia and killed Polonius he wasn't himself. This is evidence that rage and grief push his madness beyond mere appearance. When he does put on his facade of madness, everyone involved has a personal, subjective explanation: Claudius fears that Hamlet has guessed his crime; Gertrude worries that her remarriage has driven him insane; Polonius suggests that frustrated love for Ophelia has deprived him of his wits. All of them would shape Hamlet's appearance to the reality of their own attitudes.

8. **Does Hamlet find life merely a sham, with no reality or meaning at all?**

    One specific reality is discussed at great length — death, the ultimate reality. In fact, the play seems intensely preoccupied with the state of being dead. The concern is not with dying, but actually being dead, as in Hamlet's third soliloquy and in the gravedigger scene. This reality does give meaning to human experience.

9. **In Act V Hamlet says, "There's nothing either good or bad but thinking makes it so." Does each of us create his own reality then?**

    Answers here will vary. Students should realize that every individual possesses the power to shape his own reality to some extent, to influence his destiny by the attitude he takes.

Philosophy:

1. **In what way is Hamlet shaped by his environment?**

   Hamlet's personality reflects his society — he is sophisticated and articulate with a subtle, probing mind. His world reflects not the evil of a brute, savage, unformed culture, but the distortions of a complex, elaborate system which has been set on the wrong course.

2. **What is the relationship between Hamlet and the evil of his world?**

   He is surrounded by it but not really part of it. Although he is eventually driven to acts of wickedness — insulting his mother, wounding Ophelia, killing Polonius — evil exists more as a condition than as a volitional act. He is no more responsible for it than a sick man is for his illness. (A variety of figures of speech associated with sickness and infection reinforce this attitude.) Hamlet has inherited a tragic dilemma: "O cursed spite that ever I was born to set it right."

3. **Is Hamlet powerless against his destiny?**

   In Shakespeare's philosophy, nemesis does exist and a certain fatalism is in operation. However, man has the power to resist, to struggle for good. The basis of tragedy's inevitability lies within human character. It is the interplay between the individual and his environment, psychological cause and effect, which results in a cosmic order.

4. **If, as Hamlet tells Horatio in Act V, "the readiness is all," is life then reduced to dumb resignation in the face of death?**

   No, death can give meaning to life. Death's finality must be accepted if life is to be enjoyed from a mature perspective, without the turmoil of fear and worry. Man must come to terms with his own mortality, as Hamlet does when he narrowly escapes death at sea, or when he speculates with the gravediggers about the physical actuality of dying. Realizing the limits of human existence enhances the value of life, which never loses its full mystery or true sense of tragedy.

Encore: Vocabulary Words

In each group below, the main word is found in *Hamlet*. Mark the letter of the word in each group that comes closest in meaning to the main word.

1. usurp
   a. use up
   b. seize unfairly
   c. grow stale

2. avouch
   a. assert
   b. deny
   c. calm down

3. martial
   a. married
   b. military
   c. halfway

4. portentous
   a. overbearing
   b. soft
   c. ominous

5. harbinger
   a. forerunner
   b. port
   c. delay

6. dirge
   a. claim
   b. revealing look
   c. mourning song

7. impious
   a. empty
   b. unholy
   c. charming

8. jocund
   a. insistent
   b. merry
   c. careless

9. circumscribe
   a. navigate
   b. round
   c. limit

10. dalliance
    a. amorous play
    b. quiet prayer
    c. disrespect

11. perusal
    a. conclusion
    b. intention
    c. careful reading

12. precept
    a. teacher
    b. rule of conduct
    c. decide

13. extremity
    a. utmost limit
    b. very much
    c. cutting edge

14. firmament
    a. heavens
    b. strength
    c. cruelty

15. paragon
    a. identical
    b. model of perfection
    c. lover

16. gratis
    a. free
    b. thankful
    c. intentional

17. savory
    a. extravagant
    b. appetizing
    c. challenging

18. chronicles
    a. clocks
    b. curses
    c. histories

19. cleave
    a. spice
    b. split
    c. unthinking

20. malefaction
    a. evil deed
    b. homemade
    c. wrinkled skin

21. visage
    a. clothing
    b. letter
    c. face

22. consummation
    a. thought
    b. completion
    c. pleasure

23. orison
    a. prayer
    b. occupation
    c. interest

24. paradox
    a. unpleasant idea
    b. beginning
    c. apparent
       contradiction

25. calumny
    a. excitement
    b. slanderous
       accusation
    c. wonderment

26. temperance
    a. rebellion
    b. moderation
    c. forcefulness

27. buffet
    a. a blow
    b. a nod
    c. an embrace

28. purge
    a. memento
    b. insistence
    c. elimination

29. bulwark
    a. strong defense
    b. reminder
    c. departure

30. mandate
    a. resistance
    b. authoritative
       command
    c. description

31. conjecture
    a. supposition
    b. rejection
    c. worship

32. impetuous
    a. gracious
    b. impulsive
    c. unwanted

33. requite
    a. repay
    b. almost
    c. direct

34. obscure
    a. clever
    b. tidy
    c. hidden

35. bier
    a. paper
    b. coffin stand
    c. expression

36. incensed
    a. thrown out
    b. prayed
    c. enraged

37. inter
    a. magic
    b. discuss
    c. bury

38. pestilent
    a. nagging
    b. poisonous
    c. casual

39. superfluous
    a. unnecessary
    b. colossal
    c. powerful

40. importunate
    a. essential
    b. urgent
    c. regrettable

41. cudgel
    a. legal
    b. refuse
    c. heavy club

42. pate
    a. head
    b. hair
    c. intelligence

43. abhorred
    a. led
    b. sent in
    c. hated

44. prate
    a. attack
    b. babble
    c. attach

45. amity
    a. friendship
    b. consolidation
    c. interest

46. dearth
    a. length
    b. scarcity
    c. fatality

47. germane
    a. relevant
    b. unfamiliar
    c. thoughtful

48. commended
    a. praised
    b. required
    c. began

49. diligent
    a. defiant
    b. strange
    c. hard-working

50. felicity
    a. truthfulness
    b. bliss
    c. dispute

Improvisation: Student Enrichment

Research:

1. In Act II, Scene 2, Hamlet calls Polonius "Jephthah." Check the Biblical reference, Judges XI: 30-40, and write a brief report explaining Shakespeare's reference to this character.

2. Using the text as resource, organize a class debate on the subject, "Resolved: Hamlet procrastinated needlessly."

3. Read the condensation of *Hamlet* in Lambs' *Tales from Shakespeare* and note the omissions made by the Lambs to achieve brevity.

4. Henry VIII, father of Elizabeth I, used the excuse of marrying his brother's widow as grounds for annulment so he could remarry and legitimize Elizabeth. Write a short research report dealing with Henry's reasoning and legal manipulation.

5. Read another Shakespearean tragedy and compare its theme to that of *Hamlet.*

Reaction:

1. At times many modern people share Hamlet's disgust with a world that seems corrupt and "out of joint." Consider any situations in which you have felt this way. What specific circumstances prompted your reaction? Was it as difficult for you as it was for Hamlet to find cures for the situations that aroused your concern?

2. Ophelia's personality type is present even today: the sheltered, pliable person who depends on others for direction. Do you feel that persons of this type are unfit — as Ophelia was — to deal with the sometimes shattering world of real-life experience?

Imagination:

1. Write a descriptive poem or essay dealing with Hamlet's reaction to Ophelia's death.

2. Script-write or role-play a conversation between Hamlet and a friend in which Hamlet tries to explain his mood at the very beginning of the play.

3. Write a newspaper article as though it were to be published in Denmark on the same day as the deaths of Hamlet, Laertes, Claudius, and Gertrude. The article should include a full account of the happenings at the castle, as well as interviews with Horatio and Fortinbras.

4. Rewrite the Act III, Scene 1 soliloquy ("To be or not to be") in your own words.

5. When Ophelia wandered into the brook, she must have made a particularly poignant picture. Write the lyrics to "The Ballad of Ophelia" and include a description of her tragic death.

Between the Lines: Essay Test

Literal Level

1. Why is Hamlet so unhappy at the beginning of the play?

2. What conflicting emotions does the ghost rouse in Hamlet?

3. Why does Hamlet say "The readiness is all"?

4. List three characteristics of Claudius and give examples from the play to illustrate them.

Interpretive Level

1. Discuss Hamlet's relationship with Ophelia and its effect on her.

2. How does Hamlet's third act soliloquy, "To be or not to be," reveal his inner torment?

3. What are the two functions of the clowns in the graveyard scene?

Final Curtain: Objective Test

I. True—False

Mark each statement T for True or F for False.

_____ 1. Hamlet's romance with Ophelia is ended by his mother.

_____ 2. Gertrude is astonished to see the ghost.

_____ 3. Yorick had been court jester.

_____ 4. Claudius never admits his guilt to the audience.

_____ 5. Claudius killed the king by pouring poison in his ear.

_____ 6. At the end of the play, Horatio becomes king.

_____ 7. Hamlet fears that the ghost may have been sent by the devil.

_____ 8. "To thine own self be true" is part of Hamlet's soliloquy.

_____ 9. Hamlet is afraid to trust Rosencrantz and Guildenstern.

_____ 10. The ghost is in Purgatory waiting to ascend to Heaven.

_____ 11. Polonius believes that love for Ophelia caused Hamlet's madness.

_____ 12. In the "To be or not to be" speech, Hamlet discusses suicide.

_____ 13. After the players perform, the whole court knows of Claudius' crime.

_____ 14. Claudius deeply loves Gertrude.

_____ 15. Like Hamlet, Ophelia only pretends to be mad.

II. Multiple Choice

Choose the best answer to complete each statement.

16. Fortinbras is a prince of
    a. Norway.
    b. Denmark.
    c. Poland.

17. "Get thee to a nunnery" is addressed to
    a. Gertrude.
    b. Hamlet.
    c. Ophelia.

18. Hamlet resents Gertrude's marriage to
    a. her husband's brother.
    b. a complete stranger.
    c. a Norwegian.

19. Hamlet compares Polonius to
    a. Judas.
    b. Jephthah.
    c. Solomon.

20. Hamlet does not kill Claudius at prayer because
    a. the Queen is there.
    b. he is well guarded.
    c. he wants to damn the King's soul.

21. Hamlet hopes the play will
    a. win Ophelia back.
    b. cause Claudius to reveal his guilt.
    c. amuse Horatio.

22. The ghost tells Hamlet
    a. to leave the Queen alone.
    b. that Polonius was involved in his death.
    c. that he can trust Horatio.

23. Claudius hopes that Hamlet will be killed in
    a. Norway.
    b. England.
    c. the graveyard.

24. The graveyard scene shows
    a. that all are equal in death.
    b. that Hamlet killed Polonius.
    c. that the ghost is not at rest.

25. Hamlet feels Gertrude is guilty of
    a. usurping the throne.
    b. killing her brother.
    c. an incestuous marriage.

26. Ophelia dies by
    a. hanging.
    b. poison.
    c. drowning.

27. Laertes joins the dueling plot because of
    a. grief.
    b. ambition.
    c. jealousy.

28. Comic relief is provided by
    a. Laertes.
    b. the gravediggers.
    c. the players.

29. Hamlet feels he can trust only
    a. Horatio.
    b. Laertes.
    c. Gertrude.

30. Hamlet is the only one at court who
    a. still wears mourning.
    b. can read and write.
    c. drinks too much.

31. The first to see the ghost is
    a. Hamlet.
    b. Horatio.
    c. a sentry.

32. In his first soliloquy, Hamlet sees the world as
    a. generally good.
    b. generally evil.
    c. both good and evil.

33. The court is located in
    a. Oslo.
    b. Copenhagen.
    c. Elsinore.

34. The duel is planned by Laertes and
    a. Claudius.
    b. Polonius.
    c. Hamlet.

35. Hamlet kills Polonius
    a. in a duel.
    b. not knowing who it is.
    c. with poison.

III. Matching

A. Match the characters with their descriptions.

_____36. Polonius
_____37. Claudius
_____38. Hamlet
_____39. Gertrude
_____40. Ophelia
_____41. Laertes
_____42. Horatio
_____43. Gonzago

     a. once married to King Hamlet
     b. returns Hamlet's gifts
     c. names Hamlet heir to the throne
     d. feels "the readiness is all"
     e. part of "play-within-a-play"
     f. adviser to the king
     g. says "Good night, sweet prince"
     h. brother to Ophelia

B. Match the items with the proper descriptions.

_____44. Yorick
_____45. letters to England
_____46. poisoned wine
_____47. mouse trap
_____48. rapier
_____49. armor
_____50. flowers

     a. kills Gertrude
     b. skull in graveyard
     c. nickname for the "play"
     d. part of Ophelia's mad scene
     e. delivered by Rosencrantz and Guildenstern
     f. identifies the ghost
     g. kills Laertes